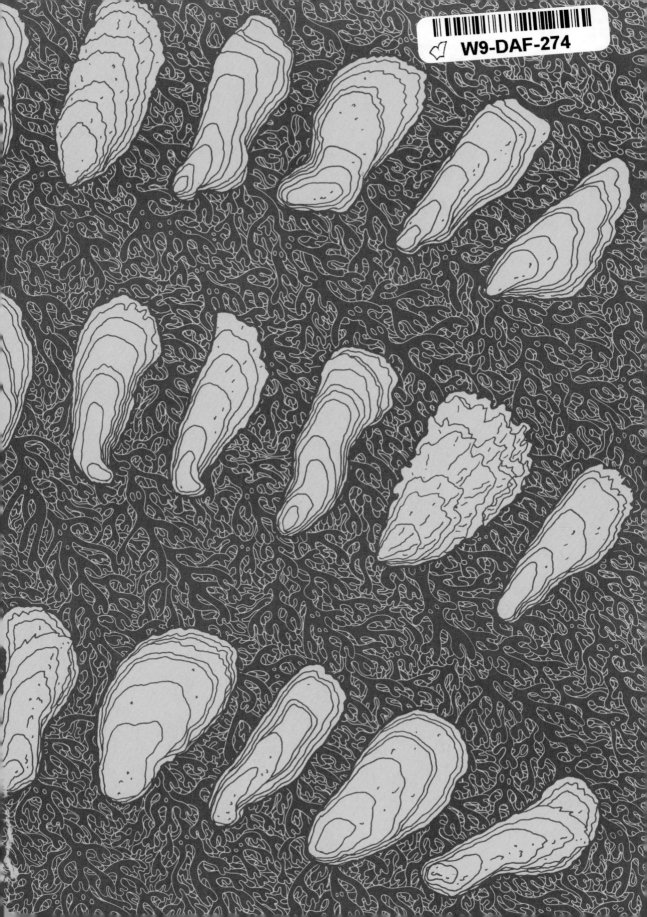

OYSTERS

OYSTERS

A CULINARY CELEBRATION

Joan Reardon
Ruth Ebling

Joan Reardon
Ruth Ebling

PARNASSUS IMPRINTS

Orleans, Massachusetts

This book and jacket were designed by Richard C. Bartlett,
who also drew the oyster portraits. Page makeup was done
by Ann Hatfield. The jacket photography is by Benjamin
Parran, and Hugo Poisson did the photographs within the
book. Crane Typesetting Service set the text in Herman
Zapf's Palatino, perhaps his finest typeface design, and
Zapf's Chancery is used for the quotations. Display faces
used are Columna Open and Raffia.
New England Book Components printed the color inserts
and the jacket, and Arcata Graphics/Halliday Lithograph
printed the text on S.D. Warren's Sebago Antique and bound
the book in Holliston's Roxite cloth.

CONTENTS

ACKNOWLEDGEMENTS

Partially surrounded by the shelter of Cotuit Bay and the expanse of Vineyard Sound, Cotuit is a generous village. For years, it has given its oysters to connoisseurs, a serendipitous way of life to its villagers, and, unusual for a seashore community, Cotuit has given a place and "space" to both year-round residents and summer people to pursue serious intellectual and creative work.

Our first thank you, therefore, is to Cotuit, to the resources and staff of the Cotuit Library, to the Cotuit Oyster Company, to all the friends and neighbors who supported our efforts and especially to Mr. and Mrs. Benjamin Parran and Mrs. Robert Downs who contributed so much to the first phase of this project.

But to write a cookbook is to incur a more far-reaching debt of gratitude. The cuisine of today is the cuisine of yesterday updated. Without the ground breaking efforts of James Beard, Julia Child, Craig Claiborne, Pierre Franey, Judith and Evan Jones, Alma Lach, and scores of other experts in the culinary field, this book could not have been written. And we wish to thank them in a more personal way than the Selected Bibliography allows. We acknowledge an even greater debt of gratitude to the comprehensive work of Marian Morash in *The Victory Garden Cookbook*, to the innovative genius of Alice Waters at Chez Panisse, and to the "daring to be delicious" spirit of *The Silver Palate Cookbook*. And a special thank you goes to the woman whose books are a continual source of inspiration to everyone who really wants to write about food in a creative and meaningful way — M. F. K. Fisher.

The Culinary Collection at the Schlesinger Library, Radcliffe, the Brown University Library, and the community libraries of Falmouth and Osterville, Cape Cod, greatly facilitated the gathering of old recipes, oyster legend and lore. We want to thank the staff at each of these libraries for their patience and assistance.

The preparation of the book, supervised by Trumbull Huntington and Ben Muse, has been a continual source of gratification. Richard Black's culinary expertise and advice were indispensable in editing the manuscript. The design and layout of the book under Richard Bartlett's direction literally transformed the typed pages into a handsome book, and the efforts of chef Edwin Woelfle at The Cranberry Moose restaurant in Yarmouthport translated certain recipes into visual delights. We wish to thank Tom Rowlands for the opportunity to photograph these dishes under such aesthetically pleasing circumstances. Our special thanks go to Hugo Poisson for the photographs and to Benjamin Parran for the cover photography.

David Nosiglia at The Smokehouse, Hyannis, Massachusetts, gave generously of his time and advice in perfecting the recipe for Oyster Sausages and supplied his own recipe for the Oysters and Sausages appetizer. We are grateful for all his efforts.

We also wish to thank Houghton Mifflin Company for permission to quote lines from Anne Sexton's *Book of Folly*.

Without Cotuit and the justly-fabled oyster that bears the village's name this book could not have been imagined; without the support of our husbands, families, friends, and neighbors it could not have been accomplished; and without the confidence of our publisher, Parnassus Imprints, it would not have become a reality.

Joan Reardon
Ruth Ebling
Cotuit, Massachusetts, 1984

OYSTERS

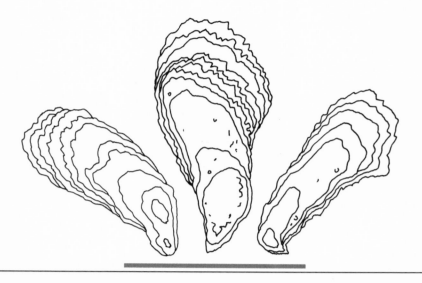

Caesar: *I have been in Britain, that western land of romance. . . . I went there in search for its famous pearls. The British pearl was a fable; but in searching for it I found the British oyster.*
Apollodorus: *All posterity will bless you for it.*
        George Bernard Shaw, *Caesar and Cleopatra*

R is for Oyster
M. F. K. Fisher

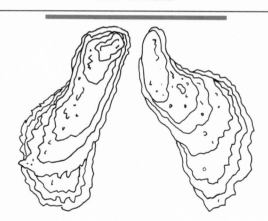

RUMORS

The history of the oyster has been told many times, in many ways, and, like a come-hither buffet table, there's a little something for everyone in the story.

Folklore enthusiasts who delight in the human dimensions of simple tales will find their share of Neolithic humor in the account of the unsuspecting man who picked up a yawning oyster, thought it a stone, and then got his index finger caught in the snapped-shut shell. The conclusion was predictable. When the man freed his finger and put it into his mouth to relieve the pain, he tasted the oyster liquor and discovered that the incredible oyster was also edible.

Oyster buffs will, no doubt, be interested in the remnants of 4,000 miles of barrier reef that since ancient times extended from Scandinavia down the Atlantic coast into the Mediterranean and along the coastline of France and Italy to Greece. The flat and smooth European oyster, *Ostrea edulis*, and a score of other shellfish bedded in the reef were a seemingly inexhaustible supply of food. The desire to learn more about these gifts from the sea motivated the Greeks to make modest forays into the practice of farming oysters. It's intriguing, moreover, to learn that as early as the fourth century, B.C., it was a known fact that oysters did not necessarily reproduce in the waters where they grew well, and that aquaculture probably began at that time.

Fascinating reading, also, are the lengths and depths *Homo faber* plumbed in order to preserve and transport this indolent mollusk. Because the Romans discovered the Breton oyster at a fairly early date, they set up ice houses between Brittany and Rome to replenish the snow and ice in the oyster carts traveling over land. During the summer months, cistern carts filled with salt water were used. And there is an amazing tale of a Roman refrigerator devised more than two thousand years ago to keep oysters and other perishable comestibles fresh during the warm weather. Basically a deep freeze set in a windowless rock wall secured by a tight door, it was a construct of vertical caves reached by a narrow wooden staircase. On the floor of the lowest cave, a wooden box was set in two or more feet of trampled, hardened snow. Cold spring water flowed underneath it and kept the oysters cold until needed.

Later on, when the Romans discovered the magnificent flavor of Colchester oysters growing in the estuaries of the Thames River, there were even more dramatic measures taken to transport oysters by boat. Seamen commandeered double-hulled galleys for the voyage which occasionally was so long that fear of spoilage necessitated pickling the oysters in vinegar, salt, and laurel berries and storing them in barrels fumigated with pitch.

Then there are the many accounts of outrageous banquets, a facet of the oyster's history that has had more than its share of notoriety. Pliny called oysters "the palm and pleasure of the table," and he savored many a bivalve. In fact, Romans consumed bushels of oysters, relishes, mushrooms, peacock's eggs, and sardines as appetizers. But oysters were so popular that they were also used as accompaniments to roasted boar and other entrées and were served throughout the entire orgy. Documented or simply rumored, there are stories that virtually every influential Roman statesman, military hero, and emperor had more than a passing interest in oysters. Perhaps Gibbons' account of the Emperor Vitellius feasting on a thousand, or some such fabulous number, sums up the situation. Freud would have had something interesting to say about that, and, no doubt, the guests at the banquet did too. But, alas, the glory that was Rome, faded away.

Although seafaring people like the Vikings ate oysters as a matter of course, the Visigoths, who had little fear of anything else, were apprehensive about oysters and acquired no taste for them. Happily in those "dark ages," however, there were a few, recorded, closet oyster lovers who were adamant about including oysters in their diet. Chronicles of the eighth century show that a certain St. Evremond ate several dozen for breakfast and lived to be at least ninety. During the years of his exile in England, the French king, Louis IV, developed a taste for British oysters, and later, when he was imprisoned in Normandy, he requested a ration of them regularly. And little more than a century later, when the Normans under the leadership of William the Conqueror invaded England, they seized the oyster beds in Kent and Essex. The British oyster was definitely one of the jewels of the crown, and fittingly, by 1319, Edward II established the custom of opening the oyster season with a feast held on the day of St. Deny's Fair.

Unfortunately, in spite of these modest Medieval examples of oyster savoring, the halcyon days of wine and peacock feathers were over, and the interest in oysters rekindled in the Renaissance had a slightly different orientation. Even though Queen Elizabeth often feasted on raw Colchesters as a first course, and oysters on the half shell were still considered important banquet fare, an era of serious oyster cookery had begun in England. Elizabethan cookbooks got down to the brisk business of pickling, stewing, roasting, and saucing the oyster.

In France, extravagance, oysters, and royalty remained inseparable. The trend-setting court of Louis XIV consumed oysters with abandon, and the king kept a private "park" at Versailles to guarantee an adequate supply for royal banquets. A hundred years later, one of the "Sun King's" less than fortunate successors, Louis XVI, stocked private beds of oysters at Etretat which supplied him and Marie Antoinette with more than one royal repast before royalty was no more.

From the mid-seventeenth century until the early nineteenth century, oysters, like power, ceased to be the private domain of the aristocracy and passed to the man in the street. The oyster became the darling of the bourgeoise, *the* fashionable food. Casanova, adventurer manqué that he was, consumed fifty a day with his evening punch. And early gastronomic authors, like Brillat-Savarin, were of the opinion that "oysters furnish[ed] very little nourishment" and did not spoil one's appetite for dining. Little wonder that by the mid-nineteenth century, Charles Monselet, another French gastronomer, admitted with some chagrin, "Oysters seem to be losing ground this year. It can't be more than a breathing spell, a bad joke of fortune."

While France lamented the difficulty of obtaining oysters, the "Rhymesmith" of the "Preston Oyster and Parched Pea Club" in Lancashire, England, expressed the satisfaction of the British middle class with the surfeit of oysters and political good fortune that they enjoyed: "Nelson has made the seas our own,/ Then gulp your well-fed oysters down,/ And give the French the shell."

During the eighteenth and nineteenth centuries, oysters were plentiful, nourishing, and available to the poor and not-so-poor in England. Gentleman's clubs and university clubs, pubs, fairs, and oyster tubs in rows, oyster girls and oyster wenches, and a certain amount of high-jinks down in the oyster cellars flourished.

The oyster was the subject of paintings, the object of amatory speculation, and a frequent topic for journalists and writers. In *All the Year Round* (1859), Dickens wrote a wonderful account of a free company of oyster dredgers who prospered in Whitstable in the mid-nineteenth century and turned oystering into a very profitable business, indeed. "Without stint or limit," they shipped the famous Whitstables to London's markets where they were always in demand. Seemingly, there was no limit to the oyster craze in England.

RECOLLECTIONS

Across the Atlantic, there was another oyster, *Crassostrea virginica*, another dining scene, and another story. Mounds of shells along the Eastern seaboard give more than enough evidence of the huge storage pools that the Indians used for oysters and other shellfish. Seven million bushels of shells were found off the coast of Maine. Remnants of a significant number of weirs were located in the marsh area that was reclaimed and now known as Boston's Back Bay. And such a heavy concentration of oyster beds and shells was found on Cape Cod that many of its bays and harbors were simply named "oyster" by the early explorers.

The changing role that oysters played in American cuisine from the wigwams of the Wampanoags to the private dining rooms of Delmonico's was definitely a saga that progressed from sheer necessity to serendipity. And even the culinary footnotes are different from the history of oyster savoring in Europe.

On both the Atlantic and Pacific coasts pre-Columbian Indians ate oysters only after they boiled them for five or six hours to make them tender. And it is fair to assume that the Indians taught the settlers to make oyster stew with different combinations of roots, vegetables, and grains in order to compensate for the absence of milk-giving animals. But necessity did little to dispel the Pilgrims' prejudice that oysters were fit only for farm animals.

Some colonists, however, adapted their taste for British oysters to the rough-shelled, different tasting American oyster. In 1607, during the Christmas season, Captain John Smith wrote that in Virginia, "we were never more merry nor fed on more plenty of good oysters . . . in England." But from Massachusetts to Maryland, their appreciation of oysters waned every spring because supplies of food dwindled and a diet of oysters was the only way to keep from starving.

In the New World, wars were even started because of oysters. When Charles I gave Lord Baltimore the area up to the highwater mark on Virginia's side of the Potomac River and the projection of that line into Chesapeake Bay, he gave Maryland the lion's share of the oyster beds. And if the colonists failed to appreciate the gift, the potential of one of the greatest oyster producing areas was soon discovered. Gun shots were and are still heard across those waters. But that's another story.

At some point in time between the years when the early settlers reluctantly dined on oysters and the years of community "oyster roasts," American attitudes changed. By 1857, Charles Mackay, an English visitor in the States, concluded that "the rich consume oysters and champaigne; the poorer classes consume oysters and *lager bier*, and that is one of the principal social differences between the two sections of the community."

Up and down the Eastern seaboard, oysters became synonymous with conviviality, profit, and regular tavern fare. Express "oyster wagons" crossed the Alleghanies to Pittsburg where, either by boat or wagon, oysters were rushed to "parlors" in Cincinnati and Chicago. As far away as downstate Illinois, Abraham Lincoln included oyster roasts in his campaign strategy.

Menus in important restaurants like New York's Astor House featured "boiled cod fish and oysters" and "oyster pie." Almost every testimonial banquet ranging from $100 to $5,000 a plate began with Lynnhavens on the half shell, and a London gentleman wrote that New York City consumed daily £3,500 worth. The Revere House in Boston used 100 gallons of oysters a week. In Philadelphia almost no oysters

were served in 1810, but by 1840, 4,000 tons were sent annually from Chesapeake Bay. And in the West, two of the costliest ingredients, eggs and oysters, were used in tandem to make what must have been the most expensive omelet in the world, presumably paid for in gold. By 1850, the oyster was the favorite of the tavern and town set. And nineteenth century cookbooks were more than generous in instructing cooks to "enrich" a modest gumbo with a hundred oysters, and add at least two quarts of them to a soup.

Perhaps this American fondness for oysters was in imitation of the craze that swept Paris and London, the twin capitols of the world known for taste and fashion. Maybe it was the inevitable adaptation of French, Italian, and Spanish cuisines to ingredients that were plentiful in the various "regions" of the country. Possibly the taste for oysters was attributable, at least in part, to the fact that many native beds of oysters were depleted as early as the 1770's and the difficult, time-consuming process of seeding and cultivation made the "oystermen" a breed apart and gave their "harvest" additional value. And there just might be another reason.

REFLECTIONS

While the androgynous oyster's own sense of romance is open to question, it is certainly no accident that the names associated with oyster lore and legend are the names of many of the world's great lovers. From rakishly Rabelaisian quips to the current psychophysiological mass market studies of human sexuality, the cult of oysters as aphrodisiacs is a story unto itself, and like all stories, it grows more suspect with each telling.

The possibilities of attribution are limitless, and wishful thinking is always open to question. If opening an oyster shell is a symbol for seducing a beautiful woman, are not all metaphors created in the imagination? If oysters on the half shell resemble female and male genitalia, isn't the comparison in the eye of the beholder? To wink and blink about Casanova's appetite for oysters and women and to talk about it in some circles is a bit gamey. And for those sporting individuals who acquire "double entendres" at an awesome rate to add a little antic behavior to the cocktail party scene, there are certainly more than a few words associated with oysters beginning with foot and *huître* to make the evening memorable. But what's one person's thrill may be another's tedium.

For a generation that has lived through the sixties and seventies, there is something dated and declassé about this sort of twittering, something demeaning to both "love food" and lover. Eating a serving of oysters on the half shell and drinking a glass of Champagne may be the beginning of an affair of the heart, but it is also a culinary affair between a food that is an acquired taste and a person who has painstakingly cultivated it. And to regard oysters as a means to an end, as a magic potion for love making, is a disservice to a food that is its own delectation and its own reward.

A closer look and a context might be helpful. And no one person has provided it with greater insight and style than M. F. K. Fisher: "Our three basic needs, for food and security and love are so mixed and mingled and entwined that we cannot straightly think of one without the others. . . ." A meal shared with someone one loves is a celebration; initiating someone into pleasures one has known is intensely human.

There is no doubt that eating a first oyster is a kind of coming of age, a rite of passage from the security of the familiar tastes associated with childhood to the unknown world of adult experience. It is a frightening and a joyous moment that prose cannot really describe as well as poetry can. Anne Sexton *saw* the dozen of oysters before her arranged on the plate like numbers on a clock, like time, and she looked from her father's satisfaction with his "clear as tears" martini and platter of oysters to her own plate of "twelve eyes . . . running with lemon and Tabasco." Like all difficult experiences, the first swallow was medicinal, "a large pudding" going down. But by the time that "one o'clock" and two were eaten, there was laughter and "I was fifteen/ and eating oysters/ and the child was defeated/ The woman won." * The initiation was complete.

Unique in a group of foods that includes truffles, lobster, artichokes, mangoes, passion fruit, and a score of other "love" foods, oysters are food for the initiated few. Often compared to a seductive woman, there is a mystery, a subtlety, a quality that defies explanation about them. No other food evokes such strong feeling of utter bliss or revulsion; no other food has been written about more eloquently or more trivially.

The history of oysters is definitely a riches to rags to riches story. As the favorite food of emperors and kings, oysters were transported with great difficulty and at great expense, devoured at banquets, synonymous with decadence and excess. Oysters were also the staple of the poor, the main ingredient in an astonishingly nutritious stew, roast, and pottage made to stave off hunger. Today, the story has come full circle. The days of plentiful, inexpensive oysters belong to the romantic days of America's past.

Oysters, along with caviar and *foie gras*, are in a class apart, the *pièce de résistance* in the menus of inspired chefs and the ultimate *tour de génie* at parties given by the most discriminating hostesses. And a cookbook devoted to oyster cookery ought to reflect something of the exclusivity and versatility of its subject, should suggest the balance and harmony of a meal, and even the combinations of ingredients that complement the delicacy of the main ingredient.

* Anne Sexton, "Oysters" from *The Book of Folly*, Houghton Mifflin Co., 1973.

RUMINATIONS

This is a "Come into my kitchen I want my oysters to meet you," kind of cookbook, written for the cook who needs no coaxing to purchase a half dozen or half peck of oysters at the local fish market, take the oyster knife out of the top drawer and shuck away. For whether served on the half shell with a bit of lemon or fried, baked, and grilled as a substantial dinner entrée, the fascination with the many possible ways of preparing oysters never wanes for the person who enjoys pampering family and friends with a dish of elegant oysters.

But this is also a cookbook written to seduce the hesitant into the wonderful world of oyster cuisine possible to everyone within the perimeters of the kitchen. The oyster enthusiast need not limit his enjoyment of oysters to expensive restaurants or dockside oyster bars. Oysters are trucked and flown to virtually every part of this country and are available twelve months of the year. Shucking is definitely neither a male nor an Amazonian prerogative; the skill can be learned quickly; practice makes short work of opening oysters. And the following six chapters, beginning with appetizers and ending with entrées are a compendium of both traditional and innovative ways to prepare and serve oysters complete with pertinent suggestions that are linked to specific cooking techniques.

Only one thing is necessary in oyster cookery, and that is a knowledge of and a certain respect for the ingredients used. Oysters differ tremendously in size, plumpness, and taste. Because an oyster pumps more than a hundred gallons of water a day through its mouth and gut and assimilates mostly sodium chloride and minerals, it will taste of salt and metals. Its taste will be a concentration of its last habitat.

Coppery, tinny, sweet, clean, intense—are all favorable descriptions and a matter of the strong personal preference of the oyster devotee. These same qualities have a different importance for the cook and signal caution. Some of the following recipes are especially suitable to the delicate flavor of warm water Gulf oysters; whereas New England and Long Island oysters are ideal in those recipes requiring raw oysters. It's always important to *know* the saltiness, texture, and taste of the oysters one is preparing, and to avoid, if possible, oysters that are not firm to the touch and indistinguishable in flavor. In every recipe the quality of the oysters used determines the success of the dish.

Hopefully, there is something for everyone in this book—legend and lore, old recipes, traditional recipes updated, unusual combinations of ingredients, menu suggestions, and the assurance that oyster cuisine is very much on-going, going-on in the eighties.

And now on to "oysters, a culinary celebration."

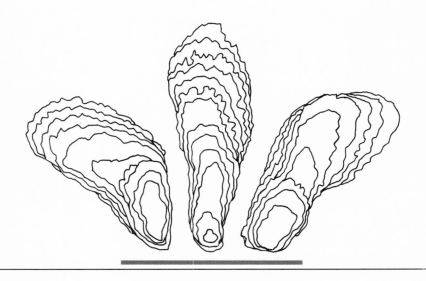

You are eating the sea, that's it!
Eleanor Clark, *The Oysters of Locmariaquer*

Four years ago—she remembered distinctly—a meal had begun with soup or oysters or lobster cocktail or an avocado with Roquefort dressing. *Something.* But now, it seemed, after large basins of Martinis-on-the-rocks (a drink she considered parvenu, as opposed to the classic Martini), you sat right down to the main course or it was served to you on your lap. Nobody alluded to the vanished first course; it was like a relation that had died and could not be mentioned.

Mary McCarthy, *Birds of America*

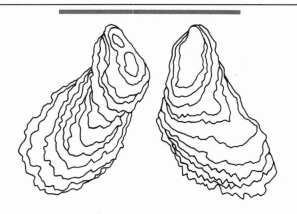

There is simply no telling if civilization will survive without a first course, but life would certainly be lacklustre without the proper prelude to a meal. An appetizer is somewhat like the tantalizing first chapter of a novel that captivates a reader's attention and compels him to turn page after page to the happy or not-so-happy end. Or perhaps it's as engaging as the beginning of a love affair—so much more scintillating than the day-to-day familiarity that eventually leads to a less than inspired good-bye. No doubt about it, first impressions are either infatuating or provoking; they can never be bland. And menus are very much the same. What diner has not glowed with delight, drinking a glass of fine Champagne and savoring a chilled briny oyster on the half shell?

Custom and history have served the oyster well and annotated such goings-on as a feast given in 50 B.C. The menu began with "sea urchins and raw oysters in profusion, giant mussels, and sea carp served on asparagus." And there was an account of the serving of roast mutton with oysters, "as a first course at the feast of the East India Company at Merchantailors' Hall, London, on January 20, 1622. Consider, also, that in Preston, England, from 1771 to 1841, there flourished the "Oyster and Parched Pea Club," whose members pledged to provide and open a barrel of oysters at exactly half past seven every Monday night during the winter season.

Perhaps it need not even be mentioned that Casanova ate at least fifty oysters per day and Louis XIV never ate less than a hundred when they appeared on the royal menu. Brillat-Savarin's observation sums it all up nicely:

> I remember that in the old days any banquet of importance began with oysters, and that there were always a good number of the guests who did not hesitate to down one gross apiece (twelve dozen, one hundred and forty-four). I always wondered what the weight of this little appetizer would be, and finally I confirmed the fact that one dozen oysters (including their juice) weigh four ounces, which makes the gross amount to three pounds. I feel quite sure, then, that these same guests, who were not at all deterred from dining well after their oysters, would have been completely surfeited if they had eaten the same weight of meat, even if it had been the delicate flesh of a chicken."

The possibilities are endless, and, it seems, have always been. Every language has a special word for the small portions of food that contribute stylistically to a meal but are literally *hors d'oeuvre*, outside the work [of the meal]. The Mandarins of ancient China called them *ti wei ping* and boasted over one thousand. The Athenians enjoyed the numerous *dolmas*; in Rome, *gustatio* came to mean a minimum of fifty tasters.

Appetizers often identify a cuisine and, because they are served in small portions, exhibit more of the innovative aspects of culinary style than the main course, where combinations of ingredients and flavors are sustained for more than a bite or a nibble. A French *hors d'oeuvre* may be a few hot stuffed mussels or a chilled rémoulade of celery root. An order of Clams Oregano or sliced Settecento Genoa salami with a cool wedge of honeydew melon or half of a fresh fig may be fitting Italian *antipasti*. A "fresh from the stream to the smoke house" platter of trout or selection of wurst can be a simple *Vorspeise* in Germany. And then there is potted shrimp in England, a *zakuski* of jellied calves' feet in Russia, and a cracked wheat salad for a Syrian *maza*.

But, despite the distinctive features of international cuisine, there are a few "constants," a few ingredients that tempt the palate with more insistence than Vegetables à la Grecque or Cocktail Chicken Wings. They are the gifts from the sea—oysters, caviar, smoked salmon, lobster, shrimp, and lump crabmeat.

Today, the menus of famous restaurants perpetuate the idea that the crisp, briny flavor of an oyster enhances the appetite. And even though the traditional favorites—Oysters Rockefeller, Bienville, and Casino—have surrendered some of their popularity to the lighter and purer taste cultivated by the practitioners of nouvelle American cuisine, fresh oysters dressed with lime juice and slivered ginger, or with a simple shallot sauce, and grilled oysters served with leeks in a pure buttery sauce are proof positive that oyster cookery does and will always reflect the taste of the moment as well as the past.

This first chapter begins with some "authentic" recipes for serving oysters as an elegant sit-down beginning to a dinner party. Freshly shucked and quivering from the sea to a bed of ice, or properly sauced and piping hot from the oven, these oyster appetizers require plates and forks and are difficult to juggle at stand-up parties or even cocktail buffets. At a sit-down dinner, Champagne or an appropriate Chablis can be leisurely sipped, lemon wedges, cracked pepper, and side dishes of sauce can be passed, and empty shells can be whisked away with the serving plates—all with great ease for the hostess and guests.

In spite of all this emphasis on serving oysters in their own shells or, as is done on the Continent, in seafood cocktail glasses, there are a few recipes that will accommodate the hostess with a penchant for serving oysters during an informal "drinks" hour. Miniature turnovers, tartelettes, profiteroles, and canapés are wonderfully attractive, delicious and easy to serve, and there is even a dip that works well with crudités, crackers, and chips—finger foods, including canapés, that will spark up any cocktail party and whet the appetite.

SUGGESTIONS:

- An appropriate appetizer complements the rest of the meal in every way but does not repeat any of the main ingredients, sauces, herbs, or preparation methods of the other courses. An elaborate first course such as Oysters au Vin de Champagne beautifully introduces a grilled rack of lamb or sirloin steak whereas raw Oysters on the Half Shell would be wonderful with a stuffed chicken breast served with Sauce Suprême.

- Six raw oysters per person are usually served as a first course. If the oysters are larger than 3½ inches and they are baked or broiled with a rich sauce or dressing, three or four per person are usually adequate.

- Raw oysters served on the half shell must always be perfectly fresh and shucked as close to serving time as possible. It is not advisable to serve bulk or frozen oysters raw. There is nothing that can equal an oyster, plucked from the depths and served immediately, but, if that is not practical, they can be kept cup-side-down in the refrigerator for at least two weeks, or shucked and then frozen for later use with a minimum loss of taste. Oysters used as a hot appetizer or finger food can be shucked in advance and refrigerated, or can be purchased by the jar or by the pint, which may be stored in the freezer if necessary.

- Oyster shells, like scallop shells, can be reused any number of times. It is convenient to have a supply on hand if the dish calls for bulk or frozen oysters.

- Oysters can never be undercooked, but can be ruined by overcooking which toughens them and diminishes their flavor. When baking an oyster appetizer, use a hot oven, from 400° to 450°, unless the other ingredients dictate a lower temperature. When broiling, place the pan 5 inches from the heat and cook for less than 5 minutes. Some recipes can be prepared most efficiently by baking for a short time and then crisping or melting (the cheese topping) under the broiler for a minute or two. When poaching an oyster, cook it only until plump or until its edges begin to curl, and remove from heat.

- Because of the irregular shape of the deep shell, lining a baking or broiling pan with rock salt is recommended to steady the shells and retain the heat. Crumpled heavy gauge aluminum foil will accomplish the same thing, but the amount of heat retained is minimal and not quite worth the effort. Shells can be placed directly in a pie pan or shallow roasting pan or on a baking sheet or broiler rack and prepared with a minimum amount of spilling. The shells retain enough heat to ensure a hot appetizer.

- Sauces for many of the hot appetizers and finger foods can be prepared in advance. Some of the recipes can also be assembled and refrigerated several hours before baking. If the prepared shells are cold, bring to room temperature before heating.

- Estimating servings of finger foods is somewhat determined by the variety of foods being served. Usually three per person are sufficient if the hostess has prepared three or four different kinds.

- Many of the recipes prepared as appetizers can also be served as the main course at a luncheon or late evening supper by adjusting the amount served.

Seven o'clock having struck, the rustle of a woman's costly robe is heard as the portières part and our hostess moves forward to survey the table while placing the beautiful and costly dinner-cards. Diamonds flash in her hair, about her neck, and on the corsage of her wonderful gown. Diamonds in front of her, diamonds at back of her, diamonds on top of her sparkle and dazzle as she goes to the salon to receive her guests.

Champagne is cooling in cracked ice, all the wines are ready, oysters on the half-shell, resting in silver plates of wondrous workmanship, garnished with artistically cut lemon, await the point of the tiny fork.

Mary E. Carter, *Millionaire Households:*
And Their Domestic Economy, 1903

COLD

On the Half Shell   16
Sauces   17
Oyster Grapefruit Cocktail   20
Oysters Borchardt   20
Unblushing Oysters   21
Oyster Spinach Rolls on the Half
    Shell   22
Oysters Flambé   24
Oysters and Sausages   25

HOT

Oysters Florentine (Rockefeller)   26
    Parmigiana   26
    Verde   27
    Gratinato   28
    al Forno   28
    Formaggio   29
Oysters Bienville   30
    Imperial   31
    au Vin de Champagne   32
    aux Écrivisses   32
Oysters Roffignac   33
Chart House Oysters   34
Oysters Casino   35
Oysters 1826   35
Oysters Forestière   36
Oysters aux Choux Brocolis   37
Oysters aux Pommes   38
Oysters Marinara   39
Gingered Oysters   39
Oysters à l'Ail   40
Stuffed Oysters   41
Stuffed Oysters Italiènne   42
Oysters Mahnomonee   43

FINGER FOOD

Angels on Horseback   44
Galloping Oysters   44
Oysters Argenteuil   45
Stuffed Mushroom Caps   46
Oyster Tartelettes   46
Oyster Beignets   47
Oyster Profiteroles   48
Oysters Parnassus   49
Oysters Scandia   50
Tasses d'Huîtres   50
Pane Imbottito   51
Whistling Oyster Dip   52

CANAPÉS

Cold

Kiss Me Canapé   53
Casino Canapé   54
Smoked Oyster Fingers   54
Oysters Lucullus   54
Oysters Lucca   54
Oysters Otero   54

Cold or Hot

Mushroom Oyster Rounds   55
Tunny Smoked Oyster Rounds   55

Hot

Zesty Oyster Canapés   56
Broiled Oyster Canapés   57
Oyster Puffs   57

COLD APPETIZERS

Oysters on the Half Shell

The ardent oyster lover, pure and undefiled by the allure of *haute cuisine*, demands his oysters pure and undefiled by any other flavor, seasoning, herb, or accompaniment that rivals the briny taste of the sea. So here is not only the obligatory recipe for savoring oysters, but also the one that perfectly exemplifies the authors' own personal conviction that in oyster cookery less is better than more.

6	oysters	Freshly cracked black pepper
2	cups crushed ice	(optional)
1/4	lemon (optional)	Wine vinegar (optional)

1. Scrub oyster shells under running cold water.
2. Shuck the oysters just before serving and strain the liquor that spills from the shell into a container.
3. Arrange the oysters in their deep shells on a bed of ice, and pour the strained liquor over them.
4. If desired, serve with a wedge of lemon, a bit of cracked pepper or a splash of vinegar.

Serves 1

It [an oyster] should be opened at street temperature in a cool month, never iced, and plucked from its rough irregular shell at once, so that its black gills still vibrate and cringe with the shock of air upon them. It should be swallowed, not too fast, and then its fine salt juices, more like the smell of rock pools at low tide than any other food in the world, should be drunk at one gulp from the shell. Then, of course, a bite or two of buttered brown bread must follow, . . . and of course a fine mouthful of a white wine.

Quoted in M. F. K. Fisher, *Consider the Oyster*

Epicurean cooks sharpen with cloyless sauce his appetite.
Shakespeare, *Antony and Cleopatra*

Sauces for Raw Oysters

If guests are less than confirmed devotees of raw oysters, the gracious hostess, mindful of the words that Shakespeare wrote about sauces many years ago, will offer one or two of them whenever she serves raw oysters either on the half shell or on a bed of shredded lettuce in a stemmed cup appropriate for seafood cocktails.

Ranging from a simple Mignonette dressing to a zesty Rémoulade, the following sauces will please some palates more than others. In all of them, the ingredients speak for themselves and, along with personal taste, should dictate the choice. Each recipe yields about a cup of sauce. Mix thoroughly and serve well chilled.

MIGNONETTE SAUCE

¼ cup finely chopped shallots
1   cup red wine vinegar (*Aceto Balsamico*)
2   teaspoons freshly ground white pepper

Variation:

¼ cup finely chopped shallots
1   cup dry white wine, or ½ cup dry white wine and ½ cup tarragon vinegar
2   Tablespoons chopped chives
2   teaspoons freshly ground white pepper

TOMATO SAUCE

1   cup chili sauce
¼ cup lemon juice
2   teaspoons Worcestershire sauce
1   teaspoon celery salt
    Tabasco

Variation:

½ cup chili sauce
½ cup tomato ketchup
1   teaspoon dry mustard
2   teaspoons lemon juice
2   teaspoons Worcestershire sauce
    Salt and freshly ground pepper

TOMATO AND HORSERADISH SAUCE

1 cup chili sauce
2 Tablespoons prepared horseradish
2 Tablespoons lemon juice
2 Tablespoons finely chopped celery

Variation:
1 cup tomato ketchup
¼ cup red wine vinegar
2 Tablespoons prepared horseradish
2 pressed garlic cloves

Variation:
1 cup chili sauce
1 Tablespoon minced onion
¼ cup lemon juice
¼ cup finely chopped celery
1 Tablespoon prepared horseradish
2 Tablespoons tarragon vinegar
Salt
Tabasco

Variation:
1 cup chili sauce
¼ cup prepared horseradish
2 Tablespoons brandy
1 teaspoon Worcestershire sauce

TOMATO AND MAYONNAISE SAUCE

½ cup mayonnaise
½ cup chili sauce
2 finely chopped hard-boiled eggs
2 teaspoons chopped chives
2 Tablespoons finely chopped green or red sweet pepper
2 Tablespoons finely chopped celery
2 teaspoons finely chopped pimiento
2 teaspoons Dijon mustard
2 teaspoons Worcestershire sauce
Salt and freshly ground pepper

Variation:
¾ cup mayonnaise
¼ cup sour cream
2 Tablespoons chili sauce
2 teaspoons lemon juice
2 teaspoons Worcestershire sauce
Paprika

Variation:
1 cup mayonnaise
2 teaspoons tomato paste
½ teaspoon anchovy paste
1 Tablespoon chopped fresh tarragon
2 Tablespoons Cognac
2 Tablespoons minced parsley

SOUR CREAM DILL SAUCE

½ cup sour cream
½ cup mayonnaise
1 Tablespoon chopped fresh dill weed

¼ cup finely chopped dill pickle
1 teaspoon finely chopped parsley

SOUR CREAM SPINACH SAUCE

1 cup finely chopped uncooked spinach
1 teaspoon finely chopped parsley
1 teaspoon finely chopped chives

1 teaspoon tarragon vinegar
½ cup sour cream
Salt and freshly ground pepper
Cayenne pepper

WHIPPED CREAM SAUCE

½ cup whipped cream
½ cup mayonnaise
1 Tablespoon tarragon vinegar
¼ cup chili sauce

1 teaspoon confectioners' sugar
1 teaspoon dry mustard
¼ cup finely chopped parsley

RÉMOULADE SAUCE

1½ cups mayonnaise
2 Tablespoons Dijon mustard
1 teaspoon anchovy paste
¼ cup chopped cornichons

1 Tablespoon capers
¼ cup minced fresh parsley
¼ cup minced fresh chervil

RÉMOULADE SAUCE NEW ORLEANS

¼ cup olive oil
½ cup Creole or Pommery mustard
½ cup tomato ketchup
1 Tablespoon white wine vinegar
3 Tablespoons lemon juice
1 teaspoon grated lemon rind
1 teaspoon paprika
2 Tablespoons red horseradish

1 Tablespoon Worcestershire sauce
1 teaspoon Tabasco
½ cup minced celery
2 Tablespoons finely chopped scallions
1 Tablespoon finely chopped parsley
Freshly ground black pepper

Good Beginnings

Although oysters are usually served icy cold on the half shell and as *au naturel* as possible, the following ideas for presenting these versatile shellfish add an innovative footnote to the fine art of using the oyster as a first course.

Oyster Grapefruit Cocktail

12	shucked oysters
1	large grapefruit
2	Tablespoons sweet Sherry

Dressing:

2	Tablespoons lemon juice
1	Tablespoon dry Sherry
	Horseradish or Tabasco

1. Drain the oysters and set aside.
2. Cut the chilled grapefruit in half, loosen the pulp from the peel, cut out the fibrous center, and remove seeds. Pour a tablespoon of sweet Sherry over each half.
3. Place 6 oysters in the center of the grapefruit and spoon the seasoned lemon and Sherry dressing over the top.
4. Serve chilled with cheese straws or canapés.

Serves 2

Oysters Borchardt

Serve this simple but utterly sensational cocktail during the early days of September when the bounty of the summer garden overflows with vine ripened tomatoes and when oysters, forgotten during the heat of the summer months, become very appealing, especially with caviar.

24	shucked small oysters
1	extra large tomato, or
	4 medium tomatoes
2	ounces American black caviar

Dressing:

2	Tablespoons olive oil
1½	Tablespoons lemon juice
1	Tablespoon finely chopped chives
1	teaspoon minced shallots
1	teaspoon Dijon mustard
	Salt and freshly ground pepper

1. Drain the oysters and set aside.
2. Peel and slice the tomato into 4 1-inch slices and arrange each slice on a glass plate. If using small tomatoes, cut off their tops, scoop out the seeds and pulp with a melon baller, and set upside down on absorbent paper to drain before arranging on plates.
3. Place 6 oysters on each tomato slice or in the cavities. Drizzle some of the dressing on each and surround with a cordon of caviar.
5. Serve well chilled.

Serves 4

Unblushing Oysters

Perhaps this oyster cocktail could introduce a dinner for two at eight?

12	shucked small oysters	1	avocado
1	small onion	1	Tablespoon lemon juice
½	cup sour cream	2	select leaves Boston lettuce
	Pinch of sugar	2	pimiento pieces
	Freshly cracked pepper		

1. Cut the onion into paper thin slices, mix with sour cream, sugar, and a generous amount of pepper. Add the drained oysters and marinate at least 24 hours before serving.
2. Cut the avocado in half, remove the pit, and peel. Brush surfaces with lemon juice. Arrange each half on a lettuce leaf and fill with the marinated oysters.
3. Cut the pimiento into a heart-shape, place on top of the oysters and serve.

Serves 2

I received a letter from the California Avocado Advisory Board which stated unblushingly, "Since we so fondly think of our avocado as an aphrodisiac, and have such experts as Mae West [sic] explaining its proof positive in this area . . . we certainly do wonder, how do you know it isn't?"

Waverley Root, *Food*

Oyster Spinach Rolls on the Half Shell

Wrapped in cold spinach leaves and teased with the subtle flavor of smoked salmon or mushroom and pimiento, these miniature *rouleaux* are eye-catching appetizers. Either place them on a bed of sour cream or nap them with homemade mustard mayonnaise or a perky hot cheese sauce, and they taste as wonderful as they look. Double the recipe and any one of them makes a luscious luncheon dish.

WITH MUSTARD SAUCE

24 shucked oysters and deep shells	4 slices smoked salmon
12 select spinach leaves	1 cup mustard mayonnaise
	Lemon wedges

1. Drain the oysters. Wash and dry deep shells.
2. Stem and wash the spinach leaves. Drop one leaf at a time in boiling salted water. Lift out immediately and refresh in cold water. Drain and pat dry. Cut each leaf in half along the central vein, discarding the vein.
3. Spread out the leaves, right side down, and arrange an oyster and a piece of salmon at the stem end of each half. Roll up in jelly roll fashion.
4. Place each roll, seam side down, on a shell and spoon mustard mayonnaise over it.
5. Serve with lemon wedges.

Serves 4

WITH MORNAY SAUCE

24 shucked oysters, liquor, and deep shells	*Sauce:*
1 cup dry white wine	$1/4$ cup oyster liquor
24 select spinach leaves	$1/2$ cup chicken stock (See p. 63)
4 large mushroom caps	$1/2$ cup light cream
24 pimiento strips	2 Tablespoons butter
	2 Tablespoons minced green pepper
	2 Tablespoons minced scallion or onion
	$1^{1}/2$ Tablespoons flour
	$1/4$ cup grated Cheddar cheese
	2 Tablespoons chopped pimiento
	Salt and freshly ground pepper
	Cayenne pepper (optional)

1. Remove the oysters from their shells; wash and dry the deep shells. Strain and reserve ¼ cup of the liquor for the sauce.
2. Poach the oysters in wine until they begin to plump, and drain.
3. Stem and wash the spinach leaves. Drop one leaf at a time into boiling salted water. Lift out immediately and refresh in cold water; drain and pat dry.
4. Slice the mushroom caps into 24 pieces.
5. Spread out the leaves, right side down, and arrange an oyster, a slice of mushroom, and a strip of pimiento in the center of each. Fold up the leaf, making a package.
6. Place each spinach package, seam side down, on a shell.
7. Mix the oyster liquor, stock, and light cream, and warm in a small saucepan.
8. Melt the butter in another saucepan and sauté the pepper and scallion until tender. Stir in the flour and cook until bubbling. Remove from the heat and whisk in the stock mixture. Return to heat and boil, stirring constantly, until the sauce thickens. Simmer at least 3 minutes.
9. Remove from the stove and whisk in the cheese, stirring until it has melted. Add the pimiento and seasoning to taste.
10. Spoon the hot sauce over the oysters and serve immediately.

Serves 6

WITH GOLDEN CAVIAR

24 shucked oysters and deep shells	*Vinaigrette sauce:*
12 select spinach leaves	1 Tablespoon finely chopped capers
8 ounces sour cream	1 Tablespoon finely chopped shallots
8 ounces golden caviar	3 Tablespoons red wine vinegar
Lemon wedges	⅓ cup olive oil
	⅓ cup vegetable oil
	Freshly ground pepper to taste

1. Remove oysters from their shells and drain. Scrub and dry the deep shells.
2. Marinate the oysters in vinaigrette for at least 30 minutes.
3. Wash spinach leaves. Drop one leaf at a time in boiling salted water. Lift out immediately and refresh in cold water. Drain and pat dry. Cut each leaf in half along the central vein, discarding the vein.
4. Spread out the leaves, right side down, and arrange an oyster at the stem end of each piece. Sprinkle with pepper and roll up in jelly roll fashion.
5. Line each shell with sour cream, add the spinach roll, seam side down, and season with a little of the vinaigrette sauce. Spoon a dollop of sour cream over each one and garnish with a generous topping of golden caviar. Serve with lemon wedges.

Serves 4

Oysters Flambé

Flambéed in a brandy snifter, an oyster cocktail rivals Broadway in show biz appeal. Serve *après théâtre* with an elegant omelet and take a bow.

24	shucked small oysters
	Salt and freshly cracked
	  pepper
	Slivered fresh ginger root
	  (optional)
		4	Tablespoons Cognac or light
			  rum
			Lime wedges

1. Drain oysters and pat dry. Sprinkle lightly with salt and pepper.
2. Arrange the oysters in brandy glasses or seafood serving glasses set on crushed ice. Sprinkle oysters with a few slivers of ginger root if desired. Keep well chilled before serving.
3. Heat the Cognac or rum. Quickly pour 1 tablespoon over the oysters and ignite. Serve with lime wedges.

Serves 4

My last meal would be cooked at home in the company of a friend or two with whom I like to cook, and we would start with French Chablis and Cotuit oysters, accompanied with very thinly sliced homemade rye bread, lightly buttered.

Julia Child, "Dinner to End All Dinners,"
Food and Wine, January, 1983

"A loaf of bread," the Walrus said,
  "Is what we chiefly need:
Pepper and vinegar besides
  Are very good indeed —
Now, if you're ready, Oysters dear,
  We can begin to feed."

Lewis Carroll, *Through the Looking Glass*

Oysters on the Half Shell (Page 16)

Oysters on the Half Shell with Four Sauces (*Pages 16-19*)

You can make a whole lunch of oysters if you eat them the way
they do in Bordeaux. Buy a dozen oysters. Fry some link sausages.
Take a bite of burning hot sausage, then soothe your mouth with
a cool oyster. Twelve times . . . .

Dr. Edouard de Pomiane, *French Cooking in Ten Minutes or
Adapting to the Rhythm of Modern Life,* 1930

Oysters and Sausages

The complementary "team up" of hot spicy sausages with ice-cold oysters is
especially worth the effort because it "kicks off" a beach party or a tailgate bash
with every assurance of success. Keep the oysters packed in ice until the sausages
are spitting on the grill. Then shuck the oysters and let the guests decide the
order for themselves — oyster-sausage, or sausage-oyster. Be sure to have an
ample supply of both.

36 freshly shucked oysters
Mignonette Sauce with Wine
(see p. 17)

28 sausages:
5 pounds lean pork butt or
shoulder
2 teaspoons salt
1 teaspoon white pepper
1½ teaspoons brown sugar

½ teaspoon freshly grated
nutmeg
½ teaspoon powdered ginger
¼ teaspoon dried sage
1 egg
¼ cup rum
10 feet sausage casing

1. Cut the pork into 1-inch cubes, be sure it is well-chilled, and coarse-grind in
a food processor fitted with the steel blade.
2. Mix in all the seasonings, egg, and rum.
3. Using a sausage stuffer, fill the casing, making each sausage about 4 inches
long. Twist and tie.
4. Cover and parboil the sausages for 5 minutes; sauté in butter or grill over
wood charcoal, turning frequently, until they are crisp outside and juicy
within.
5. Shuck and serve the oysters on ice with sauce on the side. Serve the
sausages on a hot platter or directly from the grill.

Serves 6

HOT APPETIZERS

Oysters Florentine

(OYSTERS ROCKEFELLER)

Perhaps no other oyster appetizer has become as legendary as Oysters à la Rockefeller nor subject to as much conjecture and duplication. Based on a recipe for Snails Bourguignon, the sauce was adapted to oysters by a number of enterprising New Orleans chefs and restaurateurs more than a century ago because oysters were less expensive and more readily available than snails.

Over the years, Jules Alciatore, the founder of the original Antoine's, and his successors have disclosed some of the "eighteen" ingredients—chopped celery, minced shallots, fresh chervil and tarragon, crumbs of dry bread, Tabasco, and Herbsaint, a cordial made of Southern herbs including anise—but the family-owned restaurant has consistently kept other ingredients "unknown." Whether the green color of the sauce is achieved by a combination of parsley, chervil, watercress, chives, tarragon, or, perhaps, by spinach will always be a "house secret."

Even today, the famous first course recipe remains somewhat elusive and, as usual in matters relating to personal taste, the various ingredients of the recipe are dictated by preference. But the special affinity that oysters and spinach have for each other is a given in oyster cookery. And many of the recipes called Oysters Rockefeller would more accurately be named Oysters Florentine because spinach has become the main ingredient in the sauce.

The following recipes represent the major adaptations of the appetizer that has become synonymous with affluence. Whether bread crumbs or melted cheese is preferred or whether the oyster is bedded on a spoonful of creamed spinach and then napped with a glorious Béchamel or Mornay sauce, a dash of Pernod will most certainly heighten the flavor. And a fluted glass of fine Champagne will raise the level of this first course to a celestial feast.

OYSTERS FLORENTINE PARMIGIANA

While in appearance this recipe seems to be a straightforward mixture of spinach butter melted over freshly shucked oysters, the blended flavors of Pernod, anchovies, and Parmesan cheese add a dash and daring that make it memorable.

24	shucked oysters, liquor, and deep shells	1½	teaspoons Worcestershire sauce
1	pound fresh spinach, or 1 10-ounce package frozen spinach	½	cup fresh bread crumbs Salt and freshly ground pepper
8	Tablespoons butter		Tabasco
½	cup chopped parsley	1	cup freshly grated Parmesan cheese
2	chopped anchovy fillets		
1	Tablespoon Pernod		

Oven Temperature: 450°

1. Drain the oysters and set them aside in their shells. Strain and reserve the liquor for the spinach mixture.
2. Cook, drain, and chop the spinach.
3. Melt the butter in a saucepan. Stir in the spinach, parsley, and anchovies; gradually add the Pernod, Worcestershire sauce, and bread crumbs.
4. Coarse purée the mixture in a food processor or blender, thinning with oyster liquor if necessary.
5. Season to taste with salt, pepper, and Tabasco.
6. Arrange the oysters in their shells on a baking sheet. Distribute the spinach mixture over the oysters and top with cheese.
7. Bake from 5 to 10 minutes until the cheese is melted and light brown.

Serves 4

OYSTERS FLORENTINE VERDE

A subtle blend of green vegetables and herbs makes this recipe as pleasing to the eye as it is to the palate. The food processor will make light of the work, but chopping the vegetables by hand will add an interesting texture to the taste and appearance of the dish.

24 shucked oysters in deep shells
1/2 cup finely chopped Chinese cabbage
1/4 cup finely chopped shallots
1 1/2 cups chopped fresh spinach
1 cup chopped watercress
1/2 cup finely chopped parsley
2 Tablespoons chopped fresh basil
5 Tablespoons butter

2 finely chopped anchovy fillets or 1 Tablespoon anchovy paste
2 Tablespoons dry white wine
Salt and freshly ground pepper
Cayenne pepper
1 1/2 cups shredded Port Salut or Fontina cheese

Oven Temperature: Medium Broil

1. Wash, drain, and finely chop the vegetables and herbs separately.
2. Melt the butter in a saucepan, and sauté the Chinese cabbage and shallots until tender. Add the spinach, watercress, parsley, and basil. Turn over in the melted butter until the vegetables are wilted but not faded in color. Mix in the anchovies and wine. Season to taste with salt, pepper, and cayenne.
3. Arrange the oysters in their shells on a baking sheet. Distribute the vegetable mixture over the oysters, and top generously with a semi-soft cheese.
4. Broil from 3 to 5 minutes until the cheese is bubbling and golden.

Serves 4

OYSTERS FLORENTINE GRATINATO

The green and white contrast of spinach and sauce makes this a particularly pleasing appetizer for an elegant dinner party. And if desired, the layering of sauce, spinach, oysters, and buttered crumbs also makes it a versatile recipe for individual gratin dishes or even a casserole.

24	shucked oysters, liquor, and deep shells	1	teaspoon sugar
8	Tablespoons butter	3	Tablespoons dry Sherry
1	pound fresh spinach, or 1 10-ounce package frozen spinach		Pinch of mace or nutmeg Salt and freshly ground pepper
1¼	cups cream	1½	cups buttered bread crumbs
3	Tablespoons flour		

Oven Temperature: 450°

1. Remove the oysters from their shells, drain, and set aside in a container. Strain and reserve ¼ cup of liquor for the cream sauce. Dry the shells and arrange them on a baking sheet.
2. Melt the butter in a saucepan.
3. Cook, drain, and chop the spinach in a food processor or blender. Add 4 tablespoons of the melted butter, and salt and pepper to taste.
4. Warm the cream and oyster liquor in a small saucepan.
5. Stir the flour into the remaining melted butter and cook until bubbling. Remove from heat, and whisk in the cream mixture. Return to heat and boil, stirring constantly, until the sauce thickens. Add the sugar, Sherry, and mace, and simmer for 3 minutes.
6. Line each shell with a spoonful of sauce and a layer of spinach. Add an oyster and cover with more sauce. Top with a tablespoon of the buttered crumbs.
7. Bake 5 minutes, or until the topping begins to brown.

Serves 4

OYSTERS FLORENTINE AL FORNO

The addition of bacon to an oyster-spinach appetizer is simply a descent from the sublime to the delicious. Be generous and be amply rewarded.

24	shucked oysters, liquor, and deep shells	8	Tablespoons butter
1	pound fresh spinach, or 1 10-ounce package frozen spinach	½	cup finely chopped scallions
		2	Tablespoons flour
¾	cup heavy cream	2	Tablespoons dry Vermouth
12	slices bacon		Salt and freshly ground pepper Tabasco

Oven Temperature: 450°

1. Drain the oysters and set them aside in their shells. Strain and reserve 1/4 cup of liquor for the cream sauce.
2. Cook, drain, and finely chop the spinach.
3. Warm the oyster liquor and cream in a small saucepan.
4. Quarter the bacon slices and cook in a microwave oven for 1 minute, or fry over low heat until the edges begin to curl. Set aside on absorbent paper.
5. Melt the butter in a saucepan, and sauté the scallions until tender. Stir in the flour and cook until bubbling. Remove from the heat and whisk in the cream mixture. Return to heat and boil, stirring constantly, until the sauce thickens. Simmer at least 3 minutes. Add the spinach and Vermouth.
6. Process the mixture to a smooth consistency in a food processor or blender, and season to taste with salt, pepper, and Tabasco.
7. Arrange the oysters in their shells on a baking sheet. Distribute the creamed spinach mixture over the oysters and cover each one with two pieces of bacon.
8. Bake from 5 to 10 minutes until the bacon is crisp and sizzling.

Serves 4

OYSTERS FLORENTINE FORMAGGIO

A delicate Mornay tops this quietly combined dish of spinach and oysters. A jigger of Kirschwasser or white wine may lend a little razzle-dazzle to the cheese sauce but its addition is strictly a matter of personal taste.

24	shucked oysters, liquor, and deep shells	1	cup heavy cream
8	Tablespoons butter	2	Tablespoons flour
1	pound fresh spinach, or 1 10-ounce package frozen spinach	2	egg yolks
	Salt and freshly ground pepper	1/4	cup freshly grated Gruyère, or 2 Tablespoons Gruyère and 2 Tablespoons Parmesan cheese
			Pinch of nutmeg

Oven Temperature: Medium Broil

1. Remove the oysters from their shells, drain, and set aside in a container. Strain and reserve 1/4 cup of liquor for the cheese sauce. Dry the shells and arrange them on a baking sheet.
2. Melt the butter in a saucepan.
3. Cook, drain, and chop the spinach in a food processor or blender. Add 4 tablespoons of melted butter and salt and pepper to taste.
4. Warm the oyster liquor and 3/4 cup of cream in a small saucepan.
5. Stir the flour into the remaining melted butter and cook until bubbling. Remove from heat and whisk in the warm cream mixture. Return to heat and boil, stirring constantly, until the sauce thickens. Simmer at least 3 minutes.

6. Whisk egg yolks and remaining ¼ cup of cream in a bowl. Whisk in ½ cup of the hot sauce, a spoonful at a time. Then slowly beat in the remaining sauce. Transfer the enriched sauce to the saucepan. Place over moderate heat and, stirring carefully, simmer for 3 or 4 more minutes.
7. Remove from heat and whisk in the cheese until it has melted. Add the nutmeg and salt and pepper to taste.
8. Make a bed of spinach on each shell. Cover it with an oyster and spoon cheese sauce over the top.
9. Broil from 3 to 5 minutes until the cheese is glazed and golden.

Serves 4

Oysters Bienville

Whether designated to sing the praises of legendary patriots and citizens, famous chefs, or prominent patrons, the dishes that have made New Orleans the haunt of epicureans remain the "original" oyster appetizers, possibly never improved upon, but always subjected to countless imitations.

Named in honor of the Frenchman who founded the "crescent city" in 1718, Oysters Bienville have not escaped the epigone's fancy. So, it is not surprising that the sauce associated with this well-known dish has come to include crabmeat and shrimp, bacon and mushrooms, and even Champagne as an added fillip instead of the usual white wine of the original recipe.

Giving away nothing to Rockefellers and Roffignacs in piquancy, this first course is a favorite of all those who love seafood and are willing to take the time and effort to present it with a bit of improvisation.

24 shucked oysters, liquor, and deep shells	½ cup light cream
¾ cup chicken or fish stock (See p. 63, 62)	1 cup chopped cooked shrimp and/or back fin crabmeat
4 Tablespoons butter	3 Tablespoons dry Sherry
¼ cup finely chopped mushrooms	Salt and freshly ground pepper
¼ cup finely chopped shallots	Cayenne pepper
2 Tablespoons flour	1 cup buttered bread crumbs (optional)
2 egg yolks	Paprika (optional)

Oven Temperature: 450°

1. Drain the oysters and set them aside in their shells. Strain and reserve ¼ cup of the liquor. Add it to the stock and heat in a small saucepan.
2. Melt the butter in another saucepan and sauté the mushrooms and shallots until tender. Stir in the flour and cook until bubbling. Remove from heat

and whisk in the stock mixture. Return to heat and boil, stirring constantly, until the sauce thickens. Simmer at least 3 minutes.

3. Whisk egg yolks and cream in a bowl. Whisk in ½ cup of the hot sauce, a spoonful at a time. Then slowly beat in the remaining sauce. Transfer the enriched sauce to the saucepan. Place over moderate heat and, stirring carefully, bring to a simmer.
4. Add the shrimp, crabmeat, and Sherry. Season to taste.
5. Arrange the oysters in their shells on a baking sheet. Distribute the seafood mixture over the oysters and top with buttered crumbs and paprika if desired.
6. Bake from 5 to 10 minutes until the sauce is bubbling and the bread crumbs are lightly browned.

Serves 4

OYSTERS IMPERIAL

The generous use of cream and Cognac in this sauce elevates it to the category that French gastronomes usually reserve for caviar, *foie gras* and *saumon fumé* — *hors d'oeuvre riches*. It's quite special.

24 shucked oysters, liquor, and deep shells
¾ cup heavy cream
2 Tablespoons butter
1½ Tablespoons flour
¾ cup finely chopped cooked shrimp
½ cup finely chopped cooked crabmeat

2 Tablespoons Cognac
½ teaspoon Worcestershire sauce
Salt and freshly ground pepper
Tabasco
1 cup buttered bread crumbs

Oven Temperature: 450°

1. Remove the oysters from their shells, drain, and set aside in a container. Strain and reserve ¼ cup of liquor for the cream sauce. Dry the shells and arrange them on a baking sheet.
2. Warm the oyster liquor and cream in a small saucepan. (If a richer sauce is desired, use 1 cup of cream and omit oyster liquor.)
3. Melt the butter in another saucepan. Stir in the flour and cook until bubbling. Remove from heat and whisk in the cream mixture. Return to heat and boil, stirring constantly, until the sauce thickens. Simmer at least 3 minutes.
4. Add the shrimp and crabmeat, and stir in Cognac, Worcestershire sauce, salt, pepper and Tabasco to taste.
5. Spoon some of the sauce into each shell. Add an oyster and cover with the remaining sauce. Top with buttered bread crumbs.
6. Bake from 5 to 10 minutes or until the bread crumbs are a golden brown.

Serves 4

OYSTERS AU VIN DE CHAMPAGNE

Lighter in texture than the other Bienville recipes, the subtle combination of Champagne and crabmeat makes this a wonderful first course before a grilled rack of lamb or Entrecôte au Roquefort.

24	shucked oysters, liquor, and deep shells		Salt and freshly ground pepper
1	cup Champagne	1	cup flaked back fin cooked crabmeat
2	Tablespoons finely chopped shallots	2	Tablespoons lemon juice
1	cup heavy cream		

Oven Temperature: 425°

1. Remove the oysters from their shells, reserving the liquor. Scrub and dry the shells, and place them on a baking sheet. Pat the oysters dry and set them aside.
2. Boil the Champagne and shallots in a saucepan until the liquid is reduced by half.
3. Strain and add the oyster liquor, and reduce by half.
4. Add the cream, reduce again, and season to taste. There should be about 2 cups of sauce.
5. Stir a little of the sauce into the crabmeat and distribute the mixture on the shells. Place an oyster on each shell and sprinkle with lemon juice.
6. Bake for about 2 minutes until the oysters are heated, nap with the hot sauce and serve immediately.

Serves 4

OYSTERS BIENVILLE AUX ÉCRIVISSES

Not exactly plebeian fare, but definitely zestier than the other seafood sauces, this appetizer can also double as a luncheon treat when served with a simple tossed salad and a glass of chilled white wine.

24	shucked oysters, liquor, and deep shells	2	Tablespoons flour
4	Tablespoons dry white wine	1	cup chopped cooked crayfish, shrimp, and/or crabmeat
3/4	cup light cream	2	Tablespoons chopped parsley
2	slices bacon		Salt and freshly ground pepper
2	Tablespoons butter		
1/2	cup chopped mushrooms	1	Tablespoon lemon juice (optional)
1	minced garlic clove		
1/4	cup chopped onion		

Oven Temperature: 450°

1. Drain the oysters and set them aside in their shells. Strain and reserve ¼ cup of the liquor for the sauce.
2. Warm the oyster liquor, wine, and cream in a small saucepan.
3. Cut the bacon into very small pieces, and cook in a microwave oven or fry until brown. Drain the bacon bits, reserving 1 tablespoon of fat.
4. Melt the butter in a saucepan with the bacon fat, and sauté the mushrooms, garlic, and onions until tender. Stir in the flour and cook until bubbling. Remove from heat and whisk in the warm liquids. Return to heat and boil, stirring constantly, until the sauce thickens. Simmer at least 3 minutes.
5. Add the bacon, crayfish, shrimp, and/or crabmeat, parsley, and adjust the seasoning, using a bit of lemon juice if desired.
6. Arrange the shells on a baking sheet and distribute the sauce over the oysters.
7. Bake from 5 to 10 minutes until the sauce is bubbling.

Serves 4

Oyster dear to the gourmet, beneficent Oyster, exciting rather than sating, all stomachs digest you, all stomachs bless you!
Seneca

Oysters Roffignac

Whether Oysters Roffignac properly honors an early 19th century mayor of New Orleans or is simply one of the most distinctive oyster recipes on the menu of the illustrious Roffignac restaurant matters very little. What is important about this appetizer is the introduction of red wine into the seafood and oyster sauce.

The dark color of the dish before it is baked may be somewhat disconcerting but, when it mellows in the oven, the result appeals to both the eye and the palate.

24 shucked oysters, liquor, and deep shells	1 finely chopped garlic clove
½ cup fish or chicken stock (See pp. 62, 63)	2 Tablespoons flour
¼ cup dry red wine	1 cup chopped cooked shrimp
8 Tablespoons butter	Salt and freshly ground pepper
½ cup finely chopped mushrooms	Cayenne pepper
½ cup finely chopped onions or scallions	Paprika

(Oysters Roffignac, continued)

Oven Temperature: 450°

1. Drain the oysters and set them aside in their shells. Strain ¼ cup of the oyster liquor, mix with the stock and wine, and heat in a small saucepan.
2. Melt the butter in another saucepan, and sauté the mushrooms, onions, and garlic until tender. Stir in the flour and cook until bubbling. Remove from heat and whisk in the warm liquids. Return to heat and boil, stirring constantly, until the sauce thickens. Simmer at least 3 minutes.
3. Add the shrimp and season to taste with salt, pepper, cayenne, and paprika.
4. Arrange the shells on a baking sheet and spoon the sauce over the oysters.
5. Bake from 5 to 10 minutes until the sauce has heated through and mellowed in color.

Serves 4

Who can believe with common sense,
A Bacon Slice gives God offense?
Jonathan Swift

Chart House Oysters

From the shores of Chesapeake Bay, where lump crabmeat is a birthright, comes a recipe that proves once again that serendipity is sometimes just around the corner.

24	shucked oysters in deep shells	1	cup flaked crabmeat
8	ounces cream cheese	4	Tablespoons minced shallots
4	Tablespoons mayonnaise		Tabasco
3	Tablespoons dry Sherry		Paprika (optional)
1	Tablespoon dry mustard		

Oven Temperature: 450°

1. Cream the cheese, mayonnaise, Sherry and mustard together. Combine thoroughly with the crabmeat, shallots, and a dash of Tabasco.
2. Arrange the oysters in their shells on a baking sheet. Distribute the crabmeat and cheese mixture over the oysters. Sprinkle with a bit of paprika if desired.
3. Bake for about 10 minutes until the sauce is bubbling and beginning to brown.

Serves 4

Oysters Casino

With a tip of the hat to a classic clam recipe, the combination of bacon, onions, sweet red and/or green peppers doubles as a delectable oyster appetizer. There are many variations: if it suits, top with buttered bread crumbs, Mozzarella, Parmesan, or Roquefort cheese, or tease with a jigger of Sherry or Vermouth, and garnish with lemon and parsley.* Because overheating tends to toughen oysters, bake quickly.

24	shucked oysters in deep shells	2	Tablespoons dry Sherry
12	slices bacon		Tabasco (optional)
4	Tablespoons butter		Buttered bread crumbs
¼	cup finely chopped shallots, or scallions		(optional)
¼	cup finely chopped green pepper		Freshly grated cheese (optional)
¼	cup finely chopped red pepper, or pimiento		

Oven Temperature: 450°

1. Cut the bacon slices into eighths and cook in a microwave oven for 1 minute, or fry over low heat until golden and the edges begin to curl. Remove with a slotted spoon and drain.
2. Heat 2 tablespoons of the bacon fat and the butter in a skillet. Sauté shallots, green and red pepper until tender. Stir in Sherry and season with Tabasco if desired.
3. Arrange the oysters in their shells on a baking sheet. Distribute the butter and vegetable sauce over the oysters. Top with crumbs or cheese, and bits of bacon.
4. Bake from 5 to 10 minutes until the bacon is crisp.

   * Oysters Kirkpatrick are made with tomato ketchup added to the bacon, peppers, and cheese mixture, and are named in honor of a former manager of the Palace Hotel in San Francisco.

Serves 4

Oysters 1826

Whether Daniel Webster savored Union Oyster House oysters this way or simply swooshed down a dozen or two of the famous bivalves with a tumbler of brandy and water, will never really be known. But this adaptation of the restaurant's special oysters perpetuates the fame of the oldest restaurant in continuous service in America.

24 shucked oysters, liquor, and
    deep shells
 6 slices bacon
 4 Tablespoons butter
 2 Tablespoons finely chopped
    sweet green and red
    peppers
  ¼ cup finely chopped onion

½ cup finely chopped
    mushrooms
½ cup crumbled potato chips
½ cup fresh bread crumbs
  Salt and freshly ground
    pepper
  Lemon wedges

Oven Temperature: Medium Broil

1. Drain the oysters and set them aside in their shells. Strain and reserve ¼ cup of the liquor.
2. Cut the bacon into small pieces and cook in a microwave oven for 1 minute or fry over low heat until golden. Drain, and set aside.
3. Melt the butter in a saucepan and sauté the peppers, onion, and mushrooms until tender. Add the oyster liquor, and bring to a boil. Stir in the potato chips and enough bread crumbs to absorb the liquid. The mixture should be the consistency of a stuffing. Add the bacon pieces and correct the seasoning.
4. Arrange the oysters in their shells on a baking sheet. Distribute the bacon and crumb mixture over the oysters.
5. Broil until a light crust forms over the topping.
6. Serve immediately with lemon wedges.

Serves 4

Oysters Forestière

A creamed mushroom sauce over oysters is a natural melding of two distinct but quite compatible flavors. And while the color of the sauce may be somewhat drab, the buttered bread crumb and parsley topping does wonders for this recipe.

24 shucked oysters, liquor, and
    deep shells
  ¾ cup light cream
 4 Tablespoons butter
  ¼ cup finely chopped shallots
 1 cup chopped mushrooms
 1 Tablespoon flour
 2 teaspoons Dijon mustard
 1 teaspoon Worcestershire sauce

2 egg yolks
  Salt and freshly ground
    pepper
  Tabasco
1 cup buttered bread crumbs
2 Tablespoons finely chopped
    parsley

Oven Temperature: 450°

1. Drain the oysters and set them aside in their shells. Strain and reserve ¼ cup of liquor.
2. Warm the cream in a small saucepan.
3. Melt the butter in another saucepan and sauté the shallots and mushrooms until tender. Stir in the flour and cook until bubbling. Remove from heat and whisk in the warm cream. Return to heat and boil, stirring constantly, until the sauce thickens. Simmer at least 3 minutes. Add the mustard and Worcestershire sauce.
4. Whisk egg yolk and oyster liquor in a bowl. Whisk in ½ cup of the hot sauce, a spoonful at a time. Then slowly beat in the remaining sauce. Add Tabasco and season to taste. Transfer the enriched sauce to the saucepan, and stirring carefully, bring to a simmer over moderate heat.
5. Arrange the oysters in their shells on a baking sheet. Distribute the creamed mushroom sauce over the oysters. Top with a mixture of buttered crumbs and parsley.
6. Bake for at least 5 minutes until the bread crumbs begin to brown.

Serves 4

Oysters aux Choux Brocolis

Like spinach, broccoli just works with oysters. Add to the blend a dash of curry powder, and this is a taste treat, or substitute the flavor of garlic for curry and this appetizer will definitely fly another flag.

24	shucked oysters, liquor, and deep shells	1	Tablespoon butter
½	pound fresh broccoli, or 1 10-ounce package frozen broccoli	1	Tablespoon flour
¾	cup light cream	¼	teaspoon curry powder
			Salt and freshly ground pepper
			Paprika

Oven Temperature: 450°

1. Drain the oysters and set them aside in a container. Strain and reserve ¼ cup of liquor for the cream sauce. Dry the shells and arrange them on a baking sheet.
2. Cook, drain, and coarse chop the broccoli in a food processor or blender, and set aside.
3. Warm the oyster liquor and cream in a small saucepan.
4. Melt the butter in another saucepan. Stir in the flour and curry powder and cook until bubbling. Remove from heat and whisk in the cream mixture.

Return to heat and boil, stirring constantly, until the sauce thickens. Simmer at least 3 minutes. Add the broccoli, salt and pepper to taste.

5. Spoon some of the broccoli sauce on each shell. Cover it with an oyster and distribute the remaining sauce over the oysters. Sprinkle with paprika.
6. Bake from 5 to 7 minutes until the sauce is hot and bubbling.

Serves 4

Oysters aux Pommes

An ''R'' month of briny well-chilled oysters and a ''just-picked'' bushel of apples make this a tempting late October appetizer. Build a roaring fire in the fireplace, spice up the air with the aroma of hot cider, and a weekend at the seashore is a bit of Eden.

24 shucked oysters and deep shells	¼ cup finely chopped celery
1 cup fresh bread crumbs	1 Tablespoon finely chopped summer savory, or a pinch
3 crisp tart apples	of dried savory
6 Tablespoons butter	Soy sauce
¼ cup finely chopped onion	

Oven Temperature: 400°

1. Drain the oysters and quarter if small, or cut into eighths if large in size. Put the oysters in a bowl and stir in enough bread crumbs to bind. Scrub and dry the shells.
2. Peel, core, and coarsely chop the apples.
3. Melt the butter in a saucepan and lightly sauté the apples, onion, and celery. Remove from heat and stir in the oyster and bread crumb mixture. Season to taste with savory and soy sauce.
4. Arrange the shells on a baking sheet and mound enough of the mixture in each shell to fill it.
5. Bake for about 10 minutes or until the mixture begins to brown around the edge of the shell.

Serves 4

Oysters Marinara

If first impressions are lasting ones, this colorful melding of tomato sauce, Cognac, and oysters will introduce the simplest grilled entrée with spirit. And it's so easy to do because most cooks worthy of their gardens have a supply of homemade tomato sauce tucked away in a freezer . . . just waiting.

24	shucked oysters and deep shells	¼	cup Cognac
6	Tablespoons butter	3	Tablespoons chopped parsley
1	finely chopped garlic clove	1	teaspoon paprika
1	cup thick tomato sauce		Salt and freshly ground pepper

Oven Temperature: 450°

1. Drain the oysters and cut in halves if small and quarters if large. Set aside. Scrub and dry the shells.
2. Melt 2 tablespoons of butter in a saucepan and sauté the garlic until it is tender. Stir in the tomato sauce (if it is too thin, add a spoonful of concentrated tomato paste), Cognac, parsley, paprika and cook about 2 minutes. Remove from heat and add oysters. Season to taste.
3. Arrange the shells on a baking sheet and spoon the tomato oyster sauce into each shell. Dot with the remaining butter.
4. Bake for about 5 minutes until the sauce is hot and bubbling.

Serves 4

Gingered Oysters

Often called a spice lover's spice, ginger adds a zing to any recipe. Try it imaginatively combined with *crème fraîche* and saffron in an oyster sauce, and the result is nothing short of gourmet.

24	shucked oysters and deep shells	2	cups chicken stock (See p. 63)
6	ounces fresh ginger root		Freshly ground white pepper
1	teaspoon saffron	2	cups *crème fraîche*

Oven Temperature: 350°

1. Remove the oysters from their shells, drain, and set aside. Scrub and dry the shells and arrange them on a baking sheet.
2. Peel and finely grate the ginger root. Wrap the pulp in a double thickness of cheese cloth, squeeze the juice into a bowl, and discard the pulp. There

should be about 3 tablespoons of juice. Add the saffron and allow to mellow for at least an hour.

3. Reduce the chicken stock to ½ cup; add the ginger mixture and season with pepper to taste.
4. Reduce the *crème fraîche* to 1 cup. Remove from the heat and stir in the stock mixture.
5. Spoon a little sauce into each shell, add an oyster, and divide the remaining sauce over the top.
6. Cover loosely with a sheet of heavy gauge foil, and bake about 15 minutes until the sauce is bubbling.

Serves 4

Oysters à l'Ail

The tempting Oysters à l'Ail is an adaptation of a classic French recipe for *Escargots de Bourgogne*. Serve with a fine Chablis, a loaf of crusty bread to catch up the extra melted butter, and receive a standing ovation.

    Any of the other "compound butter" variations that are made with a different combination of herbs and spices create an easy but palate provoking sauce . . . and a practical one. Keep in the refrigerator or freezer and simply use whenever needed.

24	shucked oysters and deep shells	¼	cup blanched almonds
8	sprigs parsley	½	pound butter
½	bunch watercress	1	Tablespoon Pernod
3	shallots	3	drops Tabasco
8	garlic cloves	2	Tablespoons lemon juice
4	anchovy fillets		Freshly ground pepper

Oven Temperature: 450°

1. Drain the oysters and set aside. Wash and dry the shells and arrange on a baking sheet.
2. Wash and remove the stems from the parsley and watercress. Drain and blot dry. Peel the shallots and garlic cloves.
3. Place the parsley, watercress, shallots, garlic, anchovies, and almonds in the work bowl of a food processor and chop with the steel blade for about 2 or 3 seconds.*
4. Cut the butter into eight pieces and add a piece at a time until the mixture is smooth.
5. Add the Pernod, Tabasco, lemon juice, and a pinch of pepper, process for a second more and correct seasoning.

Oysters Florentine Verde *(Page 27)*

Oysters Florentine Gratinato *(Page 28)*

Oysters Florentine al Forno *(Page 28)*

Oysters Bienville *(Page 30)*

Potage Crème d'Huîtres (Page 65)

6. Spoon some of the butter mixture into the shells, cover with an oyster, and top with more of the butter mixture.
7. Bake for about 5 minutes until the sauce begins to bubble around the edge of the shell.

* If a coarser texture is preferred, ingredients may be minced with a knife. At Steps 4 and 5, blend everything together with a fork.

Serves 4

COMPOUND BUTTER VARIATIONS:

Leek Butter Sauce: Melt 8 tablespoons of butter, add 2 medium sized leeks that have been cut into fine julienne strips and season with a dash of Tabasco. Spoon over the oysters and bake until the oysters begin to plump.

Scallion Butter Sauce: Add 1 cup of finely chopped scallions including green tops to 1 cup of *beurre blanc,* and season to taste with freshly ground pepper. Spoon over the oysters and bake until the oysters begin to plump.

Fines Herbes Butter Sauce: Combine 3 tablespoons of each of the following herbs that have been finely chopped in a processor—chives, shallots, parsley, and fresh tarragon. Add 8 tablespoons of butter, a dash of lemon juice, salt and pepper to taste and spoon over the oysters. Bake until the sauce begins to bubble around the edge of the shell.

Stuffed Oysters

To the traditionalist who believes that Thanksgiving and turkey with oyster stuffing are authentic Americana, the following recipe will raise eyebrows and pose questions, but Stuffed Oysters are a feast for all seasons and a token to those who like their oysters disguised a bit.

24	shucked oysters and deep shells	1/2	cup finely chopped parsley†
8	Tablespoons butter	1	cup fresh bread crumbs
1	Tablespoon flour	1	egg
1/2	cup finely chopped shallots		Salt and freshly ground pepper
1/2	cup finely chopped celery		Cayenne pepper
2	Tablespoons dry Vermouth*		

* If preferred, substitute Scotch whiskey or Cognac.

† For a stronger herb flavor, add 1/2 teaspoon minced fresh sage and a generous pinch of minced fresh thyme.

Oven Temperature: 375°

1. Remove the oysters from their shells, drain and coarsely chop them. Scrub and dry the shells and arrange them on a baking sheet.
2. Melt the butter in a saucepan, stir in the flour, and cook the shallots and celery until tender. Remove from the heat and stir in the Vermouth.
3. Combine the parsley and bread crumbs and add enough of this mixture to the vegetables to make a moist stuffing.
4. Beat the egg and stir it into the stuffing with a fork. Add the oysters and seasonings.
5. Distribute the stuffing in the shells.
6. Bake for about 12 minutes until a light crust forms and the stuffing is thoroughly heated. Garnish with parsley sprigs if desired.

Serves 4

Stuffed Oysters Italiènne

The Romans went to Brittany and then on to England to satisfy their taste for oysters. And to this day, their descendants have cultivated the fine art of serving them by accommodating the various herbs and seasonings that distinguish Italian cuisine to oyster cookery. The flavor of fresh basil inspires this recipe. If it is not available, try ¼ teaspoon of oregano and tarragon for an authentic variation.

24 shucked oysters and deep shells	1 Tablespoon finely chopped fresh basil
3 Tablespoons butter	1 cup toasted bread crumbs
3 Tablespoons olive oil	Salt and freshly ground pepper
1 finely chopped garlic clove	Pinch crushed red pepper
¼ cup finely chopped parsley	
¼ cup finely chopped shallots	

Oven Temperature: 375°

1. Drain the oysters and arrange them in their shells on a baking sheet.
2. Melt and cool the butter. Add all of the remaining ingredients and season with salt, pepper, and crushed red pepper to taste.
3. Mound the crumb mixture over each oyster, and cover the pan with heavy gauge aluminum foil.
4. Bake for about 15 minutes and serve immediately with sprigs of parsley for garnish.

Serves 4

Oysters Mahnomonee

This appetizer depends on the rare essentials of Minnesota wild rice and Blue Point* oysters. Serve it on the half shell with the oyster embedded in the rice, or chop the oysters, combine with the rice mixture, and stuff a squab or boneless chicken breast for an elegant entrée.

24 shucked oysters, liquor, and deep shells	¼ cup finely chopped parsley
½ cup wild rice	¼ cup slivered almonds (optional)
2 scallions	Freshly ground pepper
6 Tablespoons butter	¼ cup Sherry
2 cups chicken stock (See p. 63)	1 Tablespoon lemon juice
Salt	Paprika
1 cup coarsely chopped mushrooms	

Oven Temperature: 350°

1. Drain the oysters and set aside. Reserve ¼ cup of the strained oyster liquor. Wash and dry the shells and arrange them on a baking sheet.
2. Wash the rice thoroughly, changing the water several times. Finely chop the white bulbs of the scallions and keep separate from the stems. Cut the stems diagonally into ⅛-inch pieces.
3. Melt 1 tablespoon of the butter in a saucepan. Add the chopped white scallions and sauté until tender. Mix in the rice, stock, and ¼ teaspoon of salt; bring to a boil, stir once, and reduce heat. Cover tightly and simmer for 45 minutes until the rice is tender. Uncover and simmer until the liquid is absorbed.
4. Melt the remaining butter in a skillet; spoon off and reserve 2 tablespoons for the sauce. Sauté the scallion stems and mushrooms until tender. Mix in the parsley, almonds, and wild rice, and season to taste.
5. Spread a thin layer of the rice mixture on each shell. Cover with an oyster and mound with more of the rice. Mix the reserved butter with the oyster liquor, Sherry, and lemon juice, and drizzle the sauce over each shell. Sprinkle with a bit of paprika, and cover loosely with heavy gauge aluminum foil.
6. Bake about 20 minutes until thoroughly heated.

* Or any variety that boasts a plump body in a 3-inch shell.

Serves 6

Angels on Horseback

Better known in Victorian England as an after-dinner "savoury" to clear the palate and prepare it for Port, these bacon-wrapped oysters skewered on a cocktail pick make excellent party fare. An interesting counterpart is Devils on Horseback, prunes stuffed with chutney, wrapped in bacon, skewered, and broiled in similar fashion. Serve both for a drinks hour that's truly Paradise Lost and Paradise Regained.

24	shucked medium-sized oysters	12	slices bacon
1	cup dry white wine	24	buttered toast rounds
1	minced garlic clove		(optional)
	Freshly ground pepper		

Oven Temperature: High Broil

1. Drain the oysters and marinate them in wine, garlic, and pepper for 1 hour.
2. Cut the bacon in half and cook in a microwave oven for about 1 minute or pan fry until its edges begin to curl but it is still flexible. Drain well.
3. Wrap each oyster in bacon and secure with a damp cocktail pick.
4. Place the oysters on a broiler pan and broil on each side until the bacon is brown and crisp.
5. Serve with the cocktail pick, or the pick can be removed and the oyster placed on a buttered toast round.

Serves 8

Galloping Oysters

Galloping rather than just trotting along, this recipe is a sophisticated version of an appetizer the Australians call "Oysters on Horseback." It takes time and a commendable display of dexterity to assemble, but it is well worth the effort.

24	shucked oysters and liquor	1/4	cup vegetable oil
12	whole water chestnuts	2	teaspoons finely chopped
2	Tablespoons sugar		ginger root
1/4	cup cider vinegar	2	chopped dried chilis
1/3	cup rice wine vinegar	12	slices bacon
1/2	cup Sherry		

Oven Temperature: High Broil

1. Drain the oysters and pat dry. Reserve 1/4 cup of the oyster liquor for the marinade.

2. Cut each water chestnut into 4 round slices and marinate them with the oysters overnight in a mixture of the oyster liquor, sugar, vinegar, Sherry, oil, ginger root, and chilis.
3. Cut the bacon slices in half, and partially cook them in a microwave oven or skillet but keep the bacon pliable. Drain on absorbent paper.
4. Place an oyster between 2 slices of water chestnut and wrap with bacon. Secure with damp cocktail picks.
5. Arrange the skewered oysters on a broiler pan and broil on each side until the bacon is crisp and sizzling.

Serves 8

Oysters Argenteuil

Although this recipe can easily be adapted to spinach or broccoli, making it with asparagus is such a total *coup de partie* that the other possibilities may never become realities. The delicate flavor of fresh asparagus is so compatible with the oysters and Muenster cheese that whenever asparagus is available is exactly the right season to serve these simple, do-ahead gobbits.

1 pint oysters	1/3 cup dry bread crumbs
1 pound fresh asparagus, or 1 10-ounce package frozen asparagus	1/2 pound freshly grated Muenster cheese
2 Tablespoons butter	1/2 cup finely chopped parsley
1 finely chopped small onion	1/4 teaspoon oregano
1 garlic clove	Salt and freshly ground pepper
5 eggs	Tabasco

Oven Temperature: 350°

1. Drain and coarsely chop the oysters and set them aside.
2. Trim and peel the asparagus. Split the stalks once or twice lengthwise and cut into 1-inch pieces. Blanch in boiling salted water and drain, reserving some of the liquid.
3. Melt the butter in a skillet and sauté the onion and garlic until tender. Discard the garlic. Stir in about 2 tablespoons of the asparagus liquid.
4. Beat the eggs in a large bowl until they are frothy. Stir in bread crumbs, the butter and onion mixture, asparagus, cheese, and parsley. Add the oysters and oregano. Season to taste with salt, pepper, and Tabasco.
5. Pour into a buttered 9 by 13-inch shallow baking pan and bake for about 45 minutes until the edges begin to brown and a knife tests clean.
6. Cool for about 3 minutes and cut into 1 1/2-inch squares. Serve warm, at room temperature, or chilled, whichever is preferred. The squares may be reheated for about 10 minutes, but oysters are not at their best when baked for too long.

Yield: 48

Stuffed Mushroom Caps

If truffles are not readily available, compensate with this "drop dead elegant" mushroom hors d'oeuvre. It can be served with cocktails or, if the mushroom caps are extra large, three of them are a tasty prelude to, or a vegetable side dish with a chicken Kiev or flamed brochette of beef entrée.

1/2	pint oysters	3	Tablespoons dry Sherry
24	large mushrooms	1/4	teaspoon oregano (optional)
6	Tablespoons butter	1	Tablespoon minced parsley
1	garlic clove		(optional)
1	finely chopped onion		Salt and freshly ground
1 1/2	cups fresh bread crumbs		pepper

Oven Temperature: 400°

1. Drain and coarsely chop the oysters and set them aside.
2. Wash and stem the mushrooms. Dry the caps on absorbent paper and chop the stems.
3. Melt the butter in a skillet. Brush the caps with some of the melted butter and set them aside. Sauté the stems, garlic, and onion, and discard the garlic when the mushrooms and onions are tender. Add the bread crumbs, oysters, Sherry, and either parsley or oregano if desired. Correct the seasoning.
4. Mound each mushroom cap with the stuffing and arrange the caps on a baking sheet.
5. Bake about 5 minutes until the stuffing begins to brown.

Serves 8

Oyster Tartelettes

A platter of these tasty tartelettes is a joy to pass at any party. They certainly can be made in advance and placed into the oven the moment guests arrive or start to enjoy their second drink. The variations are endless, but a bit of smoked salmon or a dash of Parmesan cheese added to the filling would probably extend the curfew for thirty minutes or more.

1	pint oysters		Pinch of mace or nutmeg
4	Tablespoons butter	1/2	teaspoon celery seed
3	hard-boiled egg yolks		Salt and freshly ground
2	Tablespoons chopped chives		pepper
2	Tablespoons minced parsley		Cayenne pepper
1	cup fresh bread crumbs	24	baked 2-inch tartelette shells

Oven Temperature: 350°

1. Drain and coarsely chop the oysters.
2. Melt the butter in a saucepan, add the oysters and cook over low heat until the oysters begin to plump.
3. Remove the pan from the heat and stir in sieved egg yolks, chives, parsley, and enough bread crumbs to bind the mixture. Add mace or nutmeg, celery seed, salt, pepper and cayenne to taste.
4. Spoon the filling into the tartelette shells and arrange them on a baking sheet.
5. Warm thoroughly but do not overbake or brown the edges of the shells too deeply.

Yield: 24

Oyster Beignets

From the bayou comes another palate provoker—deep-fried oyster puffs just waiting to be savored with a dipping sauce of horseradish, sour cream, mayonnaise, and parsley. Serve on a silver tray with a silver porringer of sauce in the center and a special party becomes a spectacular performance.

½ pint oysters	*Sauce:*
1 cup flour	½ cup sour cream
1 teaspoon grated lemon zest	½ cup mayonnaise
6 Tablespoons butter	¼ cup finely chopped parsley
1 cup milk	2 Tablespoons prepared
4 eggs	horseradish
1 Tablespoon chopped chives or scallions	
Oil for deep frying	

1. Drain and coarsely chop the oysters.
2. Combine flour and lemon zest in a small bowl.
3. Cut the butter into small pieces and heat with the milk in a heavy 1½-quart saucepan, stirring until the butter has melted. Remove from heat and add the flour mixture all at once, beating vigorously with a wooden spoon until flour has been incorporated. Return to moderate heat and cook, beating constantly, until mixture forms a mass and begins to film the bottom of the pan.
4. Remove from heat. Add one egg at a time, beating after each addition until the paste is well blended and completely smooth.
5. Fold in oysters and chives or scallions.
6. Drop by teaspoonfuls into hot fat and fry at 375° until golden. Cook a few at a time, draining on absorbent paper. Beignets can be kept hot in a moderate

oven if they are to be served immediately, or they can be made ahead and reheated at serving time.

7.   Skewer on cocktail picks and serve with the dipping sauce.

Yield: 40

Oyster Profiteroles

Here is a nifty version of a French treat, complete with two different fillings that definitely "stand up" to these versatile *pâte à chou* miniatures. Try the zippy horseradish, caper, and vinegar filling to pique a guest's appetite. Or simply use an enriched Béchamel sauce, add Sherry to the cooking liquid, and a jigger or two of Cognac to the sauce, and bring into the eighties a "Recipe of Quality," circa 1912.

1	pint oysters and liquor	2	teaspoons grated lemon zest
1	cup chicken stock (See p. 63)	1	Tablespoon grated horseradish
½	cup cream	2	Tablespoons capers
3	Tablespoons butter		Salt and freshly ground
3	Tablespoons flour		pepper
2	egg yolks		Cayenne pepper
½	Tablespoon white wine vinegar	36	1½-inch puff shells

Oven Temperature: 400°

1.   Drain and coarsely chop the oysters, reserving ¼ cup of liquor.
2.   Warm the chicken stock and cream in a small saucepan.
3.   Melt the butter in another saucepan. Stir in the flour and cook until bubbling. Remove from heat and whisk in the stock mixture. Return to heat and boil, stirring constantly, until the sauce thickens. Simmer at least 3 minutes.
4.   Whisk egg yolks with the oyster liquor and vinegar. Whisk in ½ cup of the hot sauce, a spoonful at a time. Then slowly beat in the remaining sauce. Transfer the enriched sauce to the saucepan over moderate heat and, stirring carefully, bring to a boil.
5.   Stir in the oysters, lemon zest, horseradish, capers, and season to taste with salt, pepper, and cayenne. Cook over low heat, stirring gently, until the mixture starts to bubble. The filling may now be cooled to room temperature, or chilled.
6.   Fill the puffs shortly before serving time. Make a slit, lift off the top, and spoon the filling into the lower section. Replace top.
7.   Heat puffs in the oven for about 5 minutes and serve immediately.

Yield: 36

Oysters Parnassus

Although the Greek chefs of yesteryear served up braised squid and octopus and grilled sea bass and red snapper to perfection, they resolutely spurned the oyster. If they had only thought to wrap it up in phyllo dough and serve it with a glass of ouzo even Zeus would have been impressed and Pegasus would surely have flown a tray of them to the summit of Parnassus.

1½	pints oysters and liquor	3	ounces cream, or Feta cheese
1	cup dry white wine	1	Tablespoon lemon juice
1¼	cups melted butter		Salt and freshly ground
2	Tablespoons chopped shallots		pepper
½	cup finely chopped celery		Tabasco
½	cup finely chopped parsley	1	cup fresh bread crumbs
1	teaspoon chopped fresh dill	12	sheets frozen phyllo dough
2	eggs		

Oven Temperature: 375°

1. Poach oysters in their own liquor and wine until they begin to plump. Drain and chop.
2. Heat 4 tablespoons of the butter in a skillet, sauté shallots and celery until tender, and stir in parsley and dill.
3. Beat the eggs in a bowl and blend in the softened cheese. Stir in the sautéed vegetables, lemon juice, and oysters. Season to taste with salt, pepper, and Tabasco. Add enough bread crumbs to bind the filling.
4. Brush 2 sheets of the phyllo dough with melted butter, and layer them. Cut into 9 strips, 18 inches long and about 2 inches wide. Place a teaspoon of the filling on the bottom edge of the first strip. Fold the strip up, flag fashion, into a triangle. Brush top with butter and place on a baking sheet. Fill and fold the remaining strips, and repeat the process with two more sheets of dough. Turnovers may be chilled or frozen.
5. Bake on a buttered baking sheet 20 to 25 minutes until puffy and golden. If the pastries are frozen, allow extra baking time.

Yield: 48

The only reason for a cocktail party
For a gluttonous old woman like me
Is a really nice tit-bit. I can drink at home.
T. S. Eliot, *The Cocktail Party*

Oysters Scandia

Once these turnovers have been served at a cocktail party, a solitary tin of smoked oysters will never be the same. Keep one in the pantry at all times and experiment with either a sour cream or a cream cheese pastry dough and a dab of mustard before adding an oyster and mixing the martinis.

1	3¾-ounce tin smoked oysters	¼	pound butter
1¼	cups flour	1	egg
2	cups grated sharp Cheddar cheese		

Oven Temperature: 400°

1. Make a dough of the flour, cheese, and butter, and chill.
2. Roll the dough ⅛th-inch thick, and cut into 3-inch rounds.
3. Use half an oyster, cut lengthwise, for each turnover. Place the oyster on the round. Fold over, seal and crimp edges. Brush the top with egg beaten with 1 teaspoon of water.
4. Bake about 15 minutes until golden.

VARIATION:

Fresh oysters may be substituted. Select 30 small oysters. Shuck, drain and pat dry. Roll in 1 cup of flour, preferably corn flour, which has been seasoned with garlic. Proceed with turnovers. In Step 3, use the whole oyster and add a dash of Dijon mustard.

Yield: 30

Tasses d'Huîtres

These marvelous "melt away" bread cups are such an exciting combination of congenial ingredients that serving one will be a tease and offering guests two will be as fatal as an apple in Eden and a lot tastier. Make them with either pumpernickel or white bread and your favorite cheese.

24	shucked oysters	⅓	cup dry white wine
24	slices bread	1	halved garlic clove
¼	cup melted butter		Pinch of nutmeg
6	slices finely chopped bacon	1	cup shredded Cheddar or Gouda cheese
1	cup finely chopped shallots		Paprika
2	Tablespoons chopped chives		
2	Tablespoons chopped parsley		
¼	teaspoon thyme		

Oven Temperature: 350°

1. Drain the oysters and set aside.
2. Remove the crusts and roll bread slices with a rolling pin. Cut out 3-inch rounds and brush one side with melted butter. Press the buttered side down into the cups of a muffin pan, and bake for 5 minutes. Remove from oven.
3. Fry the bacon in a skillet until almost crisp. Remove and drain on absorbent paper. Pour off all but 2 tablespoons of the fat and sauté the shallots, chives, and parsley until wilted. Mix in the bacon and season with thyme.
4. Boil the wine and garlic in a small saucepan and discard the garlic. Remove from heat and whisk in the nutmeg and cheese, stirring until melted.
5. Divide the bacon mixture evenly in the 24 bread cups and add an oyster to each one. Spoon the cheese sauce over the oysters and sprinkle with paprika.
6. Bake about 7 minutes until the cheese is bubbling, taking care that the bottoms of the bread cups do not burn.
7. Carefully remove from the muffin pan and serve immediately.

Serves 8

Pane Imbottito

From the sunny shores of Italy comes a wonderful idea for an original antipasto. Fill a baguette with as many good things as possible and freeze until the right moment. Squisito!

1	3¾-ounce tin smoked oysters		crumbled Gorgonzola or creamed Saga
8	ounces cream cheese		
1	Tablespoon cream	2	ounces prosciutto
8	ounces combined cheese: shredded Fontina or Provolone grated Parmesan or Romano	2	ounces Genoa salami
		1	12-inch baguette or 12-inch piece of French bread

1. Drain and coarsely chop the oysters.
2. Blend the cream cheese, cream, and any combination of the other cheese in a food processor or blender until smooth, or cream with a fork.
3. Cut prosciutto and salami into fine ½-inch slivers and mix with the cheese. Add the oysters.
4. Cut the ends of the loaf, and scoop out the bread using a long, thin-bladed knife or an apple corer. Do not cut through the crust.
5. Stuff the cavity with the cheese mixture. Replace ends of loaf.
6. Wrap in foil and freeze.
7. Before serving, preheat oven to 400° and warm the loaf in its wrapper for 10 minutes. The bread will be crusty but the cheese stuffing will still be cold.
8. Cut into slices and arrange on a platter with a garnish of ripe black olives or cornichons.

Serves 4

Whistling Oyster Dip

The following recipe will summon almost everyone to a cocktail party at full speed. Serve it with chips, crackers, and crudités. Or thicken the consistency by adding more cream cheese and much less sour cream and use it to stuff cherry tomatoes, raw mushroom caps, and marinated artichoke bottoms.

12 shucked large oysters	2 Tablespoons finely chopped shallots
½ cup dry white wine	¼ cup finely chopped parsley
3 ounces soft cream cheese	1 Tablespoon capers
1½ cups sour cream	Tabasco

1. Lightly poach the oysters in wine until they begin to plump. Drain and coarsely chop them.
2. Combine cream cheese and sour cream in the bowl of a food processor or blender, and process for 1 minute. Add the shallots and parsley and process only until they are blended. For a coarser mixture, everything may be blended with a fork.
3. Scrape into a bowl and add oysters, capers, and Tabasco to taste. Cover and refrigerate for at least 4 hours.
4. Serve at room temperature.

Yield: 2 cups

On the south side of Drury Lane Theatre there was a narrow court leading out of Catherine Street and named Vinegar Yard. There, in the first half of the nineteenth century, was an oyster and refreshment room where writers and artists went, to eat and gossip. It came to be known as "The Whistling Oyster," and over the door was a hanging lamp with a big oyster painted on the sides, shown to be whistling a tune.

The shop was first opened by Mr. Pearkes, in 1825. The Daily Telegraph reported that one day in 1840, "the proprietor of the house in question . . . heard a strange and unusual sound proceeding from one of the tubs in which shell-fish lay piled in layers . . .".

Hector Bolitho, *The Glorious Oyster*

OYSTER CANAPÉS

He who plays host without giving his personal care to the repast is unworthy of having friends to invite to it.

Brillat-Savarin, "Aphorism XVIII"

A beautifully decorated tray of canapés is an absolutely sensational way to flatter guests. And these miniature bread cutouts are also an ideal finger food, a bite or two easily eaten while standing with a drink in hand. Preparation may take a little time and a little doing, but it offers endless possibilities for a creative hostess to entertain with panache.

For cold canapés, cut fresh bread into rounds, ovals, fingers, diamonds or whatever shape the event or whimsy dictates. And then layer dibs and dabs galore. Or, if hot canapés are the order of the day, toast the cutouts on one side, turn over, and add a morsel or a glorious spread. Pop it into the broiler and serve.

The following recipes are some of the traditional oyster canapés along with a few that offer a "twist and turn" slightly different from the "tried and true." While the specific name, Oyster Canapé, always properly designates a breaded fried oyster on a toast round that has been spread with a seasoned or herbed butter, the use of raw or smoked oysters in many of these recipes offers the option to serve the canapés either hot or cold.

Dainty slices of bread, square, round, oval or rectangular, usually toasted, nicely garnished and decorated.

Hering's Dictionary of Classical and Modern Cookery

COLD CANAPÉS

Kiss Me Canapé

1	3¾-ounce tin smoked oysters	3½ ounces smoked salmon caviar
30	pumpernickel bread rounds	Parsley
6	ounces sour cream	

1. Spread a thin layer of sour cream over each bread round and cover with caviar.
2. Slice the oysters in half horizontally and place a half, cut side down, on the bread rounds.
3. Garnish with a tiny parsley sprig.

Serves 10

Casino Canapé

½ pint oysters
3 slices finely chopped bacon
2 Tablespoons butter
1 Tablespoon horseradish
4 Tablespoons finely chopped
   celery

2 Tablespoons finely chopped
   pimiento
Mayonnaise
18 pumpernickel bread ovals

1. Drain the oysters and pat dry.
2. Cook bacon in the microwave oven or fry in a skillet until crisp and drain on absorbent paper.
3. Melt the butter in a skillet and lightly sauté the oysters. Drain and chop.
4. Combine the oysters, bacon, horseradish, celery, and pimiento with just enough mayonnaise to make a spreadable mixture.
5. Spread on the bread ovals and serve garnished with a bit of pimiento.

Serves 6

Smoked Oyster Fingers

1 3¾-ounce tin smoked oysters
2 Tablespoons sour cream
8 ounces cream cheese
2 Tablespoons chopped sweet
   onion
2 Tablespoons chopped parsley

1 teaspoon Pommery mustard
½ teaspoon horseradish
Salt and freshly ground
   pepper
36 pumpernickel bread fingers
3 hard-boiled eggs

1. Drain the oysters and purée in a food processor using the steel blade.
2. Add the remaining ingredients and process until smooth.
3. Cover each pumpernickel finger with a generous amount of the spread and garnish with sieved egg yolk or slivers of the egg white.

Serves 12

CANAPÉ VARIATIONS:

Oysters Lucullus: Spread rounds of toast with steak tartare, place a raw oyster in the center of each and garnish with black caviar.

Oysters Lucca: Spread oval slices of white bread with butter, top with caviar, and place a raw oyster in the center. Garnish with a sliver of lemon peel.

Oysters Otero: Spread rounds of white toast with butter, top with caviar, place a raw oyster in the center and brush with Rémoulade sauce (See p. 19)

COLD OR HOT CANAPÉS

Mushroom Oyster * Rounds

½ pint oysters and liquor
¾ cup cream
2 Tablespoons butter
1 cup chopped mushrooms
2 Tablespoons chopped shallots
1½ Tablespoons flour

1 Tablespoon chopped parsley
1 Tablespoon Cognac
Salt and freshly ground
  pepper
30 bread or toast rounds

1. Drain and quarter the oysters. Strain and reserve ¼ cup of the liquor.
2. Warm the oyster liquor and cream in a small saucepan.
3. Heat the butter in a skillet and sauté the mushrooms and shallots until tender. Stir in flour and cook until bubbling. Remove from heat and whisk in the cream mixture. Return to heat and boil, stirring constantly, until the mixture thickens. Simmer for 3 minutes.
4. Stir in the oysters, parsley, Cognac, and salt and pepper to taste. Heat until the mixture starts to bubble.
5. Cool to room temperature and chop in a food processor. The mixture should be thick with a slightly coarse texture, not a smooth paste.
6. Spread on fresh white bread rounds and garnish with thin mushroom slices if serving cold. Spread on toasted bread rounds and heat in the broiler for a minute or two if serving hot.

* This spread makes an original and very tasty pastry liner for Beef Wellington.

Serves 10

Tunny Smoked Oyster Rounds

1 3¾-ounce tin smoked oysters
1 6½-ounce can tuna in oil
3 Tablespoons sour cream
1 teaspoon Dijon mustard
2 chopped garlic cloves
8 Tablespoons unsalted butter

⅓ cup natural pistachios
1 Tablespoon lemon juice
2 Tablespoons chopped fresh
  summer savory, or parsley
  Tabasco
36 bread or toast rounds

1. Drain the oysters and purée with tuna, sour cream, mustard, and garlic in a food processor or blender.
2. Cut butter into small pieces and add gradually to the mixture. Blend thoroughly.
3. Transfer to a mixing bowl and add pistachios, lemon juice, savory or parsley, and Tabasco to taste.

4. Cover and refrigerate for at least 12 hours.
5. Allow to stand at room temperature for 15 minutes before correcting seasonings.
6. Serve on fresh white bread rounds garnished with half a pistachio nut if serving cold. Spread on toasted rounds and heat in the broiler for a minute or two if serving hot.

Serves 12

HOT CANAPÉS

Zesty Oyster Canapés

24	shucked small oysters	1	cup freshly grated Romano cheese
1/2	cup vegetable oil		Corn flake crumbs
1	teaspoon fresh tarragon		
1/2	pressed clove garlic	2	teaspoons lemon juice
1	Tablespoon chopped parsley	24	white bread rounds
8	Tablespoons butter		

Oven Temperature: 425°

1. Combine oil, tarragon, garlic, and parsley in a bowl and set aside for at least 2 hours.
2. Heat 2 tablespoons of butter in a skillet and brown the bread rounds lightly on both sides, adding more butter as needed. Drain the rounds on absorbent paper.
3. Drain oysters and pat dry. Roll the oysters in cheese, dip in the seasoned oil mixture, and roll in crumbs.
4. Place the oysters on a lightly greased baking sheet and bake for about 5 minutes until they begin to plump.
5. Melt the rest of the butter and mix with lemon juice.
6. Place a hot oyster on each toasted bread round and drizzle with some of the hot lemon butter sauce.

Serves 8

Broiled Oyster Canapés

24 shucked small oysters
6 Tablespoons butter
½ teaspoon minced garlic clove
½ teaspoon dry mustard

2 Tablespoons minced parsley
    Pinch cayenne pepper
1 teaspoon paprika
24 white bread rounds

Oven Temperature: High Broil

1. Cream the butter with garlic, mustard, parsley, cayenne, and paprika in a food processor or with a fork.
2. Toast the bread rounds lightly on one side, remove from the oven, turn over, and spread with seasoned butter.
3. Drain and dry the oysters, and place one on each bread round. Sprinkle with additional paprika.
4. Broil about 2 minutes until the oysters begin to plump.

Serves 8

Oyster Puffs

1 3¾-ounce tin smoked oysters
8 ounces cream cheese
4 Tablespoons cream
1 chopped garlic clove

¼ cup chopped shallots or scallions
½ teaspoon Worcestershire sauce
30 white bread rounds

Oven Temperature: Low Broil

1. Drain and coarsely chop the oysters.
2. Blend the cream cheese, cream, garlic, shallots or scallions, and Worcestershire sauce in a food processor until smooth.
3. Mix in the oysters with a spoon or rubber spatula. (Do not process.)
4. Toast the bread rounds on one side, turn over, and mound with the oyster spread.
5. Place under the broiler for about 2 minutes until puffy and golden.

Serves 10

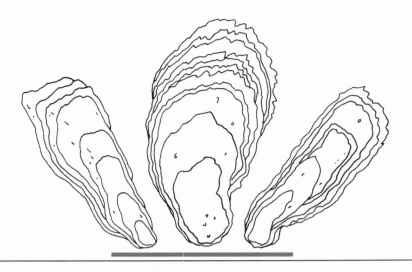

Beautiful soup! Who cares for fish, game, or any other dish? Who would not give all else for two pennyworth only of beautiful soup?

Lewis Carroll, *Alice in Wonderland*

When the cold winds begin to harp and whinny at street corners and wives go seeking among the camphor balls for our last year's overcoats, you will be glad to resume your acquaintance with a bowl of steaming bivalves, swimming in milk, with little clots of yellow butter twirling on the surface of the broth. An oyster stew, a glass of light beer and a corncob pipe will keep your blue eyes blue to any weather, as a young poet of our acquaintance puts it.

Christopher Morley, *Travels in Philadelphia*

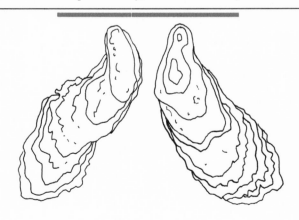

he toddler in the play room, the student home for lunch, the commuter with ten minutes until train time, the "regular" at the church supper, and the guest at an elegant dinner party—all appreciate a generous spoonful of "soup, wonderful soup." Whether served in a steaming tureen or a chilled glass bowl, soup can be many things to many people—a fond memory of grandmother's kitchen, a piquant prelude to a holiday dinner, or a complete meal in itself.

No one country possesses the secret of a particular soup for very long, even though many chowders, bisques, *potages*, and "stews" are associated with specific styles of cooking. If *bouillabaisse* originated in southern France, then Flemish fish soup, and Brazilian *bouquet do mar* are adaptations of it. And while the well-known chef, Paul Prudhomme, speaks of "chopped onions, celery, and green peppers" as the "holy trinity" of Cajun and Creole cookery, these ingredients are also liberally used in an Andalusian gazpacho and an Italian minestrone.

In the simple world of soup, borrowing is the name of the game. So, many of the recipes that follow are adaptations of soups for clams, mussels, and other kinds of seafood. In most instances, adding oysters actually improves the basic recipe because their flavor is delicate and their tenderness appreciable. In other soups, using oysters simply expands the boundaries of oyster cookery.

Recipes for oyster stew are unique and traditionally have been so. All other ingredients are so minimal that the oyster literally *is* the soup, and it is essential to use freshly shucked oysters for the ultimate in flavor. From the lightest consommé to the heartiest chowder, the secret of preparing any kind of oyster soup is subtlety.

Beethoven was undoubtedly right when he said: "Only the pure of heart can make a good soup," and a sophisticated hostess can present it with style. Bisques are served beautifully from tureens, ladled into best china with a silver *cuiller à potage*; saloon-style bowls work well with chowders. Matching sugar bowls with covers present a velouté with flair; an ample serving of oyster stew requires an adequate soup plate.

Soup is a total experience, and skill in presentation, natural instinct for garnishes, the artful use of herbs and spirits, and the test of taste will always be the cook's individual way of preserving the delicate and elusive essence of the sea captured in every oyster soup. The Spanish proverb says it well: "Of soup and love, the first is best," but, how can the two be separated?

SUGGESTIONS:

- If homemade stock is not available, the following substitutes are workable:

    Fish Stock—bottled clam juice simmered with 1 cup each of water and dry white wine, vegetables, and an herb bouquet.

    Chicken Stock—chicken broth or bouillon simmered with dry white wine, vegetables, and an herb bouquet.

    Beef Stock—beef broth or bouillon simmered with red wine, vegetables, and an herb bouquet.

- If homemade stock is to be used only for oyster soup, omit salt or use it sparingly because oysters and their liquor vary in salinity.

- Homemade stock can be made in large quantities and frozen for later use although some chefs believe that the flavor of the herbs can be reduced by freezing.

- Freshly shucked oysters make the best oyster stews, and fresh oysters, raw fish and shellfish are highly recommended for all of the recipes. However, many of the soup recipes can be made with frozen or even canned seafood with some sacrifice of flavor.

- The following herbs and spices are particularly effective in oyster soups: chives, parsley, thyme, garlic, dill weed, celery seed, cayenne pepper, mace or nutmeg, paprika, and curry.

- The following spirits will enhance the flavor of an oyster soup: white wine, Sherry, dry Vermouth, Pernod, and Cognac.

- Traditionally, Tabasco sauce, Worcestershire sauce, and lemon juice are also suitable flavorings for oyster soups.

- Many oyster soups can be prepared in advance up to the final step, and then refrigerated or frozen. If whole oysters and other fresh seafood are used, they should be added immediately before serving. And it is always wise to taste after the oysters and their liquor are added because additional salt may be unnecessary.

- Soup may be served as a first course, as a luncheon entrée, or as a complete meal. In each case the quantity of the serving will be different. The suggested serving for each recipe is about 8 ounces per person, a generous amount for a first course and an acceptable amount for a luncheon entrée. If the soup is a complete meal, the suggested amount will accommodate fewer people. Soup bowls also vary in the quantity of liquid they hold. Consequently, all of the suggested servings in the recipes are approximate.

STOCKS

In almost every instance, a superlative oyster soup, gumbo, or bisque depends on the stock used in its preparation. It is the implicit first step of every recipe, the initial challenge to the cook to use good judgment, fresh ingredients, and imagination in order to produce a satisfying soup.

Purists will opt for the classic recipe of milk or cream and oysters in their own liquor and will never be content with less than the authentic flavor of an oyster enhanced by anything more than dry white wine or Sherry. But fish stock is certainly the soul of many of the bisques and gumbos. And whenever a less intense seafood flavor is desired, chicken or vegetable stock is an excellent variation. Even beef stock, which is the essense of the steak and oyster soup, would enliven a gumbo if a congenial combination of ingredients were used.

Homemade stocks derived from fish, chicken, beef, and vegetables as well as the liquor of the oyster are to be preferred to canned broths or bouillon cubes and granules which are usually laced with salt and monosodium glutamate. These processed "essences" and bottled clam juice can be prepared in a way that makes their use a reasonable substitute but never a convincing replacement for any of the stocks that follow.

Fish Stock

4	pounds white fish frames	1	cup dry white wine
4	Tablespoons unsalted butter		Salt*
2	chopped leeks, white parts only		
2	chopped medium onions		*Herb bouquet:*
2	chopped celery stalks	2	whole cloves
1	cup chopped mushrooms (optional)	1	bay leaf
2	quarts water		Pinch of leaf thyme
		1	teaspoon fennel seed (optional)
		1	garlic clove (optional)

1. Wash the fish frames thoroughly and remove the gills. Chop the bones to accommodate the size of the pot.
2. Melt the butter in a large saucepan or stock pot and cook the vegetables, covered, over low heat until they are tender.
3. Add the fish frames, remaining ingredients, and enough water to cover. Bring to a boil and skim. Cover loosely and simmer for 30 minutes.
4. Strain through a double layer of cheesecloth; chill, and degrease the stock.
5. Taste the stock for intensity and, if necessary, boil it down to strengthen the flavor.

* If the fish stock is to be used in oyster soups, omit salt because of the salinity of oysters and their liquor.

Yield: 2 quarts

Chicken Stock

3 pounds chicken parts	*Herb bouquet:*
1 chopped medium onion	1 garlic clove
3 chopped celery stalks	6 parsley sprigs
1 chopped leek	1 bay leaf
2 chopped medium carrots	1 teaspoon thyme
2 quarts water	
1½ teaspoons salt	
Freshly ground pepper (optional)	

1. Place all the ingredients in a large saucepan or stock pot and cover with at least 1 inch of water. Bring to a boil and skim. Cover loosely and simmer gently for about 2 hours.* (Stock may be cooked in a pressure cooker for 20 minutes. Release pressure and simmer, uncovered, for 30 minutes.)
2. Strain, chill, and degrease the stock.
3. Taste the stock for flavor. Adjust the salt and season with pepper. If necessary, boil it down to correct intensity.

   * If the chicken meat is intended for another use, remove it when tender, and return the skin and bones to the stock pot.

Yield: 1½ quarts

Vegetable Stock

6 medium onions	1½ teaspoons salt
6 scallions with greens	
10 celery stalks	*Herb bouquet:*
4 medium carrots	1 bay leaf
3 tomatoes	4 parsley sprigs
6 lettuce leaves	1 whole clove (optional)
¼ pound mushrooms	1 teaspoon leaf thyme (optional)
1 bunch watercress (optional)	
4 Tablespoons butter	12 peppercorns
3 quarts water	

1. Wash unpeeled vegetables thoroughly, and cut in chunks.
2. Melt the butter in a large saucepan or stock pot and cook the onions, scallions, and celery, covered, until they are tender.
3. Add the other ingredients. Cover, and boil gently for about 2 hours. Or cook for 5 minutes in a pressure cooker. Adjust salt.
4. Strain, chill, and skim the stock.
5. Taste for intensity and boil down, if necessary, to enhance the flavor.

Yield: 2 quarts

Beef Stock

3	unpeeled onions	1	Tablespoon salt
3	celery stalks	1	6-ounce can tomato paste
3	carrots		(optional)
2	untrimmed leeks, or		
	4 scallions		*Herb bouquet:*
3	pounds beef shank and	1	bay leaf
	cracked bones	1	teaspoon thyme
2	quarts water	10	peppercorns

Oven Temperature: 450°

1. Wash the vegetables thoroughly.
2. Arrange the meat, bones, onions, and carrots in a single layer on a roasting pan and brown for 30 minutes in the center of the oven. Turn pieces occasionally to ensure even browning.
3. Transfer the ingredients to a large saucepan or stock pot. Spoon off the fat from the roasting pan and, using 2 cups of water, deglaze the pan over moderate heat. Pour all the browned juices and particles into the stock pot.
4. Add the remaining ingredients and enough water to cover by 2 inches. Bring to a boil and skim.
5. Cover loosely and simmer gently for 4 hours or longer, skimming occasionally. Add boiling water as necessary to cover ingredients.
6. Strain, chill, and degrease the stock.
7. Taste for flavor and boil down if it is necessary to increase intensity.

Yield: 1¹/₂ quarts

OYSTER SOUP

Take what quantity may be wanted of fish-stock, which must be made in this manner:

Take a pound of skate, four or five flounders, and two big eels. Cut them into pieces and put to them as much water as will cover them. Season with mace, an onion stuck with cloves, a head of celery, two parsley roots sliced, some pepper and salt, and a bunch of sweet herbs.

Cover them down close, and let them simmer an hour and a half, and then strain off the liquor for use. Being thus provided with your fish-stock, take what quantity of it you want.

Then take two quarts of oysters bearded, and beat them in a mortar with the yolks of ten eggs boiled hard. Put them to the fish-stock, and set it over the fire. Season it with pepper and salt, and grated nutmeg, and when it boils, put in the eggs and oysters. Let it boil till it be of a good thickness, and like fine cream.

Recipe of John Farley, 19th Century England

64

SOUPS

Oyster Stew

So many circumstances of time, place, and company occur to make a particular dish memorable in every way. M. F. K. Fisher has written about an oyster stew "the best in the world . . . mildly potent, quietly sustaining, warm as love and welcomer in winter." Its preparation is worth retelling.

Three copper saucepans were used and carefully tended by a young man who warmed butter in one, placed freshly shucked oysters in the other, and heated a pint of milk in the third. When the butter frothed, he poured it over the oysters, stirring them round and round in the pan for about a minute. Then he poured in the hot milk, adding a little red pepper, salt, and a few drops of Sherry, and served it—no "stewing" here, just total absorption in the task at hand for a minute or two. It's the secret of a good oyster stew.

36	shucked oysters and liquor	Worcestershire sauce
1	quart light cream	Paprika
8	Tablespoons butter	Tabasco
	Salt	

1. Remove the oysters from their shells; strain and reserve 1 cup of the liquor.
2. Heat the liquor and cream in a saucepan.
3. Melt the butter in another saucepan. When it froths, add the oysters and stir gently until they are hot and the edges begin to curl.
4. Stir in the cream mixture, season to taste, and serve immediately.

Serves 4

Potage Crème d'Huîtres

Connoisseurs of oyster stew will probably always be convinced that less is better than more. But an imaginative cook will seize the opportunity to be creative by introducing a compatible flavor or an interesting texture. Chopped leeks, shallots, scallions, or celery are congenial additions and so are many herb and spice garnishes. And who doesn't remember spooning or crushing some of those familiar oyster crackers or pilot bisquits into the steaming bowl. The possibilities are limitless and, in many cases, a matter of family tradition.

36	shucked oysters and liquor	Salt and freshly ground
3	cups milk, half-and-half, or cream	pepper
3	Tablespoons butter	
2	Tablespoons flour	

1. Remove the oysters from their shells, drain, and set aside. Strain the liquor, combine with the milk or cream and warm in a saucepan.
2. Melt the butter in another saucepan. Stir in the flour and cook until bubbling. Remove from the heat and whisk in the warm cream mixture. Return to heat and boil, stirring constantly, until the soup thickens. Simmer at least 3 minutes.
3. Add the oysters and continue to cook until the oysters plump. Salt and pepper to taste.
4. Season with celery salt, mace, or cayenne pepper, and garnish with parsley and a sprinkling of paprika if desired. Serve in warm bowls.

Serves 4

Oyster Stew aux Croûtes

From the earliest "Invalid's Tea Tray" recipes for Oyster Toast to the "pale fried sippets" recommended as accompaniments to creamy oyster stew in Victorian England, *croûtes* have been an integral part of oyster cookery.

The *croûte* may be a simple slice of thick white toast. Or, in the truly French manner, bread cases are made by hollowing out the centers of thick bread slices. All surfaces are lightly brushed with melted butter and the *croûtes* are toasted until golden in a hot oven. Either version will reinforce the comfort of an oyster stew served in an old-fashioned soup plate.

24 shucked oysters and liquor	1¾ cups heavy cream
½ cup dry white wine, or ¼ cup dry Vermouth	2 egg yolks
2 Tablespoons finely chopped shallots	Salt and freshly ground pepper
2 Tablespoons finely chopped celery	1 Tablespoon lemon juice (optional)
	4 French bread *croûtes*

1. Remove the oysters from their shells and set aside. Strain the liquor.
2. Boil the liquor, wine, shallots, and celery in a 1½-quart saucepan until the liquid is reduced to about ½ cup. Add 1½ cups of cream and simmer 5 minutes.
3. Whisk the egg yolks and the remaining ¼ cup of cream in a bowl. Whisk in ½ cup of the hot liquids, a spoonful at a time. Then slowly beat in the remaining liquids. Transfer the enriched soup to the saucepan.
4. Add the oysters, salt and pepper to taste, and lemon juice, if desired. Heat the soup, stirring carefully, until the edges of the oysters start to curl, but do not boil.
5. Place a *croûte* in each soup plate and ladle the stew over it.

Serves 4

Potage Velouté aux Huîtres

Dazzle guests with New World charm flavored with Old World elegance by adding a dash of curry, a jigger of Cognac, or a garnish of freshly-made, seasoned croutons to this enriched oyster stew. The result is not exactly "oyster bar" fare, but an inspired first course to a very special anniversary or holiday dinner.

36	shucked oysters and liquor		Salt and freshly ground
2½	cups milk or light cream		pepper
6	Tablespoons butter	2	Tablespoons Cognac (optional)
1	Tablespoon flour		Croutons (optional)
2	egg yolks		

1. Remove the oysters from their shells, drain and set aside. Strain and reserve 1½ cups of the liquor.
2. Warm the oyster liquor and 2 cups of the milk in a saucepan.
3. Melt the butter in another saucepan. Stir in the flour and cook until bubbling. Remove from heat and whisk in the warm milk. Return to heat and boil, stirring constantly, until the mixture thickens.
4. Whisk the egg yolks and remaining milk in a bowl. Stir in ½ cup of the hot mixture, a spoonful at a time. Then slowly beat in the remaining soup. Transfer the enriched soup to the saucepan and, stirring constantly, heat to just below the boiling point.
5. Add the oysters, salt and pepper to taste, and Cognac, if desired. Heat the soup until the edges of the oysters start to curl.
6. Garnish with croutons and serve immediately.

Serves 4

Holiday Oyster Stew

If there is a dinner of roast turkey with pecan and rice stuffing, rum-glazed sweet potatoes, and damson plum tarts in the oven, the ingredients for this holiday oyster stew should be ready and waiting. One spoonful says it all—either Happy Thanksgiving or Merry Christmas.

1	quart oysters and liquor	¼ cup dry Sherry
4	Tablespoons butter	Salt and freshly ground
¼	teaspoon anchovy paste	pepper
1	Tablespoon Dijon or English mustard	Paprika
3	cups finely chopped celery	Chopped parsley
1	quart heavy cream	

1. Melt the butter in a large saucepan and stir in anchovy paste and mustard. Add the celery and cook until tender.
2. Stir in the cream and bring to a boil.
3. Add the oysters, liquor, and Sherry, and heat until the edges of the oysters begin to curl. Salt and pepper to taste.
4. Garnish with paprika and parsley, and serve in warm bowls.

Serves 6

Velouté de Crevettes à la Normande

With very little effort, this tantalizing French *potage* can be served with a significant salad at a special luncheon or late evening supper. Prepared and refrigerated ahead of time, it needs only reheating and the addition of the shrimp and oyster garnish at the last minute.

16	shucked oysters and liquor	2	egg yolks
1	pound medium shrimp		Pinch of mace
1	cup fish stock (See p. 62)	1/3	cup dry Sherry
1³/₄	cups light cream		Salt and freshly ground white
2	Tablespoons butter		pepper
2	Tablespoons flour		

1. Drain the oysters and reserve the liquor.
2. Wash, peel, and devein the shrimp. Purée half of them in a food processor or blender. Reserve the remaining whole shrimp for garnish.
3. Warm the oyster liquor, fish stock, and 1¹/₄ cups of cream in a small saucepan.
4. Melt the butter in another saucepan. Stir in the flour and cook until bubbling. Remove from the heat and whisk in the warm stock mixture. Return to heat and boil, stirring constantly, until the stock thickens. Simmer at least 3 minutes.
5. Whisk egg yolks and the remaining ¹/₂ cup of cream in a bowl. Whisk in ¹/₂ cup of the hot stock, a spoonful at a time. Then slowly beat in the remaining stock. Transfer the enriched mixture to the saucepan. Mix in the mace, Sherry, and puréed shrimp. Bring to the boiling point, stirring carefully.
6. Add the oysters and whole shrimp and heat until the edges of the oysters begin to curl.
7. Season with salt and pepper and serve in warm bowls.

Serves 4

Cream of Artichoke Soup

This lightly creamed soup of artichokes, mushrooms, and oysters, should create a spurt of interest in the everyday miracles that are possible when fresh ingredients are used innovatively. *"Chacun à son gout,"* is the rule, but this recipe will please almost everybody.

1	pint oysters and liquor		Pinch of thyme
2	cooked large artichokes, or 8 frozen or canned artichoke hearts		Pinch of cayenne pepper
		3	Tablespoons butter
		1	garlic clove
3	cups chicken stock (See p. 63)	3	Tablespoons finely chopped scallions
½	pound chopped mushrooms	2	Tablespoons flour
2	Tablespoons finely chopped parsley	1	cup light cream
	Pinch of mace or nutmeg		Salt and freshly ground pepper

1. Scrape the pulp from the artichoke leaves and chop the bottoms. If frozen or canned hearts are used, rinse and chop them.
2. Bring the chicken stock to a boil in a 2-quart saucepan. Add the mushrooms, parsley, mace, thyme, and cayenne. Cover and simmer for 20 minutes. Add the artichokes and simmer 10 minutes longer.
3. Melt the butter in another large saucepan and sauté the garlic and scallions until tender. Discard the garlic.
4. Stir in the flour and cook until the roux is lightly browned. Remove from the heat and whisk in about 2 cups of the hot stock. Return to heat and boil, stirring constantly, until the mixture thickens. Stir in the remaining stock and vegetable mixture and simmer at least 3 minutes. At this point the soup may be refrigerated or frozen.
5. Stir the cream into the soup and bring to a boil. Add the oysters and liquor and heat until the edges of the oysters begin to curl.
6. Season to taste with salt and pepper, and serve immediately.

Serves 4

When I want to vary the fish soup, I often serve a sauce rouille [literally rust sauce because of paprika], which is an easily made mayonnaise-type preparation with potatoes and garlic.
Pierre Franey, *More 60-Minute Gourmet*

Plantation Pickuns

Devised to grace the buffet table of a Southern plantation, this creamy peanut and oyster soup will add a bit of antebellum nostalgia to any dinner party. It may be served with unsalted peanuts, minced parsley, or crumbled bacon, but its smooth texture and remarkable blend of flavors are quite successful without any garnish except the oysters that make it so memorable.

1	pint oysters and liquor	1/3	cup creamy peanut butter
2½	cups chicken stock (See p. 63)	2	Tablespoons dry Sherry
	½ cup heavy cream	1	teaspoon chopped fresh summer savory
1	Tablespoon butter		Salt and freshly ground pepper
2	Tablespoons chopped onions or scallions		Sour cream (optional)
3	Tablespoons flour		Crumbled bacon (optional)

1. Drain the oysters, reserving ½ cup of the liquor.
2. Warm the oyster liquor, chicken stock, and cream in a saucepan.
3. Melt the butter in another saucepan and sauté the onions or scallions until tender. Stir in the flour and peanut butter and cook until bubbling. Remove from the heat and whisk in the warm stock mixture. Return to heat and add the Sherry and savory. Boil, stirring constantly, until the mixture thickens. Simmer at least 3 minutes.
4. Add oysters, salt and pepper to taste. Heat until the edges of the oysters begin to curl.
5. Serve with a dollop of sour cream and crumbled bacon if desired.

Serves 4

East Bay Steak and Oyster Soup

This is exactly the kind of hearty soup that every sailor dreams of after an invigorating fall day on the water. Float paper-thin slices of onion or slivers of leek on the top and enjoy the full-bodied flavor of steak and oysters in the cabin or in homeport before a roaring fireplace with a dark brew and a crusty loaf.

1	pint oysters and liquor	3	cups beef stock (See p. 64)
1	pound round steak		Pinch of thyme
	1/3 cup flour		Pinch of mace or nutmeg
	Salt and freshly ground pepper		Cayenne pepper
4	Tablespoons butter		1/4 cup chopped parsley
3	Tablespoons vegetable oil		Thin onion slices or leek slivers

1. Trim meat and cut into bite-sized pieces. Dredge in flour seasoned with salt and pepper.
2. Heat butter and oil in a 2-quart saucepan and sear meat on all sides over high heat.
3. Add stock, spices, and herbs. Cover and simmer gently for an hour, stirring occasionally and adding water if necessary. Soup may be refrigerated or frozen at this point.
4. Bring to a boil, and add the oysters, liquor, and parsley. Adjust salt and pepper. Cook until the oysters are plump.
5. Serve immediately, garnished with onion rings or leek slivers.

Serves 4

*Oyster Bisque**

Sinfully extravagant are the only words for the following recipe. It captures the essence of all the oysters and vegetables that go into its making and then releases them in a deceptively simple velouté. Ladle it into fine china and add a freshly shucked oyster or two to each bowl for an elegant touch.

1½	pints oysters and liquor		Pinch of thyme
1	pint fish stock (See p. 62)		Pinch of mace or nutmeg
1½	cups dry white wine	5	Tablespoons butter
2	chopped onions	2½	Tablespoons flour
2	chopped celery stalks	2	eggs
2	chopped carrots	3	cups heavy cream
2	lemon slices		Dry Sherry
1	Tablespoon chopped parsley		Salt
12	peppercorns		Cayenne pepper

1. If oysters are large, cut them in halves or quarters.
2. Combine oysters, liquor, stock, wine, vegetables, lemon, herbs and seasonings in a large saucepan. Bring to a boil, reduce heat, and simmer, uncovered, for 45 minutes.
3. Strain through a fine sieve or cheesecloth-lined strainer. Discard the solid ingredients, and measure 5 cups of the liquid. If there is less, add stock or substitute clam juice.
4. Melt the butter in a large saucepan. Stir in flour and cook until bubbling. Remove from the heat and whisk in the hot liquid. Return to heat and boil, stirring constantly, until the mixture thickens. Simmer at least 3 minutes.
5. Whisk egg yolks and ½ cup of cream in a bowl. Whisk in ½ cup of the hot soup, a spoonful at a time. Then slowly beat in 2 more cups of the hot soup. Pour the egg mixture into the saucepan and, stirring carefully, bring to a boil. Bisque may be refrigerated or frozen.

6.   Reheat the bisque and stir in the remaining 2½ cups of cream, Sherry, salt and cayenne to taste. Garnish with freshly shucked oysters if desired.

* Derived from the same word as biscuit, bisque is a "twice cooked" regional, thick, creamy soup. One method of making bisque is to cook, strain, and then thicken the ingredients. Or the ingredients may be cooked, puréed, and then reheated.

   Because puréed oysters become an unappealing grey in color, bisque which is strained is always visually appetizing. On the other hand, the puréed bisque gives up none of the oyster flavor. The introduction of spinach or peas will resolve the color problem, and the result is a soup that is as refreshing to the eye as it is to the palate.

Serves 8

Bisque D'Épinards

While a history of the liaison between spinach and oysters is still to be written, it is a culinary "match" that seems destined to go on forever. Little wonder that this bisque is a February favorite. The stalwart green color and no-nonsense flavor make it a wonderful Lenten supper, especially when served with a loaf of homemade rye bread, a rustic Port Salut, and a glass of Vouvray—not exactly penitential, but properly subdued.

1	quart oysters and liquor		Salt and freshly ground
4	Tablespoons butter		pepper
1	cup chopped onions	3	cups heavy cream
1	cup chopped celery		Dry Sherry
2	garlic cloves		Pinch of nutmeg
1	quart chicken stock		Worcestershire sauce
	(See p. 63)		Seasoned croutons (optional)
1	cup dry white wine		
1	pound stemmed and chopped fresh spinach		

1.   Drain the oysters, reserving 1 cup of the liquor.
2.   Melt the butter in a large saucepan and sauté the onion, celery, and garlic for a few minutes; discard the garlic.
3.   Add the oyster liquor, stock, and wine to the saucepan and cook uncovered until the mixture is reduced to about 4 cups.
4.   Add the oysters and spinach, and season with salt and pepper. Heat until the edges of the oysters start to curl.
5.   Cool the mixture slightly and purée in a food processor or blender. The bisque may be refrigerated or frozen.
6.   Reheat over moderate heat but do not permit the bisque to boil. Stir in the cream, Sherry, and seasonings to taste. Serve with croutons if desired.

Serves 8

East Bay Steak and Oyster Soup (Page 70)

Oyster Saffron Bisque (Page 74)

Bisque aux Petits Pois

Petits pois are like children; you have to understand them.
James de Coquet, Food Editor of *Figaro*

There is something almost playful about the combination of ingredients in this bisque. The result is a bright and smiling luncheon treat or a whimsical transition from a cocktail hour to an entrée of roast leg of spring lamb surrounded by parsleyed new potatoes and glazed carrots. Add jonquils to the centerpiece for a perfect early spring dinner party.

1 quart oysters and liquor
6 Tablespoons butter
½ cup finely chopped onion
3 cups shelled green peas, or 2 10-ounce packages frozen peas
2 cups milk

2 cups fish stock (See p. 62)
½ cup dry white wine
Salt and freshly ground pepper
¼ cup finely chopped chives (optional)

1. Melt 2 tablespoons butter in a large saucepan and sauté the onions until tender.
2. Add the peas and milk. Cover, and simmer gently until the peas are tender.
3. Stir in the stock and wine. Bring to a boil, and add the oysters and liquor. Heat until the edges of the oysters begin to curl. Stir in the remaining 4 tablespoons of butter.
4. Allow the mixture to cool slightly and purée in a food processor or blender. Bisque may be refrigerated at this point.
5. Return to the saucepan, season with salt and pepper to taste, and heat thoroughly. Garnish with blanched fresh peas or chopped chives if desired.

Serves 8

OYSTER POTTAGE

Take some boild pease, strain them and put them in a pipkin with some capers, some sweet herbs finely chopped, some salt, and butter; then have some great oysters fryed with sweet herbs and grosly chopped, put them to the strained pease, stew them together, serve them on a clean scowred dish on fine carved sippets, and garnish the dish with grated bread.

Robert May, *The Accomplisht Cook, or the Art and Mastery of Cooking*, 1660

Oyster Saffron Bisque

Second only to beets in sugar content, carrots seem an unlikely ingredient for an oyster bisque, but spiced with saffron, the southern Mediterranean influence on this dish is unmistakable and unique. The recipe will definitely do the trick for the hostess who likes to be different.

24	shucked oysters and liquor	1/2	lemon
3	medium carrots	2	Tablespoons chopped fresh dill weed
4	Tablespoons butter		
1	cup chopped celery	1	teaspoon saffron
1	cup chopped onion	1	cup heavy cream
1 1/2	quarts vegetable stock (See p. 63)		Salt and freshly ground white pepper
1 1/2	cups diced potato		Dill sprigs

1. Drain oysters, reserving liquor.
2. Peel the carrots and chop 2 of them for the soup. Cut the remaining carrot into fine julienne strips and blanch in boiling salted water. Refresh in cold water, drain, and reserve for garnish.
3. Melt the butter in a large saucepan and sauté the chopped carrot, celery, and onion until tender.
4. Add the oyster liquor, stock, potato, lemon, dill, and saffron. Bring to a boil, cover, and simmer for 15 minutes.
5. Remove the lemon, and purée the vegetable mixture in a food processor or blender.
6. Transfer the puréed vegetables back to the saucepan, add the cream and bring to a boil.
7. Add the oysters and heat until the edges begin to curl. Season to taste.
8. Garnish with julienned carrots and snipped dill sprigs, and serve immediately.

Serves 8

LATE AUTUMN DINNER

Oyster Bisque
Crown of Pork with Wild Rice
Acorn Squash with Apple and Raisin Stuffing
Endive and Watercress Salad
Chestnut Roll
Cabernet Sauvignon '78

Oyster Chowder

A tureen of this simple but delicious chowder on a buffet table captures the essence of the new comfortable style of entertaining. Vary the recipe and make it with fresh corn-off-the-cob and heavy cream for an unforgettable vegetable and oyster combination.

1	pint oysters and liquor	1	cup diced potato
1	cup creamed corn	1	cup water
1	cup milk	1	Tablespoon finely chopped
4	Tablespoons butter		parsley
½	cup finely chopped onion		Salt and freshly ground
1	cup finely chopped celery		pepper

1. Drain the oysters and reserve liquor.
2. Heat the corn and milk in a 2-quart saucepan.
3. Melt the butter in another saucepan and sauté the onion and celery until tender. Add the potato, oyster liquor, and water, and bring to a boil. Cover and simmer until the potato is tender but firm.
4. Combine the potato mixture with the corn and milk. Add oysters, parsley, and salt and pepper to taste. Heat thoroughly, stirring carefully, until the oysters are plump. Serve immediately.

Serves 4

New England Chowder

There's nothing prissy about the flavors in this authentic chowder—salt pork, corn, and oysters. Make it as thin or as thick as desired and have a limitless supply in the *chaudière* for the seasonal clambake or a "close-up-the-beach-house party."

1	pint oysters and liquor	2	ounces finely diced salt pork
2	cups creamed corn	1	finely chopped medium onion
1	pint milk		Salt and freshly ground pepper

1. Heat the corn and milk in a 2-quart saucepan.
2. Blanch the salt pork in boiling water for 5 minutes. Pour off the water and sauté the pork until crisp. Remove the cracklings with a slotted spoon and reserve for garnish.
3. Sauté the onion until tender in 3 tablespoons of the pork drippings. Add oysters and liquor, and heat until the oysters are plump.
4. Add the oyster mixture to the corn and milk. Season to taste with salt and pepper, and serve immediately, garnished with the cracklings if desired.

Serves 4

Oyster Chowder Bonne Femme

This traditional "homey" soup can be served with or without oysters. *With*, it is definitely company fare and a subtle variation on the New England chowder theme. *Without*, that extra touch of class is missing.

1 pint oysters and liquor
6 Tablespoons unsalted butter
1 coarsely chopped medium onion
4 coarsely chopped medium leeks
3 cups diced potato

1 cup water
2 cups vegetable or chicken stock (See p. 63)
Salt
1 cup heavy cream
2 teaspoons chopped fresh parsley or chives

1. Melt 3 tablespoons butter in a large saucepan. Sauté the onion and leeks until tender.
2. Add the potato, water, stock, and ½ teaspoon salt. Bring to a boil and simmer, covered, until the potato is cooked but firm.
3. Add the oysters, liquor, and cream. Heat until the oysters ruffle. Stir in the remaining 3 tablespoons of butter and adjust salt.
4. Ladle into warmed serving bowls and sprinkle with parsley or chives.

Serves 6

Seafood Chowder

Even though the Puritans might frown a bit at the sheer luxury of this seafood chowder, there is simply no more sophisticated way to begin "Dinner at Eight." Champagne and Wedgewood service are *de rigueur*.

1 pint oysters and liquor
1 quart water
1 cup dry white wine
1 pound white fish fillets, preferably sole
1 pound raw shrimp, or 1 pound bay scallops
4 Tablespoons butter

1 cup finely chopped shallots
1½ Tablespoons flour
1½ cups heavy cream
Cognac, or Calvados
Salt and freshly ground pepper
Cayenne pepper

1. Drain oysters, reserving liquor.
2. Combine oyster liquor, water, and wine in a 3-quart saucepan and bring to a boil.
3. Use some of the liquid to poach the fish fillets in a fish poacher or large skillet. As soon as they turn opaque, remove from heat. Return the

poaching liquid to the saucepan. Cover the fillets with waxed paper and keep warm.

4. Add shrimp or scallops to the saucepan and boil for 2 minutes. Remove shellfish with a slotted spoon. Peel and devein the shrimp. Keep the shrimp or scallops warm with the fillets.

5. Reduce the poaching liquids over high heat to about 1 quart.

6. Melt the butter in a 2-quart saucepan, and sauté the shallots until tender. Stir in the flour and cook until bubbling. Remove from the heat and whisk in the hot poaching liquid. Return to heat and boil, stirring constantly, until the mixture thickens. Simmer at least 3 minutes.

7. Stir in the oysters and cream. Heat until the oysters are plump. Add one or more tablespoons of Cognac or Calvados.

8. Distribute the fillets and shrimp or scallops into heated bowls and ladle the hot chowder over them. Serve immediately.

Serves 6

Chicken and Oyster Gumbo

Through the years, Creole cooks, working in the homes of Spanish, Italian, French, and Anglo families, acquired recipes and ways of preparing food that they, in turn, handed down to their sons and daughters. Cajun and Creole cooking, therefore, is a jumble of culinary styles.

Cooks and chefs made gumbos with almost any seafood, meat, or poultry available, but they usually seasoned them with peppers, herbs, and the powder of wild sassafras they borrowed from the Indians and called filé. Added to a bowl of gumbo just before serving, filé flavors, slightly thickens, and gives a fine dark color to this legendary soup.

1 pint oysters and liquor	2 cups peeled and chopped tomatoes
2 quarts chicken or vegetable stock (See p. 63)	1/2 pound sliced fresh okra, or 1 10-ounce package frozen okra
1 cut-up frying chicken	
1 cup flour	Paprika
2 Tablespoons butter	Salt and freshly ground pepper
2 Tablespoons oil	
1/2 pound diced ham	2 Tablespoons filé powder (optional)
1 cup chopped celery	
1 cup chopped onions	4 cups cooked long-grain rice
1/2 cup chopped sweet red pepper	

1. Drain the oysters and set aside. Combine the oyster liquor and stock in a large saucepan and simmer for 15 minutes.
2. Coat the chicken pieces with flour, reserving 4 tablespoons for the roux.
3. Melt the butter and oil in a large skillet and fry the chicken until the pieces are dark brown, adding oil if necessary. Transfer the chicken to the stock pot.
4. Lightly fry the ham in the same skillet; remove with a slotted spoon and set aside.
5. Stir the remaining flour into the skillet and cook, whisking constantly, until the roux turns a rich brown color.
6. Add the celery, onions, red pepper, tomatoes, and okra, and cook for 5 minutes. Transfer to the stock pot and simmer for about 30 minutes.
7. Add the ham and oysters and continue to simmer until the edges of the oysters begin to curl. Season to taste with paprika, salt and pepper.
8. Stir in the filé powder, if used, and remove from heat.
9. Serve the gumbo over rice in individual bowls.

Serves 8

Seafood Gumbo

Although some of the famous restaurants in New Orleans serve almost twenty different kinds of gumbo,* seafood gumbo remains a favorite—the one that "tastes just like my mother made when I was growing up in Louisiana."

1 pint oysters and liquor
½ pound white fish fillets
1 pound raw medium shrimp
½ pound crabmeat
2 quarts fish stock (See p. 62)
⅓ cup dry Vermouth
1 bay leaf
   Pinch of thyme
¾ cup flour
½ cup oil
½ pound fresh okra, or 1 10-
   ounce package frozen okra
4 Tablespoons butter
1 minced garlic clove
1 cup chopped onions

½ cup chopped green pepper
½ cup chopped celery
1½ cups peeled and chopped
   tomatoes, or canned plum
   tomatoes
½ pound sliced smoked sausage
   (optional)
½ teaspoon cayenne pepper
1 teaspoon Worcestershire sauce
   Salt and freshly ground
   pepper
2 Tablespoons filé powder
   (optional)
4 cups cooked long-grain rice

1. Drain the oysters, reserving the liquor. Quarter the fillets; shell and devein the shrimp; remove the cartilage from the crabmeat, and set aside.
2. Pour the oyster liquor, stock, and Vermouth into a saucepan. Add the bay leaf and thyme, cover, and simmer for 15 minutes. Remove the bay leaf.
3. Combine the flour and oil in a large heavy saucepan. Cook, whisking constantly, until the flour turns a rich brown color. Set aside.
4. Trim and cut the okra in 1-inch pieces. Melt 2 tablespoons of butter in a large saucepan and sauté the okra until lightly browned. Remove with a slotted spoon and drain the pan.
5. Melt the remaining butter in the same saucepan, add the garlic, onions, pepper, and celery and cook until wilted. Stir in the tomatoes and stock mixture, bring to a boil and simmer for about 10 minutes.
6. Reheat the roux if it has cooled. Whisk the warm stock and vegetables into the roux. Add the okra, sausage if desired, cayenne pepper, and Worcestershire sauce. Partially cover and simmer for 1 hour.
7. Add the seafood and simmer until the edges of the oysters begin to curl. Season to taste with salt and pepper.
8. Stir in the filé powder, if used, and remove from heat.
9. Serve the gumbo over a mound of rice in individual bowls.

* The African [Bantu] name for gumbo is okra, usually one of the vegetables used in the soup. The mucilaginous texture of okra thickens any kind of liquid it is cooked in. Use it with tomatoes because their acidity cuts the gluey texture and complements the taste of the vegetable.

Serves 8

Soupe Louisiane

The addition of white wine to this recipe contributes to its light appetizing aroma. Satisfying as either a luncheon or late supper main course, it requires only a salad and a basket of *petits pains* to bring back memories of a delightful meal in a quaint café in Les Halles.

1 pint oysters and liquor	¼ cup chopped fresh dill
1 pound raw medium shrimp	½ cup finely chopped parsley
1 pound scallops	6 cups fish or vegetable stock
2 Tablespoons butter	(See pp. 62, 63)
2 Tablespoons olive oil	2 cups dry white wine, or 1 cup
2 chopped medium onions	dry Vermouth and 1 cup
1 chopped leek	water
6 chopped scallions, including	Salt and freshly ground
green parts	pepper
1 chopped green pepper	Tabasco
1 finely chopped garlic clove	

1. Peel and devein the shrimp and halve or quarter the scallops if they are large.
2. Heat the butter and oil in a large saucepan and lightly sauté the vegetables and herbs.
3. Add the stock and wine, and cover. Simmer for 30 minutes. Soup may be refrigerated at this point.
4. Reheat to boiling. Add the oysters, shrimp, and scallops. Heat until the oysters curl.
5. Season to taste with salt, pepper, and Tabasco, and serve immediately.

Serves 8

Seafood Méditerranée

The swirl of vermicelli into this unique seafood recipe is a bonus, and it absolutely guarantees a hearty supper after a busy day. If there is a supply of fish stock in the refrigerator or freezer, the soup can be simmering during the cocktail hour and served minutes after the seafood is added.

24	shucked oysters and liquor	$^1/_2$	teaspoon saffron
6	Tablespoons olive oil	1	strip orange zest
3	chopped medium leeks	1	teaspoon thyme
1	cored and chopped medium fennel bulb	1	teaspoon rosemary
1	chopped medium onion	24	raw medium shrimp
1	chopped garlic clove	$^1/_2$	pound lobster meat
6	cups fish stock (See p. 62)	1	cup cooked vermicelli
2	cups peeled and chopped tomatoes, or chopped canned tomatoes		Salt Cayenne pepper

1. Heat the oil in a large saucepan and sauté the leeks, fennel, onion, and garlic until tender.
2. Add the fish stock, tomatoes, saffron, orange zest, thyme, rosemary, and bring to a boil. Cover and simmer about 30 minutes.
3. Strain the broth through a double layer of cheesecloth. Return to the saucepan and bring to a boil.
4. Peel and devein the shrimp.
5. Add the oysters, shrimp, lobster, and vermicelli to the pot and heat until the edges of the oysters start to curl. Season lightly with salt and cayenne.
6. Adjust the seasoning and serve immediately.

Serves 6

Cioppino

The search for the perfect "one dish" meal stops here. A mélange of seafood, vegetables, herbs, spices, and full-bodied California wine makes it a perfect Sunday night supper, especially if there's a loaf of homemade bread on the sideboard, and fall in the air.

1	pint oysters and liquor		1	quart water
12	mussels in shell		2	cups Zinfandel
1/2	pound white fish fillets		1/2	cup finely chopped parsley
6	ounces lobster meat, or 6 small tails in shell		1	teaspoon basil
1/2	pound raw medium shrimp		1	teaspoon oregano
6	ounces crabmeat		2	Tablespoons sugar
3	Tablespoons olive oil			Salt and freshly ground pepper
2	chopped medium onions			
1	finely chopped garlic clove			
10	ounces tomato purée			
2	cups peeled and chopped tomatoes, or canned tomatoes			

1. Scrub and rinse the mussels, removing the beards. Cut the fillets and lobster meat into bite-sized pieces. Shell and devein the shrimp; remove cartilage from crabmeat.
2. Heat the oil in a 3-quart saucepan and sauté the onions and garlic until tender. Add the purée, tomatoes, water, wine, herbs, and sugar. Season lightly with salt and pepper. Cover and simmer for 1 hour.
3. Reheat the stock to boiling. Add the mussels and lobster tails, and simmer 2 minutes.
4. Add the fillets, shrimp, crabmeat, lobster meat (if used), and oysters. Heat until the oysters begin to curl. Adjust seasonings and serve at once.

Serves 8

CHAUDIÈRE, n. f. Copper; boiler (of a steam-engine etc.); (C) pail. (C) faire chaudière, to prepare a meal, to eat (in a forest).

The New Cassell's French Dictionary

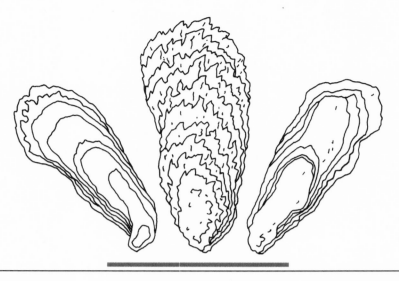

Chiffonade applies to leafy vegetables, spinach, sorrel, or lettuce, cut into shreds the width of a matchstick. The simplest way of doing this is to roll up a wad of leaves and cut them across with a sharp knife or scissors into thin slices. They will unroll into shreds. The lengths will be uneven, but this does not matter usually as a chiffonade is such a tumble of greenery.

Jane Grigson, *Vegetable Book*

I need no oyster
　　　to be in love with you,
Nor, when I roister,
　　　raw roots to chew. . . .

A. P. Herbert, *Love Song*

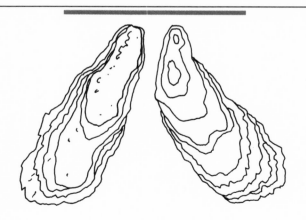

ver the past decade, salads and vegetables have come a long way from faded, overcooked, tedious, but-they're-so-good-for-you accompaniments to a meal. And, for many reasons. Vegetarianism is now popular, even chic. Fear of additives, preservatives, and chemicals motivates many amateurs to perfect their own gardening skills. And the influence of Chinese cooking and French nouvelle cuisine directs Americans into shops in search of the perfect wok for stir-frying and the most efficient food processor to slice, shred, julienne, and purée.

Urban dwellers and suburbanites alike are discovering that tending a garden of one's own or taking a deliberate detour to a country roadside stand—where bunches of brilliant dahlias and drying sea lavender mingle with baskets of zucchini, onions, peppers, and tomatoes—is a celebration of life. Indeed, the experience is a continual reminder "of the order of Nature itself: first freshness, then flavor and ripeness, and then decay." For that is the way M. F. K. Fisher describes her own efforts to purchase and prepare fruits and vegetables during the season of their "explosive rush toward ripeness and disintegration." And, doing so under the sunny skies of Provence, the effort was its own reward.

Vegetables *do* keep one in tune with the natural world. Anticipating the arrival of the first, tender, green asparagus in spring, the first peas of summer, the sun-flavored tomatoes of early fall, and the wholesome harvest of squash, potatoes, and onions *is* more meaningful *because* it is anticipated. And the memory more satisfying because gratefully remembered. With such a wealth of fresh ingredients to work with, how can anyone fail?

Let there be no more soggy salads prepared hours in advance, or gelatinous, artificially flavored molds, or "tarted up" frozen vegetables. The "fresh connection" from garden to table is here to stay, and has opened the door to a dazzling array of first course, luncheon, buffet, and side dishes. There are new and exciting possibilities with each ripe tomato, snappy bean, opulent eggplant, and bouncy bouquet of salad greens.

The recipes in this chapter are limited to those "composed" salads and vegetable dishes that simply work well with oysters. The cooking methods, blending of flavors and textures, and presentation are basically the same ones that are used in all vegetable cookery. Preserving the integrity of each ingredient and the judicious use of seasonings, herbs, and spices are essential for their success. Many of the salads and vegetable dishes are accompaniments—special fare for a special dinner. Some of the recipes will do nicely for a luncheon or a simple family meal. All of them are truly "gifts" from the sea and garden.

SUGGESTIONS:

- Freshly shucked oysters are essential for some of the salad and vegetable recipes, and bulk oysters can be used for others if oysters in the shell are not available. Frozen oysters are not recommended for any of the salad recipes.

- Fresh vegetables are a must for all of the recipes. If necessary, frozen vegetables can be used, but there is always some sacrifice of flavor. Vine-ripened tomatoes are essential for all the recipes which call for tomatoes.

- Vegetables retain their color, nutrients, and flavor when blanched in a microwave oven. Simply follow the instructions found in a basic manual regarding the amount of water and time.

- Herbs for salads should be fresh if possible because dried herbs have a slightly musty flavor.

- Tossing a salad at table is recommended because it ensures the essential fresh quality and it also designates the importance of a "salad course."

- Adding the dressing to the greens and various ingredients of a salad implies using only as much dressing as desired. A lightly dressed salad is frequently preferred to a more generously dressed one.

- Extra virgin olive oil, either a quality wine, herb, or "berry" vinegar, and a carefully selected mustard are some of the essentials of a "good" salad dressing.

- Homemade mayonnaise is always preferred to a commercial brand.

- Chilled plates are a nice touch when serving cold salads.

- Many of the recipes are for salads and vegetables that accompany an entrée. Care should be taken that all the courses of the meal complement rather than duplicate each other.

SALADS & VEGETABLES

Oh! Is For Oyster Salad

Seafood salads, once the special province of lobster, lump crab, shrimp, and the more plebeian tuna, now happily include squid, mussels, and even oysters. Perhaps it is a logical development because marinating oysters to preserve them has a somewhat eclectic history of its own.

One of the earliest Roman cookbooks, *The Apicius Book*, underscores the difficulties involved in keeping oysters fresh and mentions eating "oysters, well-seasoned with pepper, lovage, egg yolks, vinegar, broth, oil, and wine [sometimes honey]"—an interesting vinaigrette. Another Roman gastronomer describes a typical first course as "oysters, salt or pickled fish, raw onions and lettuce with various piquant sauces." And through the years "pickled" oysters customarily were eaten with brown bread, vinegar, onions, and pepper.

In America, the Indians cooked oysters and, when the colonists finally began eating them themselves rather than feeding them to their livestock, they used them in stews and stuffings. But in the South, "pickled" oysters became a common dish. *The Recipe Book of St. Anne's Parish*, Annapolis, Maryland, suggests serving "pickled" or "ripe" oysters in a salad. And by the turn of this century, such names as "Katzenjammer Salad," "Salad Tartare," and "Spanish Salad" were being used to designate the way a sauced or dressed oyster was "heaped" upon a bed of lettuce, cress, or celery.

Experience proves that pickling or marinating an oyster for a longish period of time does not always make it completely palatable, and with contemporary refrigeration there is no need to do it. But the use of a basic oil, vinegar, and herb dressing on raw or poached oysters *can* create a delectable salad, especially if the other ingredients complement the flavor and the texture of the oyster. Tangy tomato aspic, flavorful potato salad, pasta combined with crunchy vegetables bring out the oyster in oyster. It may not be a new idea but, with a slightly different zig and zag, oysters in salad can be provocative.

Whether a classic *salade verte* or a *salade composée*, a salad should be given unshared attention rather than just tucked in between the soup and entrée or somehow managed while dinner plates are being collected. The hostess should plan a special time for a salad: it should be a feast in itself. In order to do this, the salad must definitely make a statement. Ingredients should be absolutely fresh, the dressing simple, well blended, and custom-made. Above all, the timing must be perfect—only so much can be done ahead.

Anyone can follow directions for a soup or a casserole; a salad requires intuition and flair—a cook who respects, even loves, all the ingredients involved. If greens wilt, tomatoes run, watercress dangles, or croutons limp before the salad is presented, there is no remedy. If the oysters are not quite literally "quivering" right out of their shells, flavor will be lost. It's a pass-fail situation, the test of a gourmet cook, and very often the best indication of a successful meal. No wonder the French serve the salad as an "extra course."

SALADS AS ACCOMPANIMENTS

Spinnaker Salad

As colorful as a spinnaker and just as racy, this salad is an attention getter. Use perfect asparagus and let the oysters billow over the stalks in their savory dressing.

16	shucked small oysters		Salt and freshly ground white
2	pounds fresh asparagus		pepper
2	ounces Roquefort cheese		Cayenne pepper
¾	cup sour cream	12	cherry tomatoes
1	large sweet onion		

1. Remove the oysters from their shells, pat them dry and chill. Reserve the liquor for another use.
2. Wash, trim, and peel the asparagus. Plunge into boiling salted water. Bring to a boil and simmer, uncovered, for 1 minute. Refresh in ice water, drain and chill.
3. Mash the Roquefort cheese with a small amount of sour cream, and gradually add the rest of the cream.
4. Cut the onion into paper-thin slices and combine with the cheese mixture and oysters. Refrigerate until ready to use.
5. Arrange the asparagus stalks on chilled plates and spoon the oyster dressing over them.
6. Garnish with a sprinkling of cayenne and halved cherry tomatoes.

Serves 6

HOW TO BARREL UP OYSTERS, SO AS THEY SHALL LAST FOR SIXE MONETHS SWEET AND GOOD, AND IN THEIR NATURALL TASTE

Open your oisters, take the liquor of them, and mixe a reasonable proportion of the best white wine vinegar you can get, a little salt and some pepper, barrell the fish up in a small caske, covering all the Oysters in this pickle.

Sir Hugh Plat, *Delightes for Ladies*, 1609

Oyster Cucumber Boats

The alliance of oysters and cucumbers in this "place" salad has the mermaids singing. With the availability of continental cucumbers, it can be served all year long, but it is particularly tantalizing when homegrown cucumbers are ready to be picked.

12 shucked small oysters	*Dressing:*
2 5-inch cucumbers	1/2 cup plain yoghurt
Salt	1 Tablespoon lime juice
1 cup large-curd cottage cheese	2 teaspoons minced chutney
2 slices diced smoked salmon	1/2 teaspoon fennel seed
1/4 cup chopped chives	Freshly ground pepper
1 bunch watercress (optional)	
4 lime wedges (optional)	

1. Remove the oysters from their shells, drain, and pat dry. Reserve the liquor for another use.
2. Halve the cucumbers lengthwise. Remove the seeds and some of the pulp, leaving a 1/4-inch shell. Sprinkle with salt, invert, and drain on absorbent paper for about 30 minutes. Pat dry.
3. Place the oysters, cottage cheese, smoked salmon, and chives in a bowl.
4. Mix the dressing and combine with the salad, seasoning to taste with salt.
5. Fill each cucumber half with the oyster salad and garnish with watercress and lime wedges.

Serves 4

Spinnaker Salad (Page 87)

Oyster Cucumber Boats (Page 88)

Steak and Oyster Tartare (Page 235)

Concombre à la Crème Fraîche

A "cool as a cucumber" salad is especially convincing during the months when cucumbers ripen on the vine, and oysters are harvested from the deepest beds. Served on a chiffonade of iceberg lettuce or on a frilly bed of ruby lettuce, it can be both salad and vegetable with a sizzling entrée.

16 shucked small oysters	*Dressing:*
2 5-inch cucumbers	1 egg yolk
1 cup dry white wine	1/2 teaspoon Dijon mustard
Iceberg or ruby lettuce	1/3 cup vegetable or olive oil
Fennel greens or parsley	1 1/2 Tablespoons lemon juice
	1/2 cup *crème fraîche*
	Salt and freshly ground pepper

1. Remove the oysters from their shells, drain, and pat dry. Reserve the liquor for another use.
2. Peel the cucumbers and halve lengthwise. Remove the seeds and cut into 3/8-inch slices. Poach in the wine until tender but still crisp, about 3 minutes. Drain.
3. Beat the egg and mustard together and slowly whisk in the oil. Mix in the remaining ingredients of the dressing, seasoning with salt and pepper to taste.
4. Stir the oysters and cucumbers into the dressing. Adjust seasonings, and chill.
5. Serve on iceberg or ruby lettuce leaves, and garnish with chopped fennel greens or parsley.

Serves 4

Annihilating all that's made
To a green thought in a green shade.
            Andrew Marvell, "The Garden"

Most people spoil garden things by over boiling them. All things
that are green should have a little crispness, for if they are overboil'd
they neither have any sweetness or beauty.
            Hannah Glasse, *Art of Cookery,* 1747

Eggs on the Half Shell

With the array of glorious appetizers currently tempting hostesses, deviled eggs have become somewhat declassé. But, stuffed with chopped oysters, given an appropriate "bed" of greens, and "tarted up" with a rémoulade dressing, they can raise eyebrows at a buffet or bridge table luncheon. They may garnish a salad and even be stylishly served *en gelée*.

½ pint oysters and liquor
½ cup dry white wine
12 hard-boiled large eggs

Fillings:
    Sour cream
    Dijon mustard
    Worcestershire sauce
    Capers
    Chopped dill weed
    Tabasco
    Garnish: snipped dill

    Yoghurt
    Minced celery
    Minced chives
    Minced olives and pimiento
    Pommery mustard
    Tabasco
    Garnish: slivers of green
      pepper

Herb mayonnaise
Soft butter
Dry mustard
Cayenne pepper
Garnish: small shrimp or
  parsley sprigs

Mayonnaise
Curry powder
Soy sauce
Lemon juice
Garnish: chutney

Dressings: (optional)
  Tomato and Mayonnaise
  Sauce, Variation 1
  (See p. 18)

  Rémoulade Sauce (See p. 19)

1. Poach the oysters in their own liquor and wine until the edges curl. Drain and coarsely chop them.
2. Shell the eggs. Cut them in halves, and sieve the yolks into a bowl.
3. Mix together a small amount of one of the fillings, and combine with the yolks. Season lightly with salt.
4. Gently stir in the oysters, and adjust salt.
5. Mound the filling in the white halves, cover with waxed paper and refrigerate.
6. Arrange the eggs on a bed of lettuce and decorate with a garnish. Dress with one of the sauces or serve the sauce on the side.

Serves 8

OYSTERS À L'ALEXANDRE DUMAS

Place in a sauce-bowl a heaped teaspoonful of salt, three-quarters of a teaspoonful of very finely crushed white pepper, one medium-sized, fine, sound, well-peeled, and very finely chopped shallot, one heaped teaspoonful of very finely chopped chives, and half a teaspoonful of parsley, also very finely chopped up. Mix lightly together, then pour in a light teaspoonful of olive oil, six drops of Tabasco sauce, one saltspoonful of Worcestershire sauce, and lastly one light gill, or five and a half tablespoonfuls, of good vinegar. Mix it thoroughly with a spoon; send to the table, and with a teaspoon pour a little of the sauce over each oyster just before eating them.

Filippini of Delmonico's, *The Table*, 1891

Venus' Own Salad

Glowing with the color of the sun, chilled oysters emerge from their shells glistening in aspic and crisp vegetables. The rounder the shells, the more complete the novelty of this "place" salad. Season the aspic to taste, add a bit of chicken stock if desired, and these oysters will turn an ordinary meal into a love feast.

12	shucked oysters		1	Tablespoon finely chopped sweet red pepper or pimiento
24	deep 3-inch shells			
1	envelope plain gelatin			
1/4	cup dry white wine		1	Tablespoon finely chopped green pepper
8	ounces seasoned tomato juice or V-8 juice			
1	Tablespoon lemon juice Tabasco		1	Tablespoon finely chopped parsley
1	Tablespoon finely chopped celery		1	Tablespoon capers Curly lettuce

1. Cut the oysters in half and drain well, reserving the liquor for another use. Scrub and dry the shells.
2. Soften the gelatin in wine.
3. Bring the tomato and lemon juice to a boil in a small saucepan. Add the gelatin and stir until it has completely dissolved. Season with Tabasco.
4. Chill the aspic until it begins to mound. Stir in the celery, peppers, parsley, and capers.

5. Place half an oyster on each shell and cover with aspic. Chill until the aspic is firm.
6. Arrange 3 shells for each serving on a plate of curly lettuce, and garnish with parsley sprigs.

Serves 8

One of the greatest luxuries in dining is to be able to command plenty of good vegetables well served up. But this is a luxury vainly hoped for at set parties. The vegetables are made to figure in a very secondary way, except, indeed, whilst they are considered great delicacies.

Thomas Walker, *The Art of Dining*, 1835

Summerhouse Salad

Used as an individual "place" salad, or mounded in the middle of a chilled, glass serving plate, this salad will spiff up a platter of Southern fried chicken in sporting style. Perfect for a Derby Day party or for a quiet dinner on one of those brisk fall weekends at the summer cottage when the hosts and their guests settle back into lounge chairs with a little "sipping whiskey."

1 pint oysters and liquor	$^1\!/_2$ cup coarsely chopped unsalted pecans
1 cup dry white wine	
1 Tablespoon grated onion	4 Tablespoons mayonnaise
1 cup finely chopped celery	1 Tablespoon lemon juice
2 Tablespoons chopped pimiento	Salt and freshly ground pepper
	Ruby or oak leaf lettuce

1. Poach the oysters in their own liquor and the wine, drain, cut in quarters, and chill.
2. Combine the onion, celery, pimiento, pecans, and oysters in a bowl.
3. Mix the mayonnaise and lemon juice and add to the oyster mixture, using only enough mayonnaise to bind. Season to taste.
4. Arrange lettuce on the plates and mound with the oyster salad. Garnish with whole pecans if desired.

Serves 4

Love Apple Salad

Select only medium-sized perfect tomatoes for this salad, and they'll be as tempting as Fameuse apples probably were in Paradise. The stuffing is simple and certainly congenial to a few changes here and there. Use fresh basil instead of dill, fresh cucumbers from the garden rather than pickles, or spoon a little pesto sauce into the dressing. It could be seductive.

½ pint oysters and liquor
½ cup dry white wine
4 medium tomatoes
½ cup finely chopped celery
2 Tablespoons finely chopped sweet red pepper or pimiento
2 Tablespoons finely chopped cucumber pickles
2 Tablespoons capers
Parsley or watercress

Dressing:
2 Tablespoons white tarragon vinegar
1 teaspoon lemon juice
½ teaspoon dry mustard
½ teaspoon paprika
2 finely chopped scallions
Pinch of dill weed
1 garlic clove
Salt and freshly ground pepper
½ cup olive oil

1. Mix the dressing by stirring together the vinegar, lemon juice, herbs, and seasonings, using salt and pepper to taste. Slowly whisk in the oil. Allow the dressing to stand for at least 30 minutes. Discard the garlic clove.
2. Poach the oysters in their own liquor and white wine. Drain and chop the oysters. Marinate them in some of the dressing and chill.
3. Cut off the tomato tops with a serrated knife and remove the pulp and seeds, taking care not to pierce the bottoms and sides. Salt lightly, invert, and drain on a rack or on absorbent paper.
4. Combine the oysters, celery, pepper, pickles, and capers in a large bowl. Toss lightly with enough dressing to moisten. The stuffing should not be runny. Adjust salt.
5. Fill the tomato cavities with stuffing.
6. Arrange a tomato on a bed of parsley or watercress and serve as a "place" salad.

Serves 4

"The whole plant is of ranke and stinking savour," says *Gerard's Herball* under the heading "Apples of Love," which of course means "tomatoes," in reference to the aphrodisiac reputation they then enjoyed.
Waverley Root, *Food*

Oyster Mousse

Whether prepared in individual molds and garnished with cucumber and tomato slices or jelled in a quart-and-a-half ring mold and served with a mound of fresh shrimp or cherry tomatoes in the center, this oyster mousse is first class fare. But a word of caution—puréed oysters may "grey" the mousse, so add chopped oysters just before jelling and ladle an eye-dazzling sauce over the top.

1 pint oysters and liquor	*Sauce:*
¼ cup fish or chicken stock (See pp. 62, 63)	1½ cups mayonnaise
¼ cup dry Vermouth	1 Tablespoon chili sauce
2 Tablespoons butter	1 Tablespoon finely chopped tomato chutney*
1 cup sliced mushrooms	½ teaspoon A-1 sauce
1 chopped small apple	1 Tablespoon finely chopped celery
3 Tablespoons chopped onion	1 teaspoon finely chopped chives
¼ cup milk	
1 envelope plain gelatin	½ Tablespoon finely chopped green pepper
2 Tablespoons lemon juice	1 Tablespoon finely chopped pimiento
½ cup mayonnaise	
1 cup sour cream	1 Tablespoon finely chopped parsley
½ teaspoon tarragon	
Salt and freshly ground pepper	
Watercress or bibb lettuce	

1. Poach the oysters in their liquor, stock, and Vermouth until the edges begin to curl. Drain and coarsely chop the oysters, reserving ½ cup of the poaching liquid.
2. Melt the butter in a saucepan, add the poaching liquid, and cook the mushrooms until they are tender. Remove with a slotted spoon and set aside.
3. Add the apple and onion to the saucepan and simmer until tender.
4. Place the milk and gelatin in a blender or in the work bowl of a food processor and process until the gelatin is softened. Add the warm apple mixture and process again, gradually adding the lemon juice, mayonnaise, sour cream, and tarragon.
5. Stir the oysters and mushrooms into the puréed mixture, and season to taste with salt and pepper.
6. Pour into a lightly oiled 6-cup mold or individual molds and chill until firm.
7. Unmold on watercress or lettuce leaves, and serve with a sauce.

* One-half tablespoon prepared horseradish may be substituted. If it is used, add a tablespoon of chili sauce for more color.

Serves 6

Bermuda Triangle Salad

Three key ingredients—oysters, mushrooms, and watercress—are the secret of this "let's get away from it all" luncheon salad. If preferred, substitute young spinach leaves for watercress, but the slightly spicy flavor of its clover-like leaves makes watercress a great taste balancer in these uncharted waters.

24 shucked small oysters	*Dressing:*
2 bunches watercress	1 teaspoon dry mustard
8 slices bacon	1/2 teaspoon freshly ground
1/2 pound thinly sliced small mushrooms	pepper
	1 teaspoon sugar
1/2 thinly sliced red onion	2 teaspoons Dijon mustard
2 Tablespoons lemon juice	3 Tablespoons wine vinegar
1 garlic clove	Worcestershire sauce
2 sieved hard-boiled egg yolks (optional)	1/2 cup olive oil
Cherry tomatoes (optional)	Salt

1. Remove the oysters from their shells, drain, and pat dry. Reserve the liquor for another use.
2. Wash and trim the watercress. Pat the leaves dry and wrap in a towel or absorbent paper until ready to use.
3. Cook the bacon in a skillet or microwave oven until it is crisp; drain, crumble, and reserve for topping the salad.
4. Mix the ingredients for the dressing, and slowly whisk in the oil.
5. Rub the inside of a large bowl with a peeled garlic clove and lightly toss all the salad ingredients with some or all of the dressing. Adjust the salt.
6. Distribute the salad on chilled plates and sprinkle with crumbled bacon and egg yolks if desired. Garnish with cherry tomatoes or tomato wedges.

Serves 6

SPANISH SALAD

Pick over two dozen oysters, dry them carefully and put them on the ice. Rub the yolks of six hard-boiled eggs, with a fork, till they are dry and mealy; add a teaspoonful of melted butter, two tablespoonfuls of vinegar, a tablespoonful of tomato catsup, a little salt and a teaspoonful of Gebhardt's Eagle Chili powder; mix thoroughly, squeezing in the juice from half a lemon. Toss the oysters up in this sauce and serve them on shredded celery garnished with celery tops.

May E. Southworth, *One Hundred & One Ways of Serving Oysters*

Oysters Niçoise

This salad can be a cornucopia of fresh and lightly cooked ingredients, and assembling it is certainly a cook's delight. Many hostesses present the salad in a shallow, lettuce-lined, wooden bowl, arranging each ingredient in spoke-like fashion from the center. Others prefer to toss the ingredients together. Whichever arrangement is used, adding the lightly fried oysters to the center of the salad is the penultimate step to success.

16 shucked oysters	3 sliced hard-boiled eggs
1/4 cup corn flour	1/2 thinly sliced red onion
Salt and freshly ground	8 flat anchovies
pepper	8 pitted ripe Greek olives
2 eggs	
1 Tablespoon water	*Dressing:*
1/2 cup corn flake crumbs	3 Tablespoons red wine vinegar
3 Tablespoons butter	1/2 teaspoon salt
1 Tablespoon vegetable oil	Pinch of pepper
2 sliced medium tomatoes	1/2 teaspoon dry mustard
1/2 pound blanched green beans	1 Tablespoon chopped fresh
8 cooked small new potatoes	basil
(optional)	2/3 cup olive oil
1/2 head romaine lettuce	

1. Drain the oysters, reserving the liquor for another use. Pat the oysters dry, and dredge in seasoned flour. Dip in eggs beaten with the water, and roll in crumbs. Place on a plate lined with absorbent paper and chill for an hour.
2. Heat the butter and oil in a skillet and shallow-fry the oysters on both sides until golden. Drain.
3. Mix the vinegar with the salt, pepper, mustard, and basil. Slowly whisk in the oil.
4. Coat the tomatoes with the dressing and set aside. Toss the beans and then the potatoes in the dressing and set aside.
5. Assemble the salad by lining a large salad bowl with leaves of romaine, tearing some leaves into smaller pieces. Arrange the vegetables and other ingredients, placing the oysters in the center. Drizzle with some of the dressing before serving.

Serves 4

Let onion atoms lurk within the bowl
And, half suspected, animate the whole.
Lady Holland

Bamboo Hut Oyster Salad

Somewhere between Egg Drop Soup and Peking Duck, this "cold" appetizer-salad would be an exotic addition to an array of first courses (at least four) at an Oriental dinner. Or, if served at a luncheon, it could take its place with Shrimp Toast and Spring Rolls to pique the appetite but not overindulge it. A small glass of *shao hsing*, rice wine, would be the right touch.

1 pint oysters and liquor	Salt and freshly ground
½ cup dry white wine	pepper
1 large sweet red pepper	
1 8-ounce can bamboo shoots	*Dressing:*
6 ribs slivered Chinese cabbage	1 Tablespoon sesame oil
1 cup fresh bean sprouts	3 Tablespoons vegetable oil
12 pitted ripe Greek olives	1 Tablespoon lemon juice
¼ cup chopped parsley	2 teaspoons soy sauce
2 Tablespoons capers	Sugar (optional)

1. Poach the oysters in their liquor and wine until the edges curl. Drain and set the oysters aside in a large bowl.
2. Broil the pepper, turning it to char all surfaces. Cool and remove the skin, core, and seeds, and dice the pepper.
3. Drain the bamboo shoots, and cut into ⅜-inch slices.
4. Mix the dressing and add sugar if a sweet dressing is desired.
5. Combine all the ingredients with the oysters, and toss the salad with enough dressing to coat; chill for 2 hours, stir gently, and add salt and pepper if necessary.
6. Toss again before serving.

Serves 6

Oysters Madras

For an exotic foray into the special world of seafood salads, start with this subtle blend of flavors and feel free to substitute scallops and mussels for either the shrimp or the crabmeat. If the rice is prepared ahead and refrigerated, be sure to return it to room temperature before adding the seafood and tossing.

½ pint small oysters and liquor	½ pound peeled, deveined,
½ cup dry white wine	cooked shrimp
½ teaspoon saffron	½ pound lump crabmeat
3½ cups chicken stock	½ cup dried currants
(See p. 63)	Tomato or mango chutney
1½ cups long grain rice	

Dressing:

2	Tablespoons white wine vinegar	2	crushed garlic cloves
	Salt and freshly ground pepper	4	Tablespoons chopped parsley
		1	teaspoon Dijon mustard
		6	Tablespoons olive oil

1. Poach the oysters in their own liquor and wine. Drain and set aside, reserving the poaching liquid.
2. Dissolve the saffron in the poaching liquid, and combine with the stock in a large saucepan. Bring to a boil and add the rice. Cover, and simmer until the rice is tender. Drain and keep the rice warm.
3. Mix the vinegar with the herbs and spices and slowly whisk in the oil.
4. Place the warm rice in a bowl and mix thoroughly with the dressing.
5. Add the oysters, shrimp, crabmeat, and currants. Toss lightly and adjust seasonings.
6. Serve at room temperature with a sauceboat of chutney.

Serves 6

Seashell Salad

What could be more redolent of the depths of the sea than a clever combination of oysters and pasta seashells? A cool and casual luncheon dish or a gala buffet table treat, this salad will please almost every palate.

1	pint oysters and liquor		Buttercrunch or salad bowl lettuce
	Salt	1	sliced medium tomato
1½	cups maruzelle (seashells)		
	Butter or vegetable oil		*Dressing:*
1	cup dry white wine	2	Tablespoons vinegar or lemon juice
¼	cup chopped stuffed olives	½	teaspoon celery seed
3	Tablespoons chopped green pepper	½	teaspoon dry mustard
½	thinly sliced cucumber	¼	teaspoon freshly ground pepper
6	thinly sliced radishes	½	cup mayonnaise
½	cup chopped parsley		

1. Bring 2 quarts of salted water to a boil, add the pasta shells and cook until tender but firm. Drain the pasta, toss with a small amount of butter or oil, and set aside.
2. Poach the oysters in their own liquor and wine until the edges begin to curl, drain, and pat dry. If they are large, cut in halves or quarters.

3. Mix the dressing in a large bowl.
4. Stir in the olives, vegetables, parsley, and pasta. Add the oysters, and adjust the seasonings. Chill until ready to use.
5. Serve on lettuce and garnish with tomato slices.

Serves 6

As much depends upon the mixing as upon the proportions. The foolish pour in first their oil, then their vinegar, and leave the rest to chance, with results one shudders to remember. The two must be mixed together even as they are poured over the salad, and here the task but begins. For next, they must be mixed with the salad. To "fatigue" it the French call this special part of the process, and indeed, to create a work of art, you must mix and mix and mix until you are fatigued yourself, and your tomatoes or potatoes reduced to one-half their original bulk. Then will the dressing have soaked through and through them. Then will every mouthful be a special plea for gluttony, an eloquent argument for the one vice that need not pall with years.

Elizabeth Robins Pennell, *The Feasts of Autolycus*

Insalata Romana

Nuovo cucina at its most convincing, this salad can be made with almost any vegetable or combination of vegetables from the garden. Asparagus is celestial, but green peas, zucchini, and broccoli are inspired, if a little less divine.

1 pint oysters and liquor	12 pitted ripe Greek olives
1 cup dry white wine	1/2 cup coarsely chopped or
1 pound asparagus	halved walnuts (optional)
4 Tablespoons olive oil	1 1/2 Tablespoons wine vinegar
1 garlic clove	(Aceto Balsamico)
1 pound egg fettucini or egg	Salt and freshly ground
fusilli	pepper
1/4 pound julienned ham	

1. Lightly poach the oysters in their own liquor and wine, drain, and set aside.
2. Trim, peel, and blanch the asparagus in boiling salted water. Refresh in ice water and cut into 1-inch pieces.
3. Heat the olive oil in a small saucepan and cook the garlic clove for 1 minute. Discard the garlic.

4. Cook the pasta in boiling salted water until tender and drain. Transfer to a large bowl and toss with the olive oil.
5. Add the asparagus, ham, olives, oysters, walnuts, if desired, and vinegar. Toss again and adjust seasonings.
6. Serve either at room temperature or chilled.

Serves 6

Posh Potato Salad

Fried oysters add a touch of sass to a delightfully seasoned potato salad and make it a luscious luncheon meal. Served with a glass of chilled white wine, a basket of breadsticks, and some curls of sweet butter, it's simply "top drawer."

1 pint medium oysters and liquor
5 medium red potatoes
1 cup corn flour
Salt and freshly ground white pepper
Oil for deep frying
2 Tablespoons chopped parsley
2 Tablespoons chopped chives
Sour cream (optional)

Dressing:
½ cup white vinegar
1 teaspoon Dijon mustard
1 teaspoon celery seed
1 teaspoon sugar

1. Boil the potatoes in salted water, drain, and cool slightly.
2. Drain the oysters, reserving ⅓ cup of the liquor. Pat the oysters dry, dredge in seasoned corn flour, and set aside for at least 15 minutes.
3. Mix the oyster liquor, the dressing ingredients, and ¼ teaspoon salt in a saucepan, and simmer for a few minutes.
4. Deep fry the oysters in 375° oil, or pan fry over moderatedly high heat until both sides are golden. Drain on absorbent paper.
5. Peel the warm potatoes and cut into ½-inch cubes. Sprinkle with parsley and chives, and toss with the hot dressing. Adjust salt, and bind with sour cream if desired.
6. Serve the salad warm or at room temperature, garnished with the oysters.

Serves 6

Gasthof Salat

No need to travel to Germany for *Gemütlichkeit*. Just light up the charcoal grill, set out the bratwurst, knockwurst, and frankfurters, and neighbors will think there's a bit of Bavaria in the air, especially if there's some imported beer on ice.

1	pint small oysters	1	finely chopped large onion
1½	pounds potatoes		Salt and freshly ground
6	slices diced bacon		pepper
1	teaspoon flour	1	Tablespoon chopped fresh
2	Tablespoons sugar		dill weed
¼	cup chicken stock (See p. 63)		
¼	cup white wine vinegar (Sauterne)		

1. Drain the oysters and set aside. Reserve the liquor for another use.
2. Cook the potatoes in boiling salted water until they are tender. Drain and cool slightly.
3. Sauté the bacon in a saucepan until crisp. Remove the bacon with a slotted spoon and drain on absorbent paper.
4. Pour off all but 2 tablespoons of the drippings from the saucepan. Stir in the flour and sugar and cook until bubbling. Remove from the heat and whisk in the stock and vinegar. Return to heat and boil, stirring constantly, until the mixture thickens and simmers a few minutes.
5. Add the oysters and onions and cook until the edges of oysters begin to curl.
6. Peel the warm potatoes and slice them into a large bowl.
7. Add the oyster dressing and toss the salad gently. Adjust seasonings.
8. Garnish with bacon and dill before serving.

Serves 6

May I put in a good word for Dill? . . . It has many virtues, even if you do not rely upon it "to stay the hiccough, being boiled in wine," or "to render witches of their will." Amongst its virtues, apart from its light yellow grace in a mixed bunch of flowers, is the fact that you can use its seed to flavour vinegar, and for pickling cucumbers. You can also, if you wish, use the young leaves to flavour soups, sauces, and fish.

Vita Sackville-West, *Garden Book*

Pier I Salad

Perfect as a side dish for a seashore picnic of grilled hamburgers or baked ham, potato salad always waves a flag. But range a bit further and serve it with swordfish kebabs or a smoked turkey and the skipper and his crew will quickly "reach" for the finish line.

1½ pints oysters and liquor
2 pounds potatoes
    Salt
1 cup dry white wine
1 chopped medium red onion
2 cups chopped celery
1 cup chopped parsley
4 slices bacon
2 sliced hard-boiled eggs

Dressing:
½ cup mayonnaise
3 Tablespoons vegetable oil
2 Tablespoons tarragon vinegar
1 teaspoon dry mustard
1 teaspoon sugar
¼ teaspoon coarsely ground
    pepper

1. Boil the potatoes in salted water until centers can be pierced with a fork. Drain and cool slightly.
2. Poach the oysters in their own liquor and wine until the edges start to curl. Drain and pat dry. If the oysters are large, cut in halves or quarters.
3. Mix the dressing and ½ teaspoon salt in a large bowl. Stir in the onion, celery, and parsley.
4. Peel and cut the warm potatoes into ½-inch cubes.
5. Add the potatoes and oysters to the salad and bind with more mayonnaise if necessary. Season to taste, and refrigerate at least 4 hours.
6. Cook the bacon in a skillet or microwave oven until crisp, drain, and crumble. Reserve the bacon for garnish, or stir into the salad just before serving.
7. Garnish with egg slices.

Serves 8

This pretty phrase, "la salade . . . qui réjouit le coeur," is often quoted and misquoted. At the expense of being thought dully practical and unpoetical, I truthfully do not think it means that salads gladden the heart, but that they are light in the stomach and easily digested, and that they bring a feeling of easiness and comfort to the whole belly and especially to the poor overworked organ that perches on top of it, the human heart. Anything which does that is, of course, a gladsome thing.

M. F. K. Fisher, "The Translator's Glosses," *The Physiology of Taste*

VEGETABLES

Bounty of the Garden Basket

From the Food Halls of Harrods in fashionable Kensington to Quail Hollow on Cape Cod, everyone has a favorite market where tomatoes are so luscious, lettuce so fresh and crisp, in fact, all the fruits and vegetables so bursting with color and flavor that within minutes a shopping basket can be filled and rushed home to the kitchen.

And the market is all the more beguiling if it is a seasonal one. When afternoon shadows suggest fall and leaves turn a little, the aroma of pickling spices prevails in the back of the shop, and jars of "just-made" chutney, relish, and marmalade line the shelves. It's a special time of year and an inner voice says, "Please, stay a little longer," as the wind shifts from south to northeast by east.

It was during the waning days of summer and early fall that most of these vegetable and oyster recipes were tested. The oysters came from the Cotuit Oyster Company minutes away; the herbs and vegetables came from the garden or other gardens nearby. In a very real sense, the *primeurs*, or first of the crop, were used. And the results were so immediate, so tangible, that this particular cache of recipes can only be called the bounty of the garden basket.

Artichokes

The artichoke has been cultivated for centuries and has retained its identity as a "love food," the darling vegetable of the Renaissance, and the symbol of "Taste" in the visual arts. Not surprising, then, that like the oyster, the artichoke has remained "the pleasure of people who mind about good food." What can be more natural than a combination of the two? It could be called a marriage, but an *affaire de coeur* seems much more suitable for this compatible pair.

Individual servings of Artichoke Gratin and perfectly contained Stuffed Artichoke fonds are nothing short of elegant with an entrée of Veal Piquante or a Spit-Roasted Duckling.

ARTICHOKE GRATIN

1	pint small oysters and liquor	2	Tablespoons flour
3	medium artichokes	2	Tablespoons dry Sherry
½	lemon	2	Tablespoons minced parsley
	Salt	1	teaspoon chopped fresh basil
½	sliced onion		Salt and freshly ground
1	cup heavy cream		pepper
6	Tablespoons butter		Tabasco
2	garlic cloves	½	cup fresh bread crumbs

(*Artichoke Gratin,* continued)

Oven Temperature: 375°

1. Remove the stems and lower leaves from the artichokes and rub the cut edges with lemon. Add 1 teaspoon salt, the piece of lemon, and the onion slices to 1½ inches of boiling water in a saucepan large enough to hold the artichokes upright. Cover and simmer for about 40 minutes, or until the bottoms are tender when pierced with a fork. Drain and cool the artichokes.
2. Remove the leaves and scrape them, saving the pulp; discard the bristly choke and dice the bottoms.
3. Drain the oysters, reserve ¼ cup of the liquor, and warm it with the cream in a small saucepan.
4. Melt the butter in another saucepan, spoon off and reserve 2 tablespoons for the bread crumbs. Sauté the garlic cloves until tender, and discard them. Stir in the flour and cook until bubbling. Remove from the heat and whisk in the warm cream. Return to heat and boil, stirring constantly, until the mixture thickens.
5. Stir in the artichoke pulp and bottoms, Sherry, parsley, and basil, and simmer a few minutes. Remove from the heat and add the oysters. Adjust seasoning.
6. Spoon into 6 buttered scallop shells or ramekins and top with the buttered bread crumbs.
7. Bake about 15 minutes until the sauce is bubbling and the tops are golden brown.

Serves 6

STUFFED ARTICHOKES

½ pint oysters and liquor	1 teaspoon chopped fresh
6 extra large artichokes	tarragon
2 Tablespoons lemon juice	1 egg yolk
Salt	1 Tablespoon brandy
4 Tablespoons butter	Freshly ground pepper
3 Tablespoons finely chopped	Tabasco
shallots	½ cup fresh bread crumbs
1 cup heavy cream	Lemon wedges

Oven Temperature: 400°

1. Trim and discard the stems and outer leaves from the artichokes, cut off the ends of the leaves, and rub all cut surfaces with lemon juice. Add the remaining lemon juice to boiling salted water in a saucepan and cook the artichokes about 20 minutes, until they are tender when pierced with a fork. Drain, cool, and scoop out the bristly chokes, leaving a "wall" of some of the tender leaves.
2. Drain and chop the oysters, reserving the liquor.

3. Melt 3 tablespoons of butter in a heavy saucepan. Add the shallots, oyster liquor, ³⁄₄ cup of cream, and tarragon, and simmer until the mixture is slightly reduced.
4. Whisk the egg yolk in a bowl with the remaining ¹⁄₄ cup of cream. Whisk in the hot mixture, a spoonful at a time. Transfer the enriched sauce to the saucepan and, stirring carefully, cook until the mixture bubbles.
5. Add the oysters, brandy, salt, pepper, and Tabasco to taste; stir in the bread crumbs, and cook until hot.
6. Fill the artichokes, dot with the remaining butter, and arrange in a buttered baking dish.
7. Bake about 15 minutes, and garnish with lemon wedges.

Serves 6

Asparagus

Another vegetable that "manifestly provoketh Venus," asparagus is as legendary, luxurious, and love-inspiring as the artichoke. Although it can be prepared in a fraction of the time that it takes to cook its illustrious peer, asparagus, like the artichoke, can also be served with a little melted butter, a squeeze of lemon, or dressed more elegantly with a Hollandaise sauce. But asparagus has its own special allure. Napped with a light oyster and mushroom cream sauce, it works its magic in ways that even Madame Pompadour could never have imagined when she combined asparagus with eggs for her not too subtle purposes.

SAUCED ASPARAGUS

20	shucked medium oysters and liquor	1¹⁄₂	Tablespoons flour
1	cup heavy cream		Pinch of mace or nutmeg
3	Tablespoons butter	2	pounds asparagus
1	Tablespoon finely chopped scallions	1	cup sliced mushrooms
			Salt and freshly ground pepper

1. Remove the oysters from their shells, strain and reserve ¹⁄₂ cup of the liquor.
2. Warm the oyster liquor and cream in a small saucepan.
3. Melt 2 tablespoons of butter in another saucepan and sauté the scallions until tender. Stir in the flour and cook until bubbling. Remove from the heat and whisk in the cream. Return to heat, add the mace or nutmeg, and boil, stirring constantly, until the mixture thickens. Partially cover the pan with waxed paper, and set aside.
4. Trim, peel, and blanch the asparagus for 3 minutes in boiling salted water. Remove the stalks with a slotted spoon to a rack lined with a towel, and keep warm.

5. Stir the remaining tablespoon of butter into the sauce, and simmer for 3 minutes. Add the oysters, mushrooms; seasoning to taste, and heat until the edges of the oysters start to curl.
6. Arrange the asparagus spears on a serving platter or individual plates, and nap with the oyster and mushroom sauce.

Serves 4

Beans

Through the years bacon and beans have enjoyed a long and discreet relationship. In hard times, they were the staple of the British working class. In good times, they were, and still are, regular Saturday night fare in Boston. Little wonder, then, that this recipe for butter beans includes bacon. The surprise is the addition of oysters and sour cream. For those willing to put their adventurous foot forward, serve these lima beans as a foil for grilled pork chops or a crown roast of pork and don't forget a glass of hearty wine or ale.

SAUCED BUTTER BEANS

1 pint oysters and liquor	1½ cups shelled lima beans, or 1 10-ounce package frozen lima beans
4 slices bacon	
2 egg yolks	
1 cup sour cream	1 cup dry white wine
1 Tablespoon lemon juice	Salt
1 teaspoon sugar	
⅛ teaspoon white pepper	

1. Cook the bacon until crisp in a skillet or microwave oven, dry on absorbent paper, and crumble.
2. Mix the egg yolks, sour cream, lemon juice, sugar, and pepper in the top of a double boiler. Place over simmering water and cook about 5 minutes, stirring frequently, until the sauce thickens. Reduce the heat so the water no longer simmers.
3. Blanch the beans in boiling salted water until tender, drain, and combine with the sauce.
4. Poach the oysters in their own liquor and the wine until they are plump, drain, stir gently into the sauce and season to taste with salt.
5. Serve in a vegetable dish, and garnish with bacon.

Serves 4

Broccoli

Broccoli is simply a nifty vegetable to "team up" with chicken, pasta, eggs, or shellfish. Blanched for a minute or two, it has a delightful crunch; sautéed, the stems and florets retain their color, flavor, and crispness; stir-fried, it does wonders for a vegetable platter. For a little added drama, cast it as the main ingredient in a soufflé or mousse. It will perform magnificently at a matinée and steal the evening show.

BROCCOLI MOUSSE

1	pint oysters	1½ Tablespoons lemon juice
1½	pounds broccoli	4 eggs
	Salt	Freshly ground pepper
5	Tablespoons butter	1 cup blanched sliced carrots
⅔	cup heavy cream	Lemon slices

Oven Temperature: 375°

1. Wash, peel, and cut the broccoli into ¼-inch pieces, setting aside 1½ cups of coarsely chopped florets. Blanch the stalks in boiling salted water for 1 minute, drain, refresh in cold water, and drain again. Blanch and refresh the florets separately.
2. Melt 3 tablespoons of butter in a skillet, add the blanched stalks, cream, and lemon juice, and cook over moderately high heat, stirring constantly, until the cream thickens and the broccoli is well coated.
3. Purée the mixture in a food processor or blender, adding the eggs one at a time.
4. Drain and chop the oysters; stir them into the purée, seasoning to taste with salt and pepper.
5. Pour the mixture into a buttered 6-cup ring mold, and place it in a baking pan half filled with boiling water.
6. Bake for 25 minutes, or until a knife tests clean.
7. Melt the remaining 2 tablespoons of butter in a saucepan and sautée the broccoli florets and carrots until they are thoroughly heated. Season to taste.
8. Unmold the mousse on a serving dish, fill the center with the vegetables, and garnish with lemon slices. The mousse may be served hot or at room temperature.

Serves 8

"It's broccoli, dear."
"I say it's spinach,
and I say the hell with it."
James Thurber

Corn

Considered too "sweet" for continental palates, corn is a New World "vegetable" and probably one of the largest grain crops in America. Edible in its "green stage," corn quickly perishes and really should be prepared as soon after picking as possible or its sweetness becomes starchy.

While many devotees believe that "just picked" corn on the cob is the *only* way to eat this vegetable, the following recipes for a casserole and soufflé may give them second thoughts and, perhaps, if they also fancy oysters, second servings.

CORN CASSEROLE

1 pint oysters and liquor	1 egg
6 Tablespoons butter	³/₄ cup light cream
¼ cup chopped onion	1½ cups fresh bread crumbs
½ cup chopped green and red sweet peppers	
2 cups scraped corn	
½ teaspoon celery seed	
Salt and freshly ground pepper	

Oven Temperature: 350°

1. Drain the oysters, reserving ¼ cup of the oyster liquor.
2. Melt the butter in a skillet, pour off and reserve 2 tablespoons for the bread crumbs, and sauté the onions and peppers until they are tender. Remove from the heat, stir in the corn and celery seed, and season lightly with salt and pepper.
3. Whisk the egg, oyster liquor, and cream together in a bowl.
4. Spread one-third of the crumbs on the bottom of a buttered 1½-quart baking dish, distribute half of the vegetable mixture over them and half of the oysters. Repeat the three layers, and pour the egg-cream mixture over the top. Sprinkle with the remaining crumbs and melted butter.
5. Bake about 20 minutes, until the dish is thoroughly hot and the crumbs are golden brown.

Serves 6

CORN SOUFFLÉ

½ pint oysters and liquor
1   cup milk
3   Tablespoons butter
3   Tablespoons flour
½ cup grated Gouda cheese
4   egg yolks
1½ cups scraped corn

¼ cup finely chopped chives
    Salt and freshly ground
        pepper
5   egg whites

Oven Temperature: 350°

1. Drain the oysters and chop them, reserving the liquor.
2. Warm the oyster liquor and ¾ cup of milk in a small saucepan.
3. Melt the butter in another saucepan, stir in the flour, and cook until bubbling. Remove from the heat and whisk in the warm milk. Return to heat and boil, stirring constantly, until the mixture thickens. Stir in the cheese.
4. Whisk the egg yolks and the remaining ¼ cup of milk in a large bowl. Whisk in ½ cup of the hot sauce, a spoonful at a time; then slowly beat in the remaining sauce.
5. Stir in the oysters, corn, chives, salt and pepper to taste.
6. Beat the egg whites to stiff peaks, stir a third of them into the oyster mixture, and fold in the remaining whites.
7. Pour into a buttered 2-quart soufflé dish or 4 individual dishes.
8. Bake for 40 minutes, and test with a knife. When the knife blade comes out clean, remove from the oven and serve immediately.

Serves 4

Eggplant

The Syrians and Turks claim to have a thousand ways to prepare eggplant, and southern Mediterranean cuisine reflects the versatility of this vegetable. So beautiful and exotic in appearance that it provoked John Gerard to write in his Elizabethan *Herball*, "those apples have a mischievous quality," the eggplant was viewed with some suspicion in many countries, including this one, until the turn of the century when such prestigious restaurants as Delmonico's began to serve it.

Today dishes like Moussaka, Caponata, and Ratatouille are commonplace, and the suitability of eggplant in the preparation of hearty stews, cold and hot appetizers, and one-dish meals is well known.

In the south of France, a chef distinguished himself by serving poached eggs on the top of a casserole of Ratatouille. Try oysters for a subtle variation on a theme. And, if there is a little extra stuffing left over from the Stuffed Eggplant recipe, it will do wonders for a rock cornish hen or a small roasting chicken.

STUFFED EGGPLANT

1 pint oysters and liquor
4 8-ounce eggplants
  Salt
2 Tablespoons butter
½ pound finely chopped linguiça
  or kielbasa
1 minced garlic clove
1 chopped small onion
½ cup chopped celery
½ cup chopped green pepper
1 cup chopped parsley

1 cup chopped mushrooms
  (optional)
1 teaspoon Worcestershire sauce
¼ teaspoon thyme
1 bay leaf
  Freshly ground pepper
½ cup chicken stock (See p. 63)
1½ cups fresh bread crumbs
2 eggs
½ cup freshly grated Swiss
  cheese

Oven Temperature: 350°

1. Cut the unpeeled eggplants in half lengthwise, and scoop out the centers leaving ¼-inch shells. Cut the pulp into small cubes, and use 2 cups for the stuffing. Toss the cubes with salt and drain for 30 minutes.
2. Melt the butter in a large saucepan and sauté the sausage until it is partly cooked. Add the garlic, onion, celery, pepper, parsley, and mushrooms, and sauté until they are tender.
3. Drain the oysters, cut them in halves or quarters if they are large, and reserve 1/3 cup of the liquor.
4. Add the liquor, Worcestershire, thyme, bay leaf, and pepper to the sautéed vegetables. Cover and simmer for 30 minutes, adding stock if the mixture becomes dry. Remove the bay leaf, add the eggplant pulp, and cook another 10 minutes.
5. Combine the oysters and 1 cup of bread crumbs with the vegetables, and stir in the well-beaten eggs. The stuffing should be moist but not runny. Adjust seasonings.
6. Fill the eggplant shells and sprinkle with a mixture of cheese and remaining crumbs. The dish may be prepared ahead and refrigerated at this point.
7. Place the shells in an oiled baking pan and bake 30 minutes.

Serves 8

RATATOUILLE

1 pint oysters
1 16-ounce eggplant
  Salt
2 sliced 8-ounce zucchinis
½ cup olive oil
3 chopped medium onions
1 chopped large green or red
  pepper

1½ pounds peeled, seeded, and
  chopped tomatoes
2 minced garlic cloves
  Freshly ground pepper
½ cup freshly grated Parmesan
  cheese
½ cup fresh bread crumbs

Oven Temperature: 350°

1. Peel (or not as preferred) the eggplant and dice into ¹/₂-inch cubes. Toss with salt, drain for 45 minutes, and pat dry. Repeat the process with the zucchini.
2. Heat 3 tablespoons of oil in a large skillet, brown some of the eggplant cubes, drain and reserve the drippings; repeat until all the eggplant is browned, using the drippings and additional oil as needed. Set aside.
3. Add oil to the skillet if necessary and sauté the onions and pepper until tender. Add the zucchini, tomatoes, and garlic, and season to taste with pepper. Cover, and cook for 10 minutes; then uncover and cook over moderately high heat until the juices have evaporated.
4. Stir in the eggplant, adjust seasonings, and transfer to a large casserole. Cover and bake for 25 minutes.
5. Drain the oysters and pat dry, reserving the liquor for another use.
6. Remove the casserole from the oven and arrange the oysters on top of the vegetables. Sprinkle with a mixture of the cheese and crumbs.
7. Bake for 15 minutes, or until the topping is golden.

Serves 6

Fennel

Although the vegetable Florentine fennel, or *finocchio*, is another late-comer to American cuisine, Thomas Jefferson had two varieties of it in his vegetable garden at Monticello and was eloquent in its praise: "The fennel is beyond every other vegetable, delicious. It greatly resembles in appearance the largest size celery, perfectly white, and there is no vegetable equal to it in flavour"—a reputation to be envied, but deserved. Fennel can be used in soups, stuffings, and casseroles. It can be marinated or eaten raw with cheese for dessert, and its anise flavor makes it a super complement to seafood. In this simple recipe for sautéed fennel, mushrooms, and oysters, the addition of a dash of Pernod may well become an *exclamation point*.

SAUTÉED FENNEL

¹/₂ pint oysters	3 Tablespoons butter
1 1-pound fennel bulb with leaves	¹/₂ pound sliced mushrooms Salt and freshly ground
1 Tablespoon oil	pepper

1. Drain the oysters, pat dry, and coarsely chop them.
2. Cut the bulb in quarters and thinly slice, discarding the core. Finely chop about ¹/₄ cup of the leaves.
3. Heat the oil and 1 tablespoon of the butter in a large skillet, and sauté the

      mushrooms until the moisture has evaporated. Remove them with a slotted spoon and set aside.

4.   Melt the remaining 2 tablespoons of butter and add the fennel to the skillet. Cook until the fennel is tender but still crisp.

5.   Add the oysters and mushrooms, and cook, stirring gently, until the edges of the oysters start to curl. Season with salt and pepper.

6.   Stir in the chopped fennel leaves and serve immediately.

Serves 4

Mushrooms

Mysterious and multiple, mushrooms are as legendary as oysters, and like oysters can be prepared in innumerable ways. To be effective, the following recipe must be made with extra large mushrooms because each cap holds an oyster. It can be assembled in minutes, mellowed with a Madeira sauce, and served with Roast Quail or Beef Tournedos whenever the movers and shakers are gathered around the dining room table and the wine is *fine*.

STUFFED MUSHROOMS MADEIRA

12	shucked oysters	1	Tablespoon tomato paste
1	cup chicken or beef stock		Pinch of thyme
	(See pp. 63, 64)		Salt and freshly ground
5	Tablespoons butter		pepper
2	Tablespoons finely chopped	1	Tablespoon oil
	shallots	12	large mushroom caps
1	Tablespoon flour		Paprika
2	Tablespoons Madeira	2	Tablespoons chopped parsley

Oven Temperature: 350°

1.   Heat the stock in a small saucepan.

2.   Melt 2 tablespoons of butter in another saucepan and sauté the shallots until tender. Stir in the flour and cook until bubbling. Remove from the heat and whisk in the stock. Return to the heat, add Madeira, tomato paste, thyme, salt and pepper, and boil, stirring constantly, until the sauce thickens. Simmer at least 3 minutes, set aside and keep warm.

3.   Heat the oil and 2 tablespoons of butter in a skillet and sauté the mushroom caps for 3 minutes, sprinkle with salt, and arrange the caps in a buttered shallow baking dish.

4.   Remove the oysters from their shells, pat them dry, and place one in each cap. Sprinkle with pepper and paprika, and dot with the remaining butter.

5.   Bake for about 10 minutes until the edges of the oysters begin to curl.

6.   Stir the parsley into the sauce, spoon it over the mushrooms, and serve.

Serves 4

Onions

The less-than-glamorous step-sister of shallots, scallions, and leeks, the common onion can finally dress up and strut her stuff, providing, of course, her "stuff" is made of oysters. For years, minced, chopped, sliced, and cast in a secondary role in thousands of soups and stews, the onion can be presented in more fetching attire. Just bake to a light golden color, and show off in the company of veal medallions or butterflied trout.

STUFFED ONIONS

1/2 pint oysters and liquor	Salt and freshly ground
3 4-inch Spanish onions	pepper
3/4 cup cream	Buttered bread crumbs
3 Tablespoons butter	
1 1/2 Tablespoons flour	
2 Tablespoons dry Sherry	
1/2 cup blanched pearl onions, or	
sautéed chopped onion	
1/2 cup blanched green peas	
2 Tablespoons chopped parsley	

Oven Temperature: 375°

1. Drain the oysters, cut them in half if they are large, and reserve the liquor.
2. Cut the onions into halves, peel, and cut a slice from the stem and root ends so the halves will stand upright. Hollow out the insides, leaving a 3/8-inch shell.
3. Blanch the onions in boiling salted water about 2 minutes, until tender. Remove with a slotted spoon and drain upside down, reserving some of the poaching liquid.
4. Warm the oyster liquor and cream in a small saucepan.
5. Melt the butter in another saucepan. Stir in the flour and cook until bubbling. Remove from the heat and whisk in the warm cream. Return to heat and boil, stirring constantly, until the mixture thickens. Stir in the Sherry and simmer for 3 minutes.
6. Combine the oysters, pearl onions, and peas with the sauce, stir in the parsley, and season to taste with salt and pepper.
7. Fill the onion cavities, top with crumbs, and place the onions in a buttered, shallow baking dish. Pour in 1/4-inch of the poaching liquid.
8. Bake for 30 minutes; add liquid if the dish becomes dry, and cover with foil if the onions brown too quickly.

Serves 6

Peppers

For a "pick a peck of . . ." think of peppers *and* oysters, and ordinary meals will "quick like a jingle" become extraordinary ones. These stuffed peppers—so simple to make and yet so refreshingly different from the run-of-the-mill cheese-and-rice stuffed peppers—enhance a buffet table or luncheon party. The "serene presentation" of the dish necessitates choosing peppers that stand upright. So, check the bottoms and avoid picking a peck of problematic peppers. And remember to add some pine nuts for that additional flavor and texture.

STUFFED PEPPERS

½ pint medium oysters
4 green peppers
   Salt
3 Tablespoons butter
¼ cup finely chopped green
   onions
½ cup finely chopped celery
¼ cup chopped mushrooms,
   and/or chopped red sweet
   pepper
1½ cups tomato sauce
1 Tablespoon chopped fresh dill

   Tabasco
1 cup cooked rice
2 Tablespoons toasted pine
   nuts (optional)
   Freshly ground pepper
¼ cup fresh bread crumbs

Oven Temperature: 350°

1. Remove the tops, seeds, and membranes from the peppers. Blanch them in boiling salted water for 4 minutes, refresh in cold water, drain well, and pat dry.
2. Melt the butter in a skillet; spoon off and reserve 1 tablespoon for the crumbs. Sauté the onions, celery, mushrooms and pepper until tender. Add about 2 tablespoons of tomato sauce, the dill, and Tabasco.
3. Remove the skillet from the heat and add the drained oysters, rice, pine nuts, and as much sauce as necessary to make the mixture moist but not runny. Adjust seasonings.
4. Fill the peppers, distributing the oysters evenly, and cover with a mixture of the reserved melted butter and crumbs. Arrange the peppers in a shallow buttered baking dish and half fill the dish with tomato sauce.
5. Bake for about 20 minutes until the peppers are thoroughly heated and the crumbs are golden.
6. Spoon the extra sauce over the peppers before serving.

Serves 4

Potatoes

Associated with wars and famines, carried from South America to Europe and back again to North America, planted in presidents' gardens and outside the hovels of the poor, the potato is unique among vegetables. It has been fodder for animals, the food of prisoners and slaves, the delight of gourmets. And today the search is on for the perfect potato, one that has not been processed, packaged, or subjected to all the vagaries of convenience and fast food. The word is out— either grow your own potatoes or select them as carefully as asparagus, and suit the potato to the dish in terms of size, starch content, and flavor.

The following recipes are adaptations of dishes found in the tradition of potato cookery. From the Baltic "kugel" to the comforting "double-baked," these recipes have been partnered with oysters successfully. Potatoes are so neutral in taste and so exciting in adaptability that even the most conservative cook will soon recognize that the culinary potential of this alliance is limitless.

MASHED POTATOES

1½ pints oysters
4 cups mashed potatoes*
2 eggs
1 Tablespoon water
1 cup heavy cream
2 Tablespoons butter

1½ Tablespoons flour
    Salt and freshly ground white
      pepper
2 Tablespoons chopped parsley

Oven Temperature: 400°

1. Make a 1-inch thick wall of mashed potatoes inside the rim of a buttered 2½-quart baking dish or 6 individual gratin dishes. Brush the surface of the potatoes with a glaze of the eggs beaten with water.
2. Bake in the top third of the oven about 10 minutes, until the potatoes are golden; turn off the oven, leaving the door ajar.
3. Drain the oysters, reserving the liquor for another use.
4. Warm the cream in a small saucepan.
5. Melt the butter in another saucepan, stir in the flour, and cook until bubbling. Remove from the heat and whisk in the cream. Return to heat and boil, stirring constantly, until the mixture thickens. Simmer at least 3 minutes.
6. Stir in the oysters, salt and pepper to taste; heat until the edges of the oysters begin to curl.
7. Pour the creamed oysters inside the potato ring, garnish with parsley and serve immediately.

* The potatoes can be boiled in stock; garlic or an herb bouquet may be added to the potato water for flavor.

Serves 6

POTATO GRATIN

1 pint oysters and liquor	Freshly ground pepper
2 garlic cloves	1½ Tablespoons flour
1 medium onion	¼ cup freshly grated
4 medium potaotes	Parmesan cheese
Salt	¼ cup freshly grated
1 cup light cream	Gruyère cheese
6 Tablespoons butter	¼ cup corn flake crumbs
1 cup finely julienned celery	
1 cup finely julienned carrots	
1 teaspoon chopped fresh	
rosemary	

Oven Temperature: 350°

1. Simmer the garlic and peeled whole onion in boiling water for 30 minutes; add the potaotes and salt, and boil until the centers can be pierced with a fork. Drain the potatoes and set aside to cool.
2. Drain the oysters, reserving ¼ cup of the liquor; warm the liquor and cream in a small saucepan.
3. Melt 3 tablespoons of butter in another saucepan and sauté the celery and carrots for 3 minutes, season with rosemary, salt and pepper, remove the vegetables with a slotted spoon, and set aside.
4. Add the remaining butter to the pan, stir in the flour, and cook until bubbling. Remove from the heat and whisk in the warm cream. Return to the heat and boil, stirring constantly, until the mixture thickens. Whisk in the cheese, heat until it is melted, and adjust seasonings.
5. Peel and slice the potaotes, arrange them in a 2-quart buttered gratin dish, and cover with the sautéed vegetables. Distribute the oysters, pour the sauce over them, and sprinkle with crumbs.
6. Bake for 20 minutes or until the sauce is bubbling.

Serves 6

DOUBLE-BAKED POTATOES

12 shucked oysters and liquor	Salt and freshly ground
6 large baking potatoes	pepper
6 Tablespoons butter	Paprika
¼ cup finely chopped shallots	
¼ cup dry white wine	
¼ cup heavy cream	
2 Tablespoons finely chopped	
chives	

Oven Temperature: 425°

1. Bake the potatoes until the centers can be pierced with a fork; set aside to cool slightly, and reduce the oven temperature to 325°.
2. Remove the oysters from their shells, strain and reserve the liquor.
3. Melt 2 tablespoons of butter in a heavy saucepan and sauté the shallots until they are tender. Add the wine, oysters and liquor, and cook until the edges of the oysters begin to curl; remove the oysters with a slotted spoon and set aside. Add the cream and reduce the liquids to about ¼ cup.
4. Slice the top from each potato and scoop out the pulp with a teaspoon. Use a little more than half the pulp for the stuffing; mash with the remaining butter and enough of the reduced liquid to make a smooth mixture; add chives, salt and pepper to taste.
5. Half fill the potato shells, arrange 2 oysters in each, mound with the rest of the potatoes, and sprinkle with paprika.
6. Place in a baking pan and heat in a 325° oven for about 15 minutes.

Serves 6

POTATO CASSEROLE

1	pint oysters		Salt and freshly ground
1	cup *crème fraîche*		pepper
1	Tablespoon chopped fresh dill weed	4	boiled medium potatoes
4	Tablespoons butter	1	cup coarsely grated Swiss cheese
2	sliced Spanish onions	¼	cup chopped parsley

Oven Temperature: 350°

1. Drain the oysters and place them in a bowl, reserving their liquor for another use.
2. Combine ½ cup of the *crème fraîche* with the dill, mix with the oysters and marinate for at least 30 minutes.
3. Melt the butter in a skillet and sauté the onions until tender, seasoning with salt and pepper.
4. Peel the potatoes and cut them into ⅛-inch slices.
5. Spread a little *crème fraîche* in a 2-quart buttered gratin dish or casserole, cover with half the potatoes, arrange half the onions, then the oysters and marinade, and sprinkle with half the cheese. Repeat the layers of potato, onion, *crème fraîche*, and cheese.
6. Bake 25 minutes, and run under the broiler to brown the top; garnish with parsley before serving.

Serves 6

POTATO KUGEL

½	pint oysters	2	Tablespoons flour
6	medium potatoes	8	parsley sprigs
2	shallots	¼	cup diced bacon
2	eggs		Sour cream (optional)
2	Tablespoons melted butter or chicken fat		Snipped chives (optional)

Oven Temperature: 350°

1. Drain the oysters, pat them dry, and chop.
2. Peel the potatoes and shallots and coarse grate in a food processor.
3. Add the eggs, shortening, flour, and parsley to the work bowl, and process for a minute.
4. Spoon half of the potatoes into a buttered 2-inch-deep quiche dish. Distribute the oysters and bacon over the mixture, and cover with the remaining potatoes. Bake immediately or the potatoes will discolor.
5. Bake for about 40 minutes or until a golden brown crust forms over the top. Allow the kugel to stand for a short time before cutting it into wedges.
6. Serve with a garnish of sour cream and snipped chives if desired.

Serves 8

That [potatoe] which was heretofore reckon'd a food fit only for Irishmen, and clowns, is now become the diet of the most lux- uriously polite.
Stephen Switzer, 1733

At the beginning of the 14th century, [spinach] is listed in the household accounts of wealthy families, and at the end of that century the anonymous *Menagier de Paris* reported that "there is a species of chard called *espinache* which is eaten at the beginning of Lent."
Waverley Root, *Food*

Spinach

"On a bed of spinach" has come to have such lusty charm that the temptation to do it one more time cannot be overcome. Oh, *felix culpa*! The simple earthiness of a well-flavored (either ginger or garlic) layer of spinach, inlaid with oysters, and topped with cheese or pure Mornay sauce, can only be called Oysters Jezebel.

SPINACH GRATIN

24	shucked oysters and liquor	1/2	cup heavy cream
3 1/2	pounds spinach	1 1/2	Tablespoons flour
2	Tablespoons vegetable oil	1/4	cup dry white wine
4	Tablespoons butter	4	ounces grated Fontina cheese†
2	Tablespoons chopped shallots		
2	teaspoons minced ginger root*		
	Salt and freshly ground pepper		

Oven Temperature: 350°

1. Remove the oysters from their shells, pat dry, and set them aside, reserving 1/3 cup of the strained liquor.
2. Wash, stem, and cut the spinach into fine strips.
3. Heat the oil and 2 tablespoons of the butter in a large saucepan. Add the shallots and ginger and cook about 1 minute. Add the spinach, toss to coat the leaves, and cook until the spinach is just wilted. Season with salt and pepper, remove the spinach with a slotted spoon, and spread in a buttered gratin dish.
4. Warm the oyster liquor and cream in a small saucepan.
5. Melt the remaining 2 tablespoons of butter in another saucepan. Stir in the flour and cook until bubbling. Remove from the heat and whisk in the warm cream mixture. Return to heat and boil, stirring constantly, until the mixture thickens. Add the wine, season with salt and pepper, and simmer 3 minutes.
6. Arrange the oysters on the spinach, pour the sauce over them, and top with the cheese.
7. Bake for 25 minutes, then place under the broiler and lightly brown the cheese.

* Substituting any other herb or spice for the ginger root will create a different dish. Chopped garlic works particularly well in this recipe.

† For a stronger cheese flavor, use the classic Mornay sauce (Parmesan and Gruyère or Swiss cheese) over the spinach and oysters.

Serves 6

Squash

Maybe it's the autumn leaves turning pumpkiny orange and the abundance of summer and winter squash that bring the words "rustic" and "robust" to mind whenever these vegetables are displayed in mounds or heaped into over-sized baskets. Perhaps it's simply the beneficence of the generous vines that makes one want to gather all the interesting shapes and colors of squash, and either use them or hoard them. The opportunities to do so are endless.

The zucchini that has slipped notice and grown a little larger than one might wish can always be cut crosswise, scooped out, and filled with a savory oyster stuffing. More stunning in presentation, but equally delicious, is a platter of sautéed spaghetti squash with a heavenly cream sauce. And then there's acorn, butternut, patty pan and . . . . It's definitely a hoarding vegetable.

SPAGHETTI SQUASH

24 shucked oysters
1 5-pound spaghetti squash
8 Tablespoons butter
    Salt and freshly ground
       pepper
1½ cups heavy cream
⅛ teaspoon nutmeg
¼ cup grated Parmesan
    cheese

1 cup finely chopped fresh
    herbs: parsley, chives, basil,
    rosemary, watercress,
    chervil, dill
    Cayenne pepper

Oven Temperature: 350°

1   Prick the squash with a fork, and bake it about an hour until it is tender.
2. Split the squash in half when it is cool enough to handle, and remove the seeds and stringy center. Comb out the long strands of the fleshy part with a fork.
3. Melt 4 tablespoons of the butter in a large saucepan and sauté the squash strands, tossing lightly to coat, and seasoning with salt and pepper. Keep the squash warm, or reheat it just before serving time.
4. Remove the oysters from their shells and pat them dry, reserving the liquor for another use.
5. Combine the cream, remaining butter, and nutmeg in a heavy saucepan, and boil over medium heat until the sauce is reduced to about 1 cup. Whisk in the cheese until it melts.
6. Stir in the fresh herbs and oysters, and heat until the edges of the oysters start to curl, seasoning to taste.
7. Arrange the hot squash on a serving platter, pour the sauce over it and serve immediately.

Serves 6

ZUCCHINI SHELLS

1 pint oysters and liquor	3 Tablespoons dry Sherry
3 medium zucchini	Salt and freshly ground
2¼ cups light cream	pepper
6 Tablespoons butter	¾ cup fresh bread crumbs
4 Tablespoons flour	
¼ pound sliced mushrooms	
1 4-ounce jar chopped pimientos	

Oven Temperature: 350°

1. Select 9-inch zucchini that are about 3 inches in diameter. Cut them into 2-inch slices and remove the centers from each slice with a knife, melon-baller or teaspoon, leaving a ¼-inch shell with a bottom.
2. Blanch the shells by placing them upside down in an inch of boiling, salted water. Boil for 3 minutes, refresh in cold water, invert and drain on a rack.
3. Drain the oysters, cut in half if they are large, and reserve ¼ cup of the liquor.
4. Warm the oyster liquor and cream in a small saucepan.
5. Melt the butter in another saucepan. Remove and reserve 2 tablespoons for the crumbs. Stir the flour into the remaining butter and cook until bubbling. Remove from the heat and whisk in the cream mixture. Return to heat and boil, stirring constantly, until the mixture thickens. Simmer for 3 minutes.
6. Add the oysters, mushrooms, pimiento, and Sherry and season to taste with salt and pepper. Cook, stirring gently, until the mixture starts to bubble.
7. Spoon the filling into the zucchini shells. Mix the reserved butter with the crumbs and sprinkle over the tops.
8. Bake about 15 minutes until the shells are thoroughly heated and the crumbs are golden.

Serves 12

OYSTERS AND TOMATOES

Two tablespoonsful of butter, one tablespoonful of flour, one slice of onion, one cup of stewed and strained tomato, one pint of oysters, salt and pepper. Cook the onion in the butter till light brown, add the flour and brown again, add the tomato and cook and stir until thick. Add the oysters, drained, and cook until they plump up. Serve on toast.

What We Cook on Cape Cod, compiled by Amy L. Handy, 1911.

Tomatoes

If there is a surfeit of vine-ripened tomatoes in the garden, these recipes will put them to good use. Baked tomatoes are so easy, so versatile, they brighten up any meal. And as a "sizzling" counterpart to the Love Apple Salad, the stuffed tomato side dish flirts with everything from grilled cheeseburgers to a T-bone steak.

BAKED TOMATOES

1 pint oysters and liquor	Salt and freshly ground
4 Tablespoons butter	pepper
2 Tablespoons chopped onion	Tabasco
1/4 cup chopped green pepper	1/2 cup fresh bread crumbs
1 Tablespoon flour	2 Tablespoons freshly grated
2 Tablespoons Zinfandel or	Romano cheese
other full-bodied red wine	
3 cups peeled, coarsely chopped	
tomatoes	
1 teaspoon sugar	
1 Tablespoon chopped fresh	
oregano	

Oven Temperature: 375°

1. Drain the oysters, pat them dry, and set aside, reserving 1/3 cup of the liquor for the sauce.
2. Melt the butter in a saucepan; pour off and reserve 2 tablespoons for the crumb and cheese topping. Sauté the onion and green pepper until they are tender. Whisk in the flour, cook until bubbling, and stir in the oyster liquor, wine, tomatoes, sugar, Tabasco, and oregano. Season to taste. Simmer uncovered, stirring frequently, until the mixture thickens.
3. Arrange the oysters on the bottom of a buttered shallow baking dish and spread the tomato mixture over them. Combine the bread crumbs, cheese, and reserved melted butter, and sprinkle over the top.
4. Bake about 20 minutes until the crumbs are golden brown.

Serves 4

Why, then the world's mine oyster,
Which I with sword will open.
Shakespeare, *The Merry Wives of Windsor*

STUFFED TOMATOES

12	shucked small oysters and liquor	2	Tablespoons dry Vermouth
6	large tomatoes	2	cups cooked rice
	Salt and freshly ground pepper	2	Tablespoons finely chopped anchovies
2	Tablespoons butter	2	Tablespoons chopped parsley
2	garlic cloves		
2	Tablespoons chopped scallions		
1	Tablespoon chopped fresh basil		

Oven Temperature: 350°

1. Remove the oysters from their shells, strain and reserve the liquor.
2. Cut the tops off the tomatoes and scoop out the pulp and seeds, leaving a 1/2-inch shell; season with salt and pepper, and turn upside down to drain.
3. Melt the butter in a saucepan and sauté the garlic, scallions, and basil for a few minutes; discard the garlic. Add the Vermouth and oysters, and heat until they begin to plump. Remove the oysters with a slotted spoon and set aside.
4. Stir in the rice, anchovies, parsley, salt and pepper, adding a little oyster liquor if necessary to bind the filling.
5. Spoon some rice, then 2 oysters into each tomato; mound with the remaining rice.
6. Place the tomatoes in a buttered casserole and bake about 15 minutes until the stuffing is hot.

Serves 6

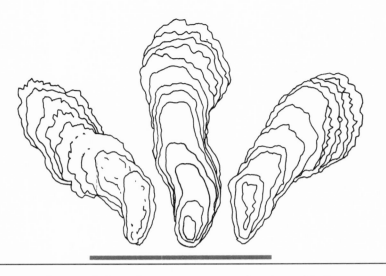

No matter how good the cooking is, it's not worth eating with the wrong people. Call it the tea ceremony, call it what you will, breaking bread is a way of making contact. It's the mass; and when we break bread we say a *barucha*. It's part of the dance between the man and the woman, the marvelous meal, the bottle of wine—the civilized way of saying I want to eat with you, I like you.

Art Buchwald, *Cuisine*, October, 1983

The French housewife does not normally make bread at home. The small restaurants ordinarily do not bake on the premises. Breads are bought from the neighborhood bakeshop. Therefore, practically no bread recipes come to us from the homes or the chefs of France. The men who work in the bakeries are all members of the bakers' guild. Their secrets of dough making are passed on to the apprentice bakers and do not become common knowledge.

Alma Lach, *Hows and Whys of French Cooking*

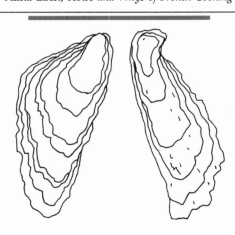

BREADS & PASTRIES

read can be leavened or unleavened, white or dark, round or two-feet long, thin as muslin or heavy and coarse-textured, and there is always a reason for these differences. Often more revealing than an archeological dig, the customs, folk-ways, even the utensils used in the preparation of bread tell the story of a people.

Baked, poached, fried, or steamed, bread has brought men to their knees in thanksgiving or supplication. The Chinese believed that wheat was a gift from heaven; the Anglo-Saxons offered to God the loaves baked from the first harvest. And Chaucer's pilgrims carried "Goddes Kechyl," a cake given as alms. Bread is eucharistic, a messianic bonding, "Take and eat for this is My Body." The antithesis to barrenness, it is also the symbol of the earth's fecundity. And bread is one of the ingredients for a perfect love feast, " A Jug of Wine, a Loaf of Bread, and Thou. . . ."

Bread has united men in the rites of communion and in battle (it is said that Norman soldiers demanded white bread for courage), in the partaking of saddlebag fare around a camp fire, and, framed in a more contemporary idiom, in the sharing of a sandwich from a lunch box or picnic hamper. But bread has also divided men. The Jews eat unleavened bread as a reminder of their expulsion from Egypt. "To know the color of one's bread" was a Roman saying that cautioned men to keep their place in society. All through Europe, the darker the bread, the poorer the family. Mixing, kneading, and baking bread was simply a "peasant" thing to do.

In the New World things were different. From early colonial cabins and the settlers' covered wagons to today's gourmet kitchens, Americans have had a tradition of baking their own bread. And the efforts of pioneer women to bake bread in heavy iron pots buried deep in hot ashes and to transport "starters" in order to turn out nourishing loaves as soon as possible after camps were set up would be an amazing tale, and one worth telling.

Using cornmeal, wheat, barley, rye, or oats in the kitchens of Plymouth, Sturbridge, and Williamsburg, or improvising with whatever was available on a Southern plantation or on the trail, colonial women and generations of their daughters have, quite literally, made America the "bread basket of the world." And that basket is filled with a dazzling list of hoe cakes, griddle cakes, steamed brown bread, beignets, rice flour and sour dough breads.

And while one may envy the French their *boulangeries* on every street corner, the sniff and whiff of bread baking in one's own oven, of tarts and muffins cooling on racks, are as American as—dare it be said?—motherhood and apple pie. In the tradition of "homemade is best," a marble slab can replace the trencher table, stainless steel bowls and not earthenware crocks can hold the rising dough, and a convection rather than a clay oven can register 375°, but the search for the perfect loaf continues. The bread box and the pie basket are never empty, and those loaves, muffins, griddle cakes, and pie shells are the substance of this chapter.

Basically hearth-and-kettle in nature, the following recipes range beyond the usual breads and pastries to include biscuits, corn sticks, vol-au-vent, and quiches that become the "serving dishes" for a variety of oyster fillings. They are the possibilities an enterprising baker can conjure up when she eyes her dough rising or when she sends some flour and shortening whirling in the work bowl of a food processor. But they are possibilities with a difference. A hollowed-out loaf can be a box for fried oysters, ordinary rolls readily become "oyster rolls," crêpes, pancakes, and waffles can be swathed in an oyster sauce.

Bread has always sustained and nourished man. While some of these recipes are tradition-bound, others are unique; but all of them feed a man's hunger if made with love.

A very exaggerated idea of the difficulty of breadmaking prevails amongst persons who are entirely ignorant of the process.
Eliza Acton, *The English Bread Book*, 1857

SUGGESTIONS:

- In some of the following recipes poached oysters may be substituted for fried oysters although the suggested method of cooking suits the recipe most effectively.

- Recipes will be greatly enhanced if made with homemade breads and pastries. The availability of specialty breads, frozen phyllo leaves, and puff pastry, however, can be helpful in preparing a given dish in a limited amount of time.

- The fresh bread removed from loaves and rolls makes excellent bread crumbs.

- If the top crust of a baked, filled loaf is too difficult to pierce with a knife, brush the crust with melted butter, cover with a damp towel, return to a warm oven for about ten minutes, and then cut into the desired number of slices.

- Traditionally, pumpernickel or rye bread is the perfect complement to oysters, but various kinds of corn breads and sour dough bread are also very compatible with the flavor of smoked and raw oysters.

- After the final rolling, classic puff pastry can be cut into scallop shells, baked, and filled with a rich oyster sauce.

- Cheese, lemon zest, and congenial "shellfish herbs" like basil, bay, dill weed, marjoram, oregano, summer savory, tarragon, and thyme can be added to bread and pastry dough to sharpen the flavor of the recipe.

- Sour cream or buttermilk, additional eggs, honey or brown sugar, and the *color* of corn flour will alter the flavor and texture of corn bread. Water-ground, white, flint corn is supposed to produce a finer sweeter loaf than most of the other varieties of corn flour. Kiln-dried, stone-ground, yellow meal is preferred by other bakers. Some recipes for corn bread call for both.

- The consistency of the filling and the quantity of the ingredients used to assemble a sandwich should guarantee ease in eating it.

- Watercress can be substituted for lettuce in pocket and club sandwiches for more comfortable bites.

- If a quiche is allowed to "rest" when removed from the oven, cutting it into serving pieces will be facilitated.

- If a quiche, pie, or tart is served as a supper course, the number of servings may be fewer than those suggested at the end of the recipe.

La Médiatrice

Nothing in New Orleans is better known than the "Peace-Maker," and it is a foolish husband who does not rely on it in case of need. In the old days when a man told his wife he was detained on business, the peace-maker was a good thing . . . and at one o'clock in the morning "La Médiatrice" remains a good thing.

Mary Moore Bremer, *New Orleans Recipes*

Whether it is associated with peace-making, with poverty, or is a treat for a frightened "po" boy matters very little. A hollowed-out, toasted bread with dozens of fried oysters inside is guaranteed to please a less than understanding wife, especially in the early hours of the morning.

A favorite way of preparing this classic loaf is to use a square or rectangular loaf, sometimes referred to as a "cottage loaf." Within its crusty cavity, the fried oysters can be "boxed" handsomely and kept warm—ideal for a "kiss and make up" situation.

Shredded lettuce, chili, tartar, or a special yoghurt sauce may be used if desired. But if the "peace loaf" must be transported, serve the garnish or sauce "on the side."

24	shucked large oysters		*Sauce: (optional)*
	Seasoned flour	1	pint plain yoghurt
1	egg	1	minced clove garlic
1	Tablespoon water	2	Tablespoons grated onion
	Fine bread crumbs	1	teaspoon chopped fresh dill
1	loaf "Cottage" bread or	1	seeded and grated cucumber
	18-inch French loaf		Salt and freshly ground
½	cup melted butter		pepper
	Oil for frying		

Oven Temperature: 400°

1. Make the sauce by combining the yoghurt, garlic, onion, and dill, and refrigerate. Just before serving, stir in the cucumber and season to taste.
2. Remove the oysters from their shells, drain, and pat them dry. Dust them with seasoned flour, dip in the beaten egg and water, and roll in crumbs. Refrigerate at least 15 minutes before frying.
3. Slice the top crust from the loaf and scoop out some of the soft bread, leaving a generous shell. Brush the cavity and lid with melted butter, bake until golden, and keep warm.
4. Heat the oil to 375° and deep-fry the oysters a few at a time, until they are golden brown. Drain on absorbent paper and keep warm until all are cooked.
5. Brush the inside of the loaf and lid with sauce if desired. Fill the loaf with the fried oysters, replace the lid, cut in half, and serve with a ramekin of sauce.

Serves 2

Not So "Po" Boy Loaf

Imagine Colchester oysters selling for eight pence a bushel two hundred years ago. Little wonder that "olde" recipe books pass along hints for "small economies in the kitchen" and provide directions for "Penny Loaves." Here are a few. Hollow out and fill a loaf with stewed oysters and a bit of lemon juice or fry the oysters in batter. And, as E. Smith suggests in the *Compleat Housewife* (London, 1739), toast the loaf in a pound of butter and season the oysters with ". . . a blade of mace, a little white pepper, a little horseradish and a piece of lean bacon, and a half a lemon."

The following recipe, slightly more expensive and elaborate than the earlier ones, is know in New Orleans as the "Po" Boy. It is highly recommended to assuage the fears of a frightened boy, or comfort the "boy" inside the man.

1	pint oysters and liquor	Pinch of thyme
2	eggs	Salt and freshly ground pepper
3	Tablespoons water	½ thinly sliced green pepper
2	medium tomatoes	½ thinly sliced sweet onion
½	cup fine bread crumbs	4 lemon wedges
8	slices bacon	
1	Vienna loaf	*Dressing*
1	cup dry white wine	½ cup mayonnaise
2	Tablespoons butter	1 teaspoon Dijon mustard
1	Tablespoon flour	1 teaspoon prepared
1	teaspoon Worcestershire sauce	horseradish

Oven Temperature: 400°

1. Separate the egg yolks from the whites, beat the yolks with 2 tablespoons of water, and beat 1 tablespoon of water into the whites.
2. Cut the tomatoes into 12 thin slices, dip in the egg yolk, coat with crumbs, and dry on a rack for 30 minutes. Reserve the remaining yolk mixture for use in the sauce.
3. Sauté the bacon in a skillet until crisp, and drain on absorbent paper.
4. Fry the tomato slices in the bacon drippings until brown on both sides; remove and drain.
5. Cut off the top of the loaf, scoop out the bread leaving a ¼-inch shell. Brush the inside of the loaf and top with the egg whites. Bake both pieces for about 10 minutes until they are golden.
6. Lightly poach the oysters in their own liquor and wine; drain, reserving ⅔ cup of the poaching liquid.
7. Melt the butter in a saucepan, stir in the flour, and cook unti bubbling. Remove from the heat and whisk in the warm poaching liquid. Return to heat and boil, stirring constantly, until the mixture thickens.
8. Whisk the hot mixture into the reserved egg yolks, a spoonful at a time. Transfer the enriched sauce to the saucepan, season with Worcestershire

and thyme and, stirring carefully, bring to a boil. Gently stir in the oysters and adjust seasonings.

9. Assemble the loaf by layering half the tomato slices on the bottom, spread the oyster mixture, pepper and onion slices, another layer of tomatoes and the bacon. Replace the upper crust.
10. Wrap the loaf in foil and bake for 20 minutes.
11. Unwrap, cut off the ends, and slice with a serrated knife. Garnish with lemon wedges and serve the dressing in a side dish.

Serves 4

Carnival Loaf

Ideal for a "Mardi Gras" buffet and a "trumpet tooting" loaf for hundreds of other occasions, this picture-perfect stuffed oyster and spinach loaf can be prepared hours in advance, stored in the refrigerator, and popped into the oven about forty-five minutes before serving. A round *pain Italien* perks up the appearance, but a traditional Vienna or Italian loaf is equally festive.

1 pint medium oysters	2 cups cooked chopped spinach
6 slices diced bacon	Pinch of mace
1 10-inch round bread loaf	Salt and freshly ground
4 Tablespoons butter	pepper
1 minced garlic clove	2 sliced medium tomatoes
3 eggs	1/2 cup freshly grated Parmesan
3/4 cup mayonnaise	cheese

Oven Temperature: 350°

1. Cook the bacon in a skillet or microwave oven until crisp and brown, drain on absorbent paper.
2. Drain the oysters, pat them dry, and set aside.
3. Slice off the top of the loaf and hollow out the center, leaving a 1/2-inch shell. Process the soft bread in a blender to make crumbs. Spread the inside of the loaf and top with creamed garlic butter.
4. Whisk the eggs in a bowl with the mayonnaise; stir in the spinach, bacon, mace, salt and pepper to taste.
5. Arrange half the oysters on the bottom of the loaf, cover with half the spinach mixture, half the tomatoes, a layer of crumbs and half the cheese. Repeat the layers, and replace the upper crust.
6. Wrap the loaf in foil and bake for 45 minutes.
7. Cut into 6 wedges with a serrated bread knife, garnish with parsley sprigs, and serve hot.

Serves 6

Oyster Bay Club

Not at all limited to any "clubby masculine enclave," these oyster sandwiches are sporting fare for anyone who revels in a spicy Bloody Mary and a club sandwich after a game of tennis or an invigorating swim at—where else?—the Oyster Bay Club.

1	pint oysters			Mayonnaise
1	cup seasoned corn flour		6	lettuce leaves
12	slices bacon		12	thin slices tomato
6	Tablespoons clarified butter			Salt and freshly ground
18	slices white or rye toast			pepper

1. Drain the oysters, pat dry, coat them in flour, and chill for at least 15 minutes.
2. Cut the bacon slices in half, sauté in a large skillet until crisp, and drain.
3. Pour off all but 2 tablespoons of the drippings from the skillet and add a tablespoon of butter. Fry the oysters, about 6 at a time, in hot fat until both sides are golden brown, adding butter as needed. Drain the oysters on absorbent paper.
4. Cut crusts from the toast and spread 6 slices of the toast with mayonnaise. Layer with the lettuce, tomatoes, more mayonnaise, and sprinkle lightly with salt and pepper. Cover with another slice of toast, the oysters, bacon, and top with a slice of toast spread with mayonnaise. Secure with toothpicks, and cut each sandwich into quarters or triangles.
5. Serve with crisp dilled pickles or cornichons.

Serves 6

- -

A Book of Verses underneath the Bough,
A Jug of Wine, a Loaf of Bread—and Thou
Beside me singing in the Wilderness—
Oh, Wilderness were Paradise enow!
Rubaiyat of Omar Khayyam

- -

SCALLYWAG OYSTER SANDWICHES

The picture-perfect and painstakingly decorated "open-faced" sandwiches that distinguish Continental cuisine are a tribute to the careful preparation that goes into the simplest snack. And while Americans do not usually serve "knife and fork" sandwiches, it might be a delightful thing to do, especially with oysters. Those "scallywags" are open to anything.

Rye, Please

24	shucked oysters	1	cup grated Port Salut cheese
8	slices rye bread	4	Tablespoons bread crumbs
4	Tablespoons butter	1	teaspoon grated lemon zest
1	teaspoon anchovy paste	4	lemon wedges

Oven Temperature: 400°

1. Toast the bread, remove crusts, and spread with the butter creamed with anchovy paste.
2. Remove the oysters from their shells, pat dry, and coarsely chop them, reserving the liquor for another use.
3. Combine the cheese with 2 tablespoons of the bread crumbs and lemon zest, and mix with the oysters; spread on the toast, and sprinkle with the remaining crumbs.
4. Place on a lightly buttered baking sheet, bake for 10 minutes, and place under the broiler to brown the crumbs. Serve with lemon wedges.

Serves 4

Make Mine Danish

2	3¾-ounce tins smoked oysters	1	large tomato
4	slices firm pumpernickel bread	½	green pepper
2	Tablespoons butter	2	hard-boiled eggs
1	Tablespoon finely chopped chives		Salt and freshly ground pepper
3	Tablespoons finely chopped parsley		

1. Drain and rinse the oysters; drain again, pat dry, and chill.
2. Remove the crusts and spread the bread with butter creamed with the chives and 1 tablespoon of parsley.
3. Cut the tomato into 8 thin slices; slice the pepper lengthwise into thin strips. Halve the eggs, press the yolks through a sieve, and cut the whites into thin lengthwise strips.
4. Arrange 2 tomato slices on each piece of bread, sprinkle lightly with salt and pepper; place the oysters on the tomatoes, sprinkle with egg yolks, and cut each sandwich diagonally in half.
5. Garnish with the pepper and egg white strips, and sprinkle the remaining parsley over the top.

Serves 4

Oyster Croque Monsieur

A seaside version of this crispy French toasted sandwich can be achieved by using a toasting iron in the form of a scallop shell. And for the ultimate variation on a theme, serve these showy hot sandwiches with marinated mushrooms, curried fruit salad, or herbed cole slaw heaped into side dishes of 4-inch scallop shells.

6	freshly shucked small oysters	4	thin slices white bread
	Seasoned flour	2	slices ham
1	egg	6	Tablespoons freshly grated
1	teaspoon water		Gruyère cheese
½	cup corn flake crumbs		Cornichons (optional)
	Oil for frying		Cherry tomatoes (optional)
	Soft butter		

1. Remove the oysters from their shells and pat them dry; dredge in flour, dip in the egg beaten with water, and roll in crumbs. Refrigerate for 15 minutes.
2. Heat the oil to 375° and deep-fry the oysters; drain on absorbent paper.
3. Butter the bread on both sides, line the iron with 2 pieces; place a slice of ham, 3 oysters, and a generous sprinkling of cheese on each piece. Cover with another slice of bread, close the iron, and heat on the top of the stove. Remove the sandwiches when they are golden brown.
4. Garnish with cornichons, cherry tomatoes, or serve with a "place salad."

Serves 2

Glyder Oysters

'Tis said that in Cornwall when the one-hundred-year-old oyster boat, Glyder, sails down the Helford River with partying dignitaries aboard, the oyster season officially begins. This simple oyster-on-toast recipe can inaugurate the season with style anytime, anyplace. But a weekend in September would be ideal.

24	shucked small oysters	1	teaspoon Worcestershire sauce
3	slices diced bacon		Tabasco
2	Tablespoons butter		Salt and freshly ground
2	Tablespoons chopped onion		pepper
2	Tablespoons chopped celery	4	slices white toast
1	Tablespoon lemon juice	2	Tablespoons chopped parsley

Oven Temperature: 400°

1. Remove the oysters from their shells and pat them dry, reserving the liquor for another use.
2. Sauté the bacon until crisp in a skillet, remove with a slotted spoon, and drain on absorbent paper.

3. Pour off all but 1 tablespoon of the drippings from the skillet, add the butter, and sauté the onion and celery until tender; stir in the lemon juice, Worcestershire, Tabasco, and season to taste.
4. Trim the crusts and place the toast slices on a lightly buttered baking sheet. Arrange 6 oysters on each slice and spoon the sautéed vegetables and some of the pan juices over them.
5. Bake about 10 minutes until the oysters begin to curl.
6. Garnish with the bacon and parsley, and serve immediately.

Serves 4

Oysters Derring-Do

Although Welsh Rarebit can bring many contrasting sensations into play, it always looks *good*, smells *good*, tastes *good*, and is adaptable. In Gloucester, England, cooks add a little mustard and ale to the "baked" cheese and serve it over thick brown toast. In Portugal, a rarebit is made with a little tomato purée and topped with sardines. Indian recipes call for some mango chutney and curry powder. And, way down South, sautéed onions and tomatoes are added to the cheese before it is spooned over fried bread. So, for a little "derring-do," layer tomato slices, fried oysters, and crumbled bacon. It's a truly "rare-bit."

16	shucked large oysters	½	pound grated sharp Vermont Cheddar cheese
1	egg		
1	Tablespoon water	3	Tablespoons grated Asiago cheese
	Corn flake crumbs		
8	slices bacon	2	Tablespoons Kirsch
	Oil for frying	8	slices white toast
1	teaspoon dry mustard	8	thin slices tomato
1	teaspoon Worcestershire sauce		Parsley sprigs
6	ounces evaporated milk		

1. Remove the oysters from their shells, pat them dry; dip in the beaten egg mixed with water, roll in crumbs, and chill at least 15 minutes.
2. Cook the bacon until brown and crisp in a skillet or microwave oven, drain on absorbent paper, and crumble.
3. Fry the oysters, a few at a time, in 375° oil until they are golden on both sides; set aside on absorbent paper, and keep warm.
4. Mix the mustard, Worcestershire, milk, cheese, and Kirsch in the top of a double boiler; cook over boiling water, stirring constantly, until the mixture is hot, smooth, and thick. Add milk if a thinner consistency is desired.
5. Trim the crusts from the toast, place a tomato slice and 2 oysters on each piece, nap with the rarebit, and top with bacon.
6. Serve immediately garnished with parsley sprigs.

Serves 8

Pita and Oyster Panache

The Middle East housewife mixed her own "flat bread" at home, and frequently marked it with a private symbol to set it apart from "other" loaves when she sent it to the village oven to be baked.

Definitely in the "personalized" tradition, these oyster and melted Brie pita pockets make a distinctive "signature" for the lady of the house whenever she chooses to serve them.

24	shucked oysters	½ pound herbed Brie, or crushed
1	cup seasoned corn flour*	black peppercorn Brie
	Oil for frying	cheese
6	6-inch pita loaves (white or wheat)	

Oven Temperature: 400°

1. Remove the oysters from their shells, drain, and pat them dry, reserving the liquor for another use. Dredge the oysters in the flour and refrigerate for 15 minutes.
2. Heat the oil to 375° and fry the oysters, a few at a time, until they are golden, and drain on absorbent paper.
3. Cut across the pita near the edge, and open the pocket. Slice the Brie and fill each pocket with 4 oysters and cheese, distributing the cheese evenly.
4. Place the pockets on a baking pan, heat just long enough to melt the cheese, and serve immediately.

* Oregano, parsley or basil, salt, and cayenne pepper.

Serves 6

(SUGGESTIONS FOR BAKING OYSTER PIE)

If you think the oysters will be too much done by baking them in the crust you can substitute for them pieces of bread, to keep up the lid of the pie.

Put the oysters with their liquor and the seasoning, chopped egg, grated bread, &c. into a pan. Cover them closely, and let them just come to a boil, taking them off the fire, and stirring them frequently.

When the crust is baked, take the lid neatly off (loosening it round the edge with a knife) take out the pieces of bread, and put in the oysters. Lay the lid on again very carefully.

75 Receipts, by a Lady of Philadelphia, 1830

Bermuda Triangle Salad (Page 95)

Oysters Benedict (Page 140)

Le Bon Bun

Petits pains filled with fried oysters in a tangy sauce are simply a little triumph. Self-contained and copy-book-perfect, these stuffed rolls make a superlative luncheon dish or a late evening supper, especially if a crisp green salad and a glass of Chablis are added for optimum effect.

24	shucked oysters and liquor	3	peeled, chopped, medium tomatoes
8	large hard rolls		
8	Tablespoons melted butter	1	Tablespoon brown sugar
1/4	teaspoon mace	1	teaspoon chopped fresh basil
	Salt and freshly ground pepper	1	cup diced cooked chicken
			Oil for frying
2	eggs		Cranberry chutney (optional)
2	Tablespoons milk		
1	finely chopped garlic clove		
1	chopped small onion		
1/2	cup chopped green pepper		
1/2	cup chopped celery		
1/2	cup sliced mushrooms		

Oven Temperature: 400°

1. Slice the top crusts from the rolls, remove the soft bread, brush the insides and tops with melted butter, and bake about 10 minutes until golden. Reduce oven temperature to 300°.
2. Process the soft bread in a blender to make crumbs, and season them with mace, salt and pepper.
3. Remove the oysters from their shells, strain, and reserve the liquor.
4. Beat the eggs and milk in a bowl; one at a time, dip the oysters in the egg, roll in the crumbs, and chill the oysters for at least 15 minutes.
5. Sauté the garlic, onion, pepper, and celery in the remaining butter in a skillet. Add the mushrooms, 1/4 cup of the oyster liquor, the drained tomatoes, sugar, basil, and seasoning to taste; simmer uncovered until most of the liquids have evaporated. Stir in the chicken, and keep the sauce warm.
6. Fry the oysters, several at a time, in 375° oil until both sides are golden brown, drain, and keep warm until all are cooked.
7. Spoon some sauce into each roll, add 3 oysters, and divide the rest of the sauce among the rolls. Replace the tops.
8. Heat the rolls a few minutes in a 300° oven, and serve with a sauceboat of cranberry chutney.

Serves 8

Rolls Royale

Oysters take a cream sauce exceptionally well, and these piping hot rolls can be a "royal" luncheon in seconds. Or, better yet, entertain a prince charming after the theater or concert. With oysters, who needs four and twenty blackbirds?

1	pint oysters and liquor	1	Tablespoon dry Vermouth
½	cup cream		Salt and freshly ground white
4	slices diced bacon		pepper
2	Tablespoons butter	4	French or Italian hard rolls
2	Tablespoons chopped shallots		Lemon wedges (optional)
	or scallions		Parsley sprigs (optional)
1	garlic clove		
1	Tablespoon flour		

Oven Temperature: Medium Broil

1. Drain the oysters and set aside. Combine ¼ cup of the oyster liquor with the cream and warm in a small saucepan.
2. Cook the bacon until golden in a skillet or for about 1 minute in a microwave oven; drain on absorbent paper.
3. Melt the butter in a saucepan and sauté the shallots and garlic until tender, discard the garlic; stir in the flour, and cook until bubbling. Remove from the heat, and whisk in the cream. Return to heat and boil, stirring constantly, until the mixture thickens; simmer for at least 3 minutes.
4. Add the oysters, Vermouth, and season to taste; heat until the edges of the oysters begin to curl.
5. Slice the rolls in half lengthwise, hollow out the centers, and arrange the tops and bottoms on a baking sheet. Distribute the oyster sauce evenly in the bottoms and sprinkle with bacon.
6. Place the baking sheet under the broiler and heat until the rolls and bacon begin to brown. Remove from the broiler and replace the roll tops.
7. Serve immediately with a lemon wedge or garnish with parsley.

Serves 4

SEALED PACKAGE

Cut the top from a round loaf of bread and dig out all the crumb; butter the inside of the crust and brown in the oven. Fill with hot creamed oysters and put the cover back on. Cover the entire loaf with beaten egg yolk and put in the oven to glaze.

May E. Southworth,
One Hundred & One Ways of Serving Oysters

Foggy Bottom Oysters

A first course of creamed smoked oysters on corn sticks made with stone-ground cornmeal can certainly make Maryland a "merry land" during the holidays. Adding some scraped corn to the batter will ensure a moist center and using the traditional cast-iron molds guarantees a crust that will stand up to the creamed oysters. All other matters pertaining to cheer depend on the customary comestibles.

2	3¾-ounce tins smoked oysters		Salt and freshly ground white
3	Tablespoons minced shallots		pepper
⅔	cup dry white wine	16	corn sticks*
2	cups heavy cream		
1	Tablespoon lemon juice		
2	Tablespoons chopped parsley		

1. Drain the oysters, rinse, and drain again.
2. Simmer the shallots and wine in a heavy saucepan until the wine has almost evaporated. Stir in the cream and cook uncovered until the sauce is reduced by one third.
3. Add the oysters, lemon juice, parsley, and seasoning to taste. Cook until piping hot.
4. Slice the corn sticks in half lengthwise, and arrange 2 on each plate; cover with the oyster sauce, and top with the remaining halves.

* For additional flavor and texture, add 1 cup scraped corn to a standard corn stick recipe, grease the pans with bacon fat, and heat the corn sticks befroe assembling the dish.

Serves 8

Three truths keep bubbling to the surface in a search for a good piece of corn bread.

Southerners like their corn bread thin—about one inch deep in the pan. They want it made with white cornmeal. White looks pure.

The North likes a thick corn bread—sometimes three to four inches deep in the pan—and made with yellow cornmeal. Yellow looks rich.

Few Europeans care for corn in any form. They consider it a "gross food."

Bernard Clayton, Jr., *The Complete Book of Breads*

Oysters Narragansett Bay

Rhode Islanders are particular about their corn bread and Jo(h)nny Cake. Rightly so, since "whitecap flint" corn is grown and milled exclusively in the Ocean State. For a total effect, spoon creamed oysters and chicken over this corn bread. You might hear the mermaids singing, or, maybe, it will only be the sound of all those water-powered buhrstones grinding away.

1	pint oysters and liquor	2	cups diced cooked chicken
2¼	cups chicken stock	3	Tablespoons chopped parsley
	(See p. 63)		Salt and freshly ground
½	cup heavy cream		pepper
4	Tablespoons butter		Tabasco
4	Tablespoons flour		Hot corn bread
2	Tablespoons lemon juice		

1. Drain the oysters and warm ¼ cup of the oyster liquor with the stock and cream in a small saucepan.
2. Melt the butter in another saucepan, stir in the flour, and cook until bubbling. Remove from the heat and whisk in the stock mixture. Return to heat, add the lemon juice, and boil, stirring constantly, until the sauce thickens. Simmer at least 3 minutes; add the chicken and parsley, and cook until thoroughly heated.
3. Add the oysters, season to taste, and cook until the oysters begin to curl.
4. Cut the corn bread into serving-sized pieces, split them, and spoon the oyster mixture over each bottom piece. Set the tops in place and cover with the remaining sauce.
5. Garnish with carrot curls or radish roses.

Serves 6

Oysters Benedict

Certainly no traitor to the cause of regional cuisine, this adaptation of Eggs Benedict must be "found out" as soon as possible. The Hollandaise sauce sets off the oysters admirably, but the thickened Oyster Bisque sauce or an elegant Champagne sauce would probably make the hostess punishable for the high crime of over-indulging her guests.

16	shucked large oysters and	1	Tablespoon dry Sherry
	liquor	2	Tablespoons finely chopped
8	rashers lean bacon or		shallots
	Canadian bacon		Freshly ground white pepper
4	English muffins	1½	cups warm Hollandaise sauce*
2	Tablespoons butter		

Oven Temperature: High Broil

1. Remove the oysters from their shells, strain, and reserve ¼ cup of the liquor.
2. Cut the bacon slices in half, cook in a skillet or microwave oven until brown, and drain. Or, lightly sauté the slices of Canadian bacon in butter.
3. Split the English muffins and toast them in the broiler.
4. Heat the butter, oyster liquor, and Sherry in a saucepan and simmer the shallots until tender; add the oysters, season with pepper, and cook until the oysters are hot and plump.
5. Place 2 muffin halves on each plate, distribute the bacon, oysters, and some of the pan juices. Nap generously with Hollandaise and serve immediately.

    * Thickened Oyster Bisque (See p. 71) can be a very effective substitute for Hollandaise in this recipe.

Serves 4

Bourbon Street Benedict

The improvisatory style of this recipe is a definite plus. A stingingly sharp Creole mustard "wakes up" the Hollandaise sauce. And if a little more swing is wanted, serving a poached egg on one half of the muffin and oysters on the other half would be as jazzy as Bourbon Street.

24	shucked oysters	12	slices ham or Canadian bacon
1	cup seasoned corn flour	1½	cups warm Hollandaise sauce
	Oil for frying	2	Tablespoons Meaux mustard*
6	English muffins		Paprika
2	Tablespoons melted butter		Lime wedges

Oven Temperature: 450°

1. Remove the oysters from their shells, drain and pat them dry; dredge in the flour, and refrigerate for 15 minutes.
2. Heat some oil in a skillet and pan fry the oysters, a few at a time; turn frequently until both sides are golden brown. Remove with a slotted spoon, drain on absorbent paper, and keep warm until serving time.
3. Split the English muffins and place open-faced on a baking sheet in the oven for about 3 minutes until they are hot. Correct the oven setting to Low Broil.
4. Brush the cut sides of the muffins with melted butter, place a slice of ham or bacon on each, and broil until the slice is thoroughly heated.
5. Arrange 2 muffin halves on each plate, divide the oysters on the muffins, and spoon the Hollandaise sauce over them. Garnish with a sprinkling of paprika and a wedge of lime.

    * Pommery mustard mixed with a small amount of white wine vinegar is a reasonable substitute for Meaux mustard.

Serves 6

Oysters Newport News

In the South these biscuits might be made with sour milk, but using buttermilk or yoghurt will also guarantee a biscuit that is flaky and crisp on the outside and moist within. Perfect for a luncheon on the patio, simply split these little wonders in half, ladle creamy oysters over them, and serve with fresh asparagus or spiced apple rings.

1	pint oysters and liquor	2	egg yolks
1¼	cups medium cream	2	Tablespoons dry Sherry
5	Tablespoons butter		Salt and freshly ground
1½	Tablespoons flour		pepper
	Pinch of ground cloves	4	large baking powder biscuits
	Pinch of mace		Lemon wedges
2	Tablespoons finely chopped scallions		

1. Drain the oysters and set aside; combine ¼ cup of the liquor with ¾ cup cream and warm in a small saucepan.
2. Melt 3 tablespoons of the butter in another saucepan, stir in the flour, cloves, mace, and scallions, and cook until the scallions are tender. Remove from the heat and whisk in the cream. Return to heat and boil, stirring constantly, until the mixture thickens; simmer for 3 minutes.
3. Beat the egg yolks and the remaining ½ cup of cream in a bowl. Whisk in ½ cup of the hot mixture, a spoonful at a time. Slowly beat in the remaining hot mixture, then transfer the enriched sauce back to the saucepan and, stirring carefully, bring to a boil.
4. Add the oysters and Sherry, season to taste, and cook until the edges of the oysters start to curl.
5. Split and butter the warm biscuits. Put the bottoms on individual plates and ladle over a portion of the oyster sauce; replace the tops and cover with the remaining sauce. Garnish with lemon wedges.

Serves 4

Many of the old fashioned rusks were made with yeast dough. Rusks have come to have an entirely different meaning from what they had several generations ago. Today a rusk is looked upon as a dried sweetened bread, not unlike toast.

Imogene Wolcott, *The New England Yankee Cook Book*

Merry Olde Oyster Pye

Deep dish and "savoury" best describe the "main course" pies that England justifiably boasts. Topped with herbed biscuits or a flaky crust, this pie will surely prove that simple is best.

1	pint oysters and liquor		Salt and freshly ground
1½	cups light cream		pepper
8	Tablespoons butter	6	partially baked 2-inch biscuits*
6	Tablespoons flour		Paprika
3	Tablespoons Madeira		

Oven Temperature: 425°

1. Drain the oysters; measure ¼ cup of the liquor and warm it in a saucepan with the cream.
2. Melt the butter in another saucepan, stir in the flour, and cook until bubbling. Remove from the heat and whisk in the warm liquids. Return to heat, add the Madeira, and boil, stirring constantly, until the mixture thickens. Simmer for 3 minutes.
3. Stir in the oysters, season to taste, and heat until the oysters are plump.
4. Pour the hot oysters into a 1-quart buttered casserole, arrange the biscuits on top, and sprinkle with paprika.
5. Bake about 10 minutes until the biscuits are completely cooked and golden brown.

* Use a standard recipe for baking powder biscuits and mix ½ teaspoon tarragon and pinch of mace with the dry ingredients. Roll the dough ½-inch thick and bake the biscuits for only 8 minutes.

Serves 4

OYSTER PIE

Line a deep dish that will hold rather more than a quart, with a good pie-crust nearly half an inch thick. Strain the liquor from a quart of oysters. Put in the bottom of the dish a layer of fine cracker or bread crumbs; then add the oysters, with bits of butter and mace, a little pepper and salt, and a part of the liquor. The liquor should fill the dish only about one-half. Over the oysters put another layer of fine crumbs, and cover with pie-crust. Cut an opening in the top of the crust, and ornament with leaves of pastry. Bake about an hour. Brown gradually. Serve the pie hot. A pie containing a pint, or a pint and a half of oysters, is large enough for a family of two or three.

(Mrs.) M. H. Cornelius, *The Young Housekeeper's Friend*, 1871

Nip and Tuck Griddle Cakes

With a little forethought and on-the-spot dexterity, these oyster griddle cakes can be made while the Sunday morning coffee is brewing. Tuck into place on a serving tray, and nip with a bit of horseradish sauce for a breakfast in bed that succeeds entirely.

12 shucked large oysters and liquor	*Sauce:*
¾ cup Champagne	1 cup sour cream
1 chopped small onion	¼ cup mayonnaise
½ cup bread crumbs	¼ cup medium cream
2 eggs	2 Tablespoons prepared horseradish
3 Tablespoons melted butter	2 teaspoons minced chives
¼ cup milk	
¾ cup sifted flour	
1 teaspoon baking powder	
Salt	
Vegetable oil	

1. Combine the sour cream, mayonnaise, cream, horseradish, and chives in a mixing bowl and whisk until smooth; refrigerate until the pancakes are ready.
2. Remove the oysters from their shells; strain ¼ cup of the liquor.
3. Heat the oyster liquor and Champagne in a saucepan and lightly poach the oysters.
4. Pour the oysters and poaching liquid into the work bowl of a processor fitted with the steel blade; add the onion, bread crumbs, eggs, butter, milk, flour, baking powder, and salt, and process until smooth. Add a little milk to the mixture if it is too thick to make thin pancakes.
5. Heat a griddle or skillet until a drop of water sizzles on the surface and brush with vegetable oil. Use 2 tablespoons of batter for each pancake, or enough to make a 4-inch cake. When bubbles form on top, turn the pancakes, and brown the other side. Keep warm in the oven until all are fried.
6. Serve with butter and a silver porringer of sauce.

Serves 4

Old Dominion Pancakes

Definitely in the "carry me back to ole Virginny" tradition, these ham-and-oyster-topped cornmeal pancakes are the essence of "country cookin." And, if there are a few pancakes to spare, be sure to have a pitcher of syrup nearby, and *be tempted*.

1	pint oysters	1/4	teaspoon celery salt
20	4-inch thin cornmeal cakes		Paprika
5	Tablespoons clarified butter	4	thin slices baked ham
2	teaspoons Worcestershire sauce	1	cup melted butter

1. Place pieces of waxed paper between the corn cakes, arrange them in stacks on an oven-proof platter, cover loosely, and heat in a warm oven.
2. Drain the oysters, reserving the liquor for another use.
3. Heat 4 tablespoons of butter, Worcestershire sauce, and celery salt in a skillet, and pan-fry the oysters, a few at a time, turning them often. Sprinkle with paprika, remove with a slotted spoon, and keep warm until all are cooked.
4. Melt the remaining tablespoon of butter and pan-fry the ham slices until hot.
5. Stack 5 corn cakes on each plate, top with a ham slice and a portion of the oysters. Serve immediately with a sauceboat of hot melted butter.

Serves 4

Waffles High Hampton

A winter holiday breakfast with a festive glass of sparkling wine or a poolside brunch with Sangria are engaging alternatives for these crowd pleasers. Either way, oysters and waffles are a feast for all seasons.

1	pint oysters and liquor	6	egg yolks
4	Tablespoons butter		Salt and freshly ground pepper
1/4	pound sliced mushrooms		Paprika
1 1/2	cups cream	4	large hot waffles
1/4	cup dry Sherry		
2	Tablespoons brandy		

1. Drain the oysters, reserving 1/3 cup of the liquor.
2. Melt the butter in a 1 1/2-quart saucepan, stir in the oysters and mushrooms, and cook until the oysters are plump; remove the oysters and mushrooms with a slotted spoon and set aside.

3. Add the oyster liquor, 1 cup cream, the Sherry and brandy to the saucepan and simmer, uncovered, for 3 minutes.
4. Whisk the egg yolks in a bowl with the remaining $1/2$ cup of cream. Beat in $1/2$ cup of the hot mixture, one spoonful at a time; then slowly whisk in the remaining hot mixture. Transfer the enriched sauce to the saucepan and, stirring carefully, bring to a boil. Add the oysters, mushrooms, and seasoning to taste, and heat thoroughly.
5. Spoon over the waffles and serve garnished with cucumber slices, carrot curls, and watercress sprigs, or serve with a fresh fruit salad.

Serves 4

Piedmont Oysters

When the sun comes up over the Blue Ridge Mountains, rise and shine in style with a platter of Piedmont waffles. They're a world apart from ordinary breakfast fare and will certainly encourage lingering awhile.

1 pint oysters and liquor	1 Tablespoon lemon juice
$13/4$ cup chicken stock (See p. 63)	Salt and freshly ground
4 Tablespoons butter	pepper
2 Tablespoons chopped onion	4 large hot waffles
1 crushed garlic clove	Lemon slices
3 Tablespoons flour	Parsley sprigs
$1/4$ pound sliced small	
mushrooms	
$1/2$ cup diced cooked ham	

1. Drain the oysters, reserving $1/4$ cup of the liquor; warm the liquor and chicken stock in a small saucepan.
2. Melt the butter in another saucepan and sauté the onion and garlic until tender; discard the garlic. Stir in the flour and cook until bubbling. Remove from the heat and whisk in the hot liquids. Return to heat and boil, stirring constantly, until the mixture thickens; simmer 3 minutes.
3. Stir in the mushrooms, ham, and lemon juice, and boil 1 minute. Add the oysters and cook until they begin to curl; season to taste.
4. Spoon the ham and oysters over the hot waffles; garnish with lemon slices and parsley sprigs before serving.

Serves 4

East India Company Crêpes

Not a staple of Indian cuisine, oysters have, nevertheless, benefited from the range of spices and culinary styles exported from that country. The light curry flavor of these crêpes is a tempting "trade-off" for ordinary luncheon fare, especially if served with pineapple rings frosted with coconut.

1½	pints oysters and liquor	2	Tablespoons flour
12	6-inch entrée crêpes	½	teaspoon curry powder
½	pound sliced mushrooms	2	egg yolks
1	cup dry white wine		Salt and freshly ground
1	cup medium cream		pepper
4	Tablespoons butter		

1. Place pieces of foil between the crêpes and stack them on a heatproof plate; cover, and keep warm over boiling water or in the oven.
2. Simmer the mushrooms in the wine for 5 minutes; remove with a slotted spoon and keep warm in a bowl.
3. Add the oysters and their liquor to the wine and cook until the edges begin to curl; remove them with the slotted spoon and, if they are large, cut in quarters, and set aside with the mushrooms.
4. Reduce the poaching liquid to 1 cup; add ¾ cup of cream and reheat.
5. Melt the butter in another saucepan; stir in the flour and curry powder and cook until bubbling. Remove from the heat and whisk in the hot liquids. Return to heat and boil, stirring constantly, until the mixture thickens; simmer for at least 3 minutes.
6. Beat the egg yolks in a bowl with the remaining ¼ cup of cream. Whisk ½ cup of the hot mixture into the yolks, a spoonful at a time; slowly beat in the remaining hot mixture. Transfer the enriched sauce to the saucepan, season to taste with salt and pepper, and, stirring carefully, bring to a boil.
7. Stir some of the sauce into the oysters and mushrooms to bind them and place 2 tablespoons of the filling on each crêpe. Roll the crêpes and arrange them, seam side down, on individual serving plates. Nap with the remaining hot sauce, and serve immediately.

Serves 6

Oysters Hamilton Place

A century ago, this short avenue was where some of Boston's wealthiest families resided in "luxury and calm." Appropriately named, the following dish combines creamed oysters, paper-thin crêpes, and a whipped cream garnish to continue the tradition of elegance associated with the location, architecture, and distinguished past of Hamilton Place.

1	quart oysters and liquor		Salt and freshly ground
1	cup light cream		pepper
3	Tablespoons butter	16	7-inch crêpes*
2	Tablespoons flour	1	cup whipping cream
4	egg yolks		Chopped parsley
1	Tablespoon lemon juice		

1. Layer pieces of foil between the crêpes and stack them on an ovenproof plate; cover, and heat over boiling water or in a warm oven.
2. Drain the oysters, reserving ½ cup of the liquor. Warm the liquor and ¾ cup of the cream in a small saucepan.
3. Melt the butter in another saucepan, stir in the flour, and cook until bubbling. Remove from the heat and whisk in the cream. Return to heat and boil, stirring constantly, until the mixture thickens; simmer for 3 minutes.
4. Beat the egg yolks and remaining ¼ cup of cream in a bowl. Whisk in ½ cup of the hot mixture, a spoonful at a time; then slowly beat in the remaining hot mixture. Transfer the enriched sauce to the saucepan, place over moderate heat, and, stirring carefully, simmer for a minute.
5. Stir in the oysters, lemon juice, and seasoning to taste. Cook until the edges of the oysters begin to curl.
6. Place two tablespoons of the filling on each crêpe; roll the crêpes and arrange them, seam side down, on a serving platter or on individual plates.
7. Serve immediately, garnished with whipped cream and parsley.

* To the basic crêpe recipe, add 2 teaspoons grated lemon zest.

Serves 8

Chumley's Crêpes

Served in some of the finest seafood restaurants, these "classic" Coquilles St. Jacques crêpes never go out of style. With a little ingenuity and a pint of oysters, this shellfish delight can be savored at home and go far in establishing the reputation of "Chez . . . ."

1	pint oysters and liquor		3	Tablespoons flour
1	cup dry white wine		2	egg yolks
³/₄	pound bay scallops			Salt and freshly ground white pepper
1	cup chicken or fish stock (See pp. 63, 62)			Cayenne pepper
1	cup light cream		12	entrée crêpes*
4	Tablespoons butter		¹/₂	cup freshly grated Parmesan cheese
2	Tablespoons finely chopped shallots			
¹/₂	cup finely chopped green pepper (optional)			

Oven Temperature: 400°

1. Poach the oysters in their own liquor and the wine until they are plump, remove with a slotted spoon; if they are large, cut in quarters, and set aside in a bowl.
2. Poach the scallops in the same liquid for about 1 minute, drain, and reserve with the oysters.
3. Strain 1 cup of the poaching liquid and warm it in a saucepan with the stock and ¹/₂ cup cream.
4. Melt the butter in another saucepan and sauté the shallots and green pepper until tender. Stir in the flour and cook until bubbling. Remove from the heat and whisk in the stock. Return to heat and boil, stirring constantly, until the mixture thickens; simmer at least 3 minutes.
5. Beat the egg yolks in a bowl with the remaining ¹/₂ cup of cream. Whisk in ¹/₂ cup of the hot mixture, a spoonful at a time; slowly beat in the remaining hot mixture. Transfer the enriched sauce to the saucepan, season to taste with salt, pepper, and cayenne, and, stirring carefully, bring to a boil.
6. Spoon enough of the sauce into the oysters and scallops to make them moist. Place 2 tablespoons of the shellfish filling on each crêpe; roll, and arrange the crêpes, seam side down, in a shallow buttered baking dish; nap with the remaining sauce and sprinkle with cheese.
7. Cover with foil and bake 3 minutes; uncover and run under the broiler until cheese is hot and bubbling.

* Use a standard recipe, and add ¹/₄ teaspoon mace if desired.

Serves 6

Chartwell Oyster Crêpes

These "do ahead" crêpes are the passport to a perfect party. No need for the hostess to busy herself with anything more than tossing a salad and opening the bottles of wine when guests arrive.

1	quart oysters and liquor	1/3	cup dry Vermouth
3	cups chicken stock	1	pint *crème fraîche*
	(See p. 63)	1 1/2	cups freshly grated Fontina
3	pounds broccoli		cheese
	Salt and freshly ground	24	7-inch crêpes
	pepper	3	Tablespoons capers
1	cup butter		
1/2	cup flour		

Oven Temperature: 350°

1. Drain the oysters and place them in a large bowl, reserving 2/3 cup of the liquor. Warm the liquor and chicken stock in a saucepan.
2. Wash, peel, and blanch the broccoli in boiling salted water or in a microwave oven for 3 minutes; refresh in cold water, drain, and chop into 1/4-inch pieces.
3. Melt 4 tablespoons of butter in a large saucepan and toss the broccoli until it is well coated, season with pepper, remove with a slotted spoon, and set aside with the oysters.
4. Melt the remaining butter, stir in the flour, and cook until bubbling. Remove from the heat and whisk in the stock. Return to heat and boil, stirring constantly, until the sauce thickens. Add the Vermouth, 1/2 cup *crème fraîche*, and simmer for 10 minutes.
5. Stir enough of the sauce into the oysters and broccoli to bind them, and adjust seasonings.
6. Mix the remaining *crème fraîche* and 1 cup of cheese, and spread it on the bottom of a large shallow, buttered baking pan. Fill each crêpe with about 2 tablespoons of the oyster mixture; roll up the crêpes and arrange them in one layer, seam side down, in the pan. Add the capers to the sauce, pour it over the crêpes, and top with the remaining cheese.
7. Cover with foil, bake 30 minutes, and serve immediately.

Serves 12

PASTRIES

Oysters La Nacelle

Up, up, and away in these puffy-pastry baskets. What oyster wouldn't feel on top of the world in this cream sauce brimming with mushrooms, peppers, and spirits?

1	pint oysters and liquor		Salt and freshly ground
1	cup light cream		pepper
4	Tablespoons butter	6	large puff-pastry shells
3	Tablespoons finely chopped celery		Lime slices
2	Tablespoons finely chopped green pepper		Parsley sprigs
2	Tablespoons flour		
2	Tablespoons Cognac		
½	cup sliced mushrooms		
1	Tablespoon chopped pimiento		

1. Drain the oysters, pat dry, and cut them in halves or quarters. Warm ¼ cup of the strained oyster liquor and the cream in a small saucepan.
2. Melt the butter in another saucepan and sauté the celery and pepper until tender. Stir in the flour and cook until bubbling. Remove from the heat and whisk in the cream. Return to heat and boil, stirring constantly, until the mixture thickens. Simmer for 3 minutes and stir in the oysters, Cognac, mushrooms, pimiento, and seasonings; heat until the edges of the oysters start to curl.
3. Spoon the sauce into warm pastry shells and serve at once. Garnish with lime slices or parsley.

Serves 6

. . . secret and self-contained, and solitary as an oyster.
Charles Dickens

Twelfth Night Oyster Tarts

These Cognac-and-wine-laced tarts are exactly right for the wind-down of the Christmas holidays when a little heavy orchestration is needed for the last gathering of the season. Be traditional and hide a pistachio nut in three of them in honor of the Three Kings. The buttered breadcrumb topping hides all.

1	pint oysters and liquor	2	egg yolks
1½	cups dry white wine	2	Tablespoons Cognac
½	pound raw medium shrimp		Salt and freshly ground
¼	pound sliced small		pepper
	mushrooms	6	4½-inch baked tart shells
6	Tablespoons butter	¼	cup fresh bread crumbs
1½	Tablespoons flour		
1	cup medium cream		

Oven Temperature: 425°

1. Poach the oysters in their own liquor and the wine until they are plump; remove with a slotted spoon, pat dry, and set them aside.
2. Rinse the shrimp and poach for 1 minute in the same liquid; refresh in cold water, shell, devein, and set aside in a bowl.
3. Keep the poaching liquid boiling and cook the mushrooms for a minute; remove them and add to the shrimp. Reduce the liquid to 1 cup, and strain it.
4. Melt the butter in a saucepan; spoon off and reserve 2 tablespoons for the bread crumbs. Stir in the flour and cook until bubbling. Remove from the heat and whisk in the hot poaching liquid. Return to heat, add ½ cup of cream and boil, stirring constantly, until the mixture thickens; simmer for 3 minutes.
5. Beat the egg yolks in a bowl with the remaining ½ cup of cream. Whisk in ½ cup of the hot mixture, a spoonful at a time. Slowly beat in the remaining hot mixture and transfer the enriched sauce to the saucepan. Add the Cognac and, stirring carefully, bring to a boil.
6. Stir in the shrimp and mushrooms, and adjust seasonings.
7. Assemble the tarts by spooning some of the shrimp and mushroom sauce into the shells. Distribute the oysters, the rest of the sauce, and sprinkle with the buttered crumbs. (The tarts may be refrigerated or frozen at this point.)
8. Bake for about 5 minutes, or longer if the tarts are cold. As soon as they are thoroughly hot and golden brown on top, remove from the oven, and serve on plates garnished with a holly sprig.

Serves 6

Chartwell Oyster Crêpes (Page 150)

Oysters with Seafood Mayonnaise (Page 167)

Society Hill Tart

In a class of its own, this elegant seafood *croustade* is nothing short of *soignée*—"adj. Carefully done, well got up, smart; (colloq.) remarkable, first-rate." *New Cassell's French Dictionary*

1 quart oysters and liquor	4 egg yolks
2 cups light cream	½ pound cooked, shelled, deveined, medium shrimp
2 cups fish stock (See p. 62)	½ pound lump crabmeat
8 Tablespoons butter	1 cup sliced small mushrooms
1 garlic clove	Salt and freshly ground pepper
1 cup finely chopped scallions	20 sheets phyllo dough*
¼ cup finely chopped green pepper	Warm melted butter
¼ cup finely chopped celery	
4 Tablespoons flour	
¼ cup dry Vermouth	
Pinch of thyme	

Oven Temperature: 350°

1. Drain the oysters, reserving ½ cup of the liquor. Warm the liquor, 1½ cups of cream and the fish stock in a saucepan.

2. Melt the butter in a large saucepan and sauté the garlic, scallion, green pepper, and celery until tender; discard the garlic. Stir in the flour and cook until bubbling. Remove from the heat and whisk in the stock mixture. Return to heat and boil, stirring constantly, until the sauce thickens. Add the Vermouth and thyme, and simmer about 15 minutes.

3. Beat the egg yolks with the remaining ½ cup of cream in a bowl. Whisk in ½ cup of the hot mixture, a spoonful at a time; then slowly beat in the rest of the hot mixture. Transfer the enriched sauce back to the saucepan; stir carefully over moderate heat until the sauce thickens.

4. Stir in the oysters, shrimp, crabmeat, mushrooms, and season to taste.

5. Butter a 13 x 9-inch baking pan and spread the bottom with a sheet of phyllo dough, brushing it with melted butter. Repeat until there are 10 sheets of dough. Spread the oyster mixture evenly and cover with another 10 buttered sheets of phyllo.

6. Bake for 40 minutes, covering with foil if the crust becomes too brown.

* Defrost frozen dough in the refrigerator, unroll on the work table, and cover with a moist towel to prevent cracking during the layering process.

Serves 10

Governor's Oyster Pie

If this recipe brings Williamsburg to mind, then little will be lost in the translation of colonial Virginia's hospitality into a more contemporary idiom. Set the out-of-the-brick-oven pie on a King's Arms trivet, lay out the best "Queen's Ware," and light the tapers in the supper room—"That the Future May Learn From the Past."
Colonial Williamsburg Foundation

1½ pints oysters and liquor	1 Tablespoon lemon juice
1 cup cream	1½ cups sliced mushrooms
4 Tablespoons butter	Salt and freshly ground
4 Tablespoons flour	pepper
Pinch of mace	Cheddar cheese pastry dough
¼ cup dry Sherry	for a 2 crust 9-inch pie*

Oven Temperature: 400°

1. Drain the oysters, reserving ½ cup of liquor. Mix the liquor and cream, and warm in a small saucepan.
2. Melt the butter in another saucepan, stir in the flour and mace, and cook until bubbling. Remove from the heat and whisk in the cream mixture. Return to heat, add the Sherry and lemon juice, and boil, stirring constantly, until the mixture thickens. Simmer at least 3 minutes.
3. Add the oysters and mushrooms, and season to taste.
4. Roll the pastry ⅛-inch thick, and line the bottom of the pie pan, spread the oyster mixture evenly, and cover with a pastry lid. Seal the edges and pierce the top with a sharp knife.
5. Bake about 40 minutes until the crust is golden brown.

* Substitute 1 cup freshly grated Cheddar cheese for 3 ounces of the regular shortening.

Serves 6

SOTTERLEY OYSTER PYE

Take a quart of large oysters, parboil them in their liquor, a little bread grated, an onion and savoury spices. When the Pye is baked, take out the onion from the oysters, pour them in the Pye, lay on butter and close it with your Paste.

Miss Ann Chase's Book, Annapolis, 1811

Dockside Pizza

This adaptation of a French provincial recipe goes a long way toward transforming the plebeian image of pizza into a chic, dockside, luncheon treat. Add a bit of pesto sauce instead of the herbs and spices, or substitute goat cheese for the anchovy fillets, and a new wave of pizza possibilities comes rolling in.

1	pint oysters		Salt	
1	pound raw medium shrimp		Pinch of cayenne pepper	
3	Tablespoons olive oil		Dough for 2 12-inch pizzas	
1/4	pound sliced mushrooms	1/2	cup pitted and sliced Greek olives (optional)	
1	28-ounce can peeled tomatoes	12	anchovy fillets (optional)	
2	Tablespoons tomato paste	1/2	cup sautéed onion rings (optional)	
1/2	teaspoon chopped fresh thyme	2	cups shredded Mozzarella cheese	
1/2	teaspoon chopped fresh oregano			
1	bay leaf			
1/4	teaspoon lemon juice			
1	garlic clove			

Oven Temperature: 400°

1. Drain the oysters, pat them dry and set aside. Rinse, shell and devein the shrimp.
2. Heat 2 tablespoons olive oil in a skillet and sauté the mushrooms over moderately high heat, stirring frequently, until the liquid has evaporated. Remove from the heat and reserve.
3. Chop the tomatoes and combine them in a heavy 1½-quart saucepan with 1 tablespoon olive oil, tomato paste, thyme, oregano, bay leaf, lemon juice, garlic, salt to taste, and cayenne. Cook, uncovered, over medium heat about 30 minutes until the sauce is thick. Discard the bay leaf and garlic.
4. Roll the dough into two 12-inch circles and place on a greased baking sheet. Cover with tomato sauce; arrange the oysters, shrimp, mushrooms, olives, anchovies, and onion rings on top,* and sprinkle each pizza with a cup of cheese.
5. Bake in the center of the oven about 20 minutes until the crust is golden brown and the cheese is completely melted.
6. Serve hot or at room temperature.

*The ingredients used should be attractively arranged over the top of the pizza either like the spokes of a wheel or in a circular pattern.

Serves 8

QUICHE

Recent popularity notwithstanding, *quiche* has long been a convenient and customary word in Continental cuisine. Spelled *kechel* in old English, it meant a small cake. And when Chaucer, who was as interested in his characters' dining habits as he was in their tales, used it as a "Goddes Kechyl or trype of cheese," he probably had in mind a cake given as alms. While neither Escoffier nor Francatelli mention quiche in their cookery books, at some point in time the word quiche became useful to describe an egg-and-bacon flan popular in Lorraine and the three-cheese, open-faced pie associated with Valenciennes.

Even today, quiche is thought of as *regional*—the English Cheddar flan, the New York smoked-salmon-and-dill quiche; as *rags-to-riches*—any ingredient from the lowly onion to the opulent oyster will do; and as just *right* for a luncheon or supper entrée.

The following recipes roam and range a bit, adding compatible spirits, herbs, vegetables, and cheese to the basic egg and cream mixture. In all of them, the extravagance of using oysters has been its own reward.

Yankee Clipper Quiche

1	pint oysters and liquor	½ cup chopped parsley
3	eggs	½ cup sautéed chopped scallions (optional)
6	ounces cream cheese	
1½	cups half-and-half	1 cup grated Swiss cheese
2	Tablespoons flour	3 Tablespoons grated Parmesan cheese
	Pinch of nutmeg	
	Salt and freshly ground pepper	
1	10-inch unbaked pastry shell	
½	cup chopped chives	

Oven Temperature: 375°

1. Drain the oysters, pat them dry, and cut in halves or quarters if they are large; strain and reserve ¼ cup of the oyster liquor.
2. Beat the eggs in a mixing bowl and blend in the softened cream cheese, oyster liquor, half-and-half, flour, and seasoning to taste.
3. Arrange the oysters on the chilled pastry shell, cover with chives, parsley, and scallions, and grated cheese. Pour the egg mixture on top.
4. Bake about 45 minutes, until the custard is set and the top a golden brown; remove from oven and cool for 5 minutes before serving.

Serves 6

Chatham Walk Quiche

½ pint oysters
2 Tablespoons butter
1 Tablespoon finely chopped shallots
1 cup sliced mushrooms
1 partially baked 9-inch pastry shell
½ cup grated Gruyère cheese
3 eggs

1½ cups medium cream
¼ cup brandy
½ teaspoon salt
¼ teaspoon freshly ground white pepper
Parsley sprigs

Oven Temperature: 375°

1. Drain the oysters and pat them dry; if they are large, cut them in halves. Reserve the liquor for another use.
2. Melt the butter in a skillet and lightly sauté the shallots and mushrooms; remove with a slotted spoon and distribute in the pastry shell.
3. Add the oysters to the shell and sprinkle the grated cheese over them.
4. Beat the eggs lightly in a bowl and stir in the cream, brandy, and seasonings; pour over the filling in the shell.
5. Bake in the upper third of the oven about 30 minutes until the top is golden brown. When a knife, inserted near the edge, comes out clean, remove from the oven and let stand for 5 minutes.
6. Garnish the individual servings with parsley sprigs.

Serves 4

Kettle Cove Quiche

1 pint oysters
4 thin onion slices
1½ cups light cream
3 eggs
3 Tablespoons dry Sherry
  Salt and freshly ground pepper
3 Tablespoons diced smoked salmon
1 partially baked 9-inch pastry shell
½ cup freshly grated Gruyère or Swiss cheese

Herb bouquet:
½ bay leaf
1 whole clove
  Pinch of celery salt
  Pinch of thyme

Oven Temperature: 375°

1. Add the herb bouquet and onion slices to the cream and scald in a saucepan; discard the herbs, remove the onions with a slotted spoon, and set aside. Allow the cream to cool.
2. Beat the eggs in a bowl until frothy, whisk in the cream and Sherry, and season to taste.
3. Arrange the diced salmon on the pastry shell, add the oysters, and top with onion slices. Sprinkle with cheese, and pour the egg and cream mixture into the shell.
4. Bake in the upper third of the oven about 30 minutes until a knife, inserted near the edge, comes out clean.
5. Remove from oven and allow the quiche to stand for about 5 minutes before cutting into wedges.

Serves 4

Quiche Capri

½ pint medium oysters
4   thin slices ham or prosciutto
2   Tablespoons butter
¼ cup finely chopped shallots or scallions
1   cup chopped cooked spinach
1   partially baked 9-inch pastry shell

½ cup grated Gruyère cheese
3   eggs
1½ cups light cream or half-and-half
¼ teaspoon nutmeg
½ teaspoon salt
¼ teaspoon freshly ground white pepper

Oven Temperature: 375°

1. Drain and pat the oysters dry.
2. Cut the ham into strips and sauté in butter with the shallots until the shallots are tender; stir in the spinach.
3. Distribute the spinach mixture in the pastry shell, add the oysters, and cover with cheese.
4. Beat the eggs lightly in a bowl, stir in the cream and seasonings, and pour over the filling.
5. Bake in upper third of the oven 25 minutes and remove when a knife tests clean. Let the quiche rest for 5 minutes before cutting.

Serves 4

Aegean Fare

1 pint oysters and liquor	1 cup crumbled Feta cheese
1 10-ounce can artichoke hearts	3 Tablespoons freshly grated
1 Tablespoon butter	Parmesan cheese
1 teaspoon chopped fresh	4 eggs
oregano	3 Tablespoons flour
1 teaspoon chopped fresh	1 pint half-and-half
rosemary	Salt and freshly ground
1 chopped medium onion	pepper
¼ cup pitted and chopped Greek	
olives	
1 unbaked 10-inch pastry shell	

Oven Temperature: 375°

1. Drain the oysters, pat dry, and cut them in halves or quarters if they are large. Reserve ⅓ cup of the liquor for the custard.
2. Rinse half the artichoke hearts, drain, and cut them into ½-inch cubes; set aside the remaining hearts for another use.
3. Melt the butter in a skillet, add the oregano and rosemary, and sauté the onion until tender. Remove from the heat; stir in the artichokes and olives.
4. Arrange the oysters in the pastry shell, spread the artichoke mixture, and sprinkle with the cheese.
5. Beat the eggs in a bowl, whisk in the flour, oyster liquor, half-and-half, and season with ½ teaspoon salt and ¼ teaspoon pepper.
6. Bake about 45 minutes until the top is brown and the custard has set. Turn the heat off, remove from the oven, and let stand for 5 minutes before cutting into wedges.

Serves 6

SHORTCAKE

Make a rich biscuit shortcake as for berries. Pick over the oysters carefully; strain the liquor, season and cook the oysters in this. Just as the shortcake comes from the oven split it and butter both inside crusts lavishly; lift the oysters with a fork and lay thick on the under buttered cake; season with pepper and salt and cover with the top crust. Thicken the gravy with flour rubbed smooth with butter; add cream and pour it hot over the shortcake the last moment before serving.

May E. Southworth, *One Hundred & One Ways of Serving Oysters, 1907*

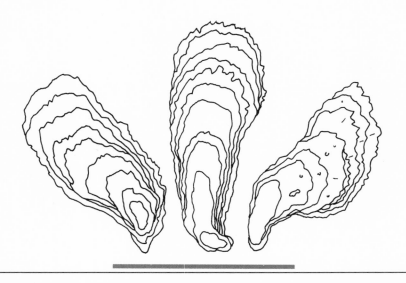

At an oyster supper, it is usual to have all the various preparations of oysters, fried, stewed, broiled, roasted, raw and in patties. Potatoes mashed, and browned, are generally added. The roasted oysters are served in the shell, on very large dishes, and brought in 'hot and hot,' all the time, as they are generally eaten much faster than they can be cooked. Small buckets (usually of maple or stained wood, with brass hoops) are placed on the floor, for the purpose of receiving the shells, beside the chairs of the gentlemen; as the business of opening the oysters mostly devolves on them. At the right hand of each plate is placed a thick folded towel and an oyster knife, which is used only to open the shell; at the other side of the napkin, fork, bread, tumbler, wine-glasses, etc. On the side-table let there be plenty of plates, knives and forks to change with; a basket of bread or light rolls; pitchers of water; bottles of port and cider; decanters of wine being on the table. Several butter plates, with a knife to each, should be set along the table. Sometimes the butter is made into the shape of a pineapple or basket of flowers.

Miss Leslie's House Book, 1841

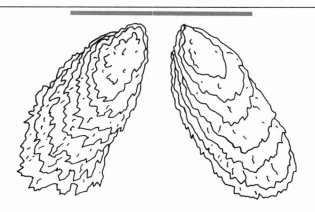

OYSTER ENTREES

arly accounts of "oyster suppers" at which bushels of "fried, steamed, boiled, roasted and [pattied]" oysters were consumed sound capricious today and thoroughly out of tune with the culinary trends, life style, and dining habits of the eighties. Except for the regional once-a-year oyster festivals that are sponsored along the Eastern seaboard, all the tales of the surfeit of oysters enjoyed at Roman banquets, in Dickensian oyster bars, and at late evening suppers by the Diamond Jim Bradys of this world are simply reminders of a time long gone, the never-never wonderland of the Walrus and Carpenter and "oysters four," or four hundred.

No longer plentiful, threatened by complex, coastal, pollution problems, the oyster has literally become the "pearl of great price." And, like the pearl, it is valued, even treasured, and usually shown off to its greatest advantage. The celebrated celebrate with freshly shucked oysters on the half shell or with the legendary and luxurious Rockefellers. High life below the stairs at Grand Central Station means a bowl of creamy oyster stew. And *de rigueur* for the wee hours of Mardi Gras morning is a "po" boy loaf and a cup of *café brulot*.

Curiously, oysters as the main course in a well-orchestrated meal will not be found in the hallowed halls of haute cuisine, but seem to be the "regulars," the Fried Oyster entrée, featured in the fish and chip restaurants that line the harbors and piers of major ports.

It may be an image problem, and, perhaps, a culinary one as well. Seneca wrote that oysters, "are not really food, but are relished to bully the sated stomach into further eating." Evidence of the absence of *cuisine minceur* in ancient Rome or at the court of Louis XIV are the bushels of oysters swallowed as a *prelude* to a meal, as appetite teasers but never as the main course.

Fortunately, a fresh new wind, gaining momentum on both the Atlantic and Pacific coasts, is blowing the briny scent of oysters across the land today. Lighter meals, low-sodium diets, simple sautéed and stir-fried methods of preparation, encourage greater use of the oyster as an elegant entrée.

The "secret and self-contained, and solitary oyster" like a demanding lover wants more than its share of time and attention in the kitchen. And its needs must be anticipated and respected. If neglected, an oyster will overcook in a split second or wallow in a soggy batter. Oysters resist steaming for so long that they are tough before their shells pop open. And, while stove-top, liquid cooking may be a brief and necessary first step in some recipes, poaching is not generally an effective way to prepare and serve oysters as a main course. Caution is "writ large" when planning an oyster entrée: careful timing and the fundamentals of each cooking technique should realistically be considered before selecting the mode of preparation.

French-frying virtually guarantees a succulent juicy oyster hidden within a firm tasty coating, providing the frying is done with the proper ingredients, utensils, and skill. The advantages of stir-frying, on the other hand, extend to the last-minute alliance of freshly shucked oysters and tender-crisp vegetables.

Sautéeing or pan frying results in a crisper and tastier oyster dish than the "panned" or "mock roasted" cooking method of yesterday, which often resulted in overcooked or "stewed" oysters. And spooning a lightly-thickened or reduced sauce over the oysters *after* frying instead of heating them in a sauce really enhances the flavor of all the ingredients used and keeps the oysters from sagging.

The benefits of baking oysters in a loaf or a simple crumb mixture effectively states the case that less is better than more when cooking this favorite mollusk of emperors and kings. "Scalloped Oysters," served *en casserole* or in the traditional scallop shell, continues to be a classic way of preparing oysters, and a delicious one.

Whether the oysters are grilled on wood charcoal, or skewered and single-layered in a broiling pan, or kept on the half shell and laced with a bit of butter, the speed and intensity of broiling make this technique a "sorceror's magic" way to transform raw oysters into an exciting entrée. Enhanced with a delicate, wine-scented, reduced sauce, they retain every ounce of flavor.

This chapter suggests that modern ovens, woks, deep-fryers, indoor and outdoor grills, and rotisseries are viable alternatives to the hot coals of colonial fireplaces and wood-burning stoves. And, while "Oyster Roasts" will never be elegant dining, a menu planned around an oyster entrée and an important bottle of Chablis can be a significant "visiting card" to a home where the old traditions have been transformed and yet respected.

SUGGESTIONS:

- Bulk oysters may be considerably smaller than oysters purchased in the shell which can be selected for size. An average-sized Eastern oyster is 3 to 4 inches long, a large oyster is about 5 inches. Pacific oysters are larger and "knife and fork" oysters are as large as a plate. In all cases the size of the oyster determines the appropriate number needed for a "main course" serving. Average-sized oysters are used in determining the number of servings suggested in the recipes unless large are specified.

- The amount of seasoning in a coating, batter, or "seasoned" crumb mixture depends on the saltiness of the oysters being prepared. Test the oyster liquor as a gauge of salinity.

- Oven temperature and thermostats vary considerably. The temperatures listed in the recipes may have to be regulated or adjusted to suit a specific unit.

- High-heat methods of cooking oysters result in a tastier dish if a marinade, basting sauce, simple coating, or a batter is used in their preparation. The lighter the coating the better.

- When frying oysters, use polyunsaturated oils that have a high "smoke point." They are superior to olive oil, butter, lard, and other shortenings that have a "low smoke" point or temperature at which the oil begins to break down. 360°—375° is the ideal range for most recipes.

- The amount of oil depends on the fryer or pan. A commercial French-fryer is ideal but, lacking this, a saucepan can be used if filled at least half full of oil. Too much oil can make the oyster "greasy;" too little oil causes burning or rapid browning. Use enough oil to permit the oysters to "swim."

- Certain coatings need "basket" frying, and batter coatings require "dropping" into hot oil. The temperature of the oil will drop when the oysters are added. Care should be taken not to crowd the fryer. And the second and third "batches" will have a tendency to brown faster if the temperature is not carefully regulated.

- Fried foods should be placed on absorbent paper to drain and be kept warm in a moderate oven until served. Do not stack or cover, and always serve on hot plates because cold plates cause condensation.

- Fritters are traditionally French-fried, but they can also be fried on a lightly coated griddle or in a skillet if a flat or "pancake" type of fritter is desired.

- French-fried oysters are usually served with sauces from the mayonnaise or Hollandaise family, or with one of the hot butter sauces.

- At a typical Chinese meal, at least four entrées are served. For ease in preparation, a soup and one or two steamed dishes will facilitate the preliminaries and last minute cooking of the stir-fried dish.

- All the ingredients of a stir-fry dish should be similar in size and shape to accommodate the short cooking time.

- Rice served with stir-fried oysters should be unsalted.

- Stir-fry recipes cannot be doubled unless a second wok is used.

- When sautéeing, it is important to use enough butter to prevent the coated oysters from sticking to the bottom of the skillet.

- Use clarified butter or butter fortified with 1/3 the amount of vegetable oil.

- To keep the oysters crisp, sauce the dish just before serving. If a sauce has enough consistency, spoon it on the plate first and then place the oysters in the center of the sauce.

- A *large* grilling surface is essential to accommodate the number of oysters-in-the-shell needed for an entrée and for the heating pans required to keep them warm.

- Tongs and heavy gloves are helpful when taking the oysters from the grill and removing the top shell.

- Even when threaded through the adductor muscle, oysters resist skewering. It is advisable to wrap the oyster in bacon, leek leaves, or a layer of onion to keep it in place when grilling kebabs.

FRENCH-FRY

Possibly no cooking technique has suffered more from abuse than French-frying or "deep-frying." Even the ingredients associated with it—oil, lard, fat, grease—make one shudder at the thought of calories, cholesterol, and corpulence. But nothing with "French" on the label can be *all* bad. Who hasn't savored a perfect potato puff teasingly placed next to a double-grilled lamb chop, or a heavenly hot plate of just-fried scallops rushed to the table with a wreath of parsley, or a perfectly French-fried oyster—thin-coated and crisp without, moist and delicious within? There is definitely something to be said about this import.

The current popularity of polyunsaturated oils and the convenience of commercial "deep-fryers," also, have gone a long way to dispel visions of sizzling grease, floating burnt particles, and heavy soggy food. Actually a "dry" method of cooking, French-frying is a plus in the preparation of many foods, especially the oyster. It seals in the natural flavor and juices, cooks the oysters quickly and uncompromisingly, and makes them the *pièce de résistance* of any supper or dinner menu.

The following recipes include simple coatings as well as batter coatings and a variety of cold and warm sauces. Many purists believe that a superlatively French-fried oyster needs little more than a wedge of lemon for its success, although tartar sauce is a classic accompaniment and other sauces can also offer either a stingingly sharp piquancy or a delicate embellishment. Preference is the key to use. Planning and preparation is all.

SOUPER INTIME

	Consommé Julienne
LE VIN:	*Huîtres Frites*
Pommard Blanc	*Sauce Tartare*
	Fonds d'Artichauts à la Duxelles
	Salade Verte
	Pain Ordinaire
	Glace au Citron
	Café

French-Fried Oysters with Tartar Sauce

24 shucked large oysters
    Vegetable or peanut oil for
      frying
    Lemon Wedges

Simple coating:
1½ cups flour
2   egg whites
    Fine dry bread crumbs

Tartar sauce:
1   cup mayonnaise
3   Tablespoons minced sweet
      pickles
1   minced shallot
2   Tablespoons snipped chives
2   Tablespoons minced parsley
1   Tablespoon minced fresh
      tarragon
1   Tablespoon capers
    Dijon mustard (optional)
    White wine vinegar (optional)

1. Make the sauce by combining all the ingredients and adding mustard and/or vinegar to taste. Refrigerate for at least two hours before serving.
2. Remove the oysters from their shells, drain, and pat dry, reserving the liquor for another use.
3. Dip the oysters in flour. Whip the egg whites until foamy and dip the floured oysters in the froth. Roll in bread crumbs and set aside. Repeat the process, whipping the egg whites to a froth between dippings.
4. Heat the oil to 375° in a deep fryer or heavy-gauge saucepan.
5. Lay a few of the oysters in the bottom of a fryer basket, taking care not to crowd it. Lower the basket into the hot fat and fry the oysters until they are golden brown, not dark brown. Remove, drain on a baking sheet lined with absorbent paper, and keep warm in a hot oven until all the oysters are fried.
6. Serve immediately with lemon wedges and a sauceboat of tartar sauce.

Serves 3

French-Fried Oysters with Seafood Mayonnaise

24 shucked large oysters
    Vegetable or peanut oil for
      frying
    Lemon wedges

Simple coating:
    Melted butter
    Fine dry bread crumbs

Seafood mayonnaise:
1   cup mayonnaise
¼   cup chili sauce
1   Tablespoon lime juice
1   Tablespoon drained
      horseradish
2   teaspoons dry Sherry

1. Make the sauce by combining all the ingredients. Refrigerate for at least two hours before serving.
2. Remove the oysters from their shells, drain, and pat dry, reserving the oyster liquor for another use.
3. Dip the oysters in melted butter. Draw between the thumb and index finger to remove excess butter, roll in bread crumbs, and set aside.
4. Heat the oil to 360° in a deep fryer or heavy-gauge saucepan.
5. Place a few oysters at a time in the bottom of a fryer basket. Lower it into the hot oil, and fry the oysters until they are golden brown. Remove and drain on a baking sheet lined with absorbent paper. Keep warm until all the oysters are fried.
6. Serve immediately with lemon wedges and a sauceboat of seafood mayonnaise.

Serves 3

French-Fried Oysters with Andalouse Sauce

24 shucked large oysters
Vegetable or peanut oil for frying
Lemon wedges

Simple coating:
2 eggs
¼ cup milk
1 Tablespoon vegetable oil
Salt and freshly ground pepper
¾ cup corn flour
Fine dry bread crumbs

Andalouse sauce:
¼ sweet red pepper
¼ green pepper
1 Tablespoon olive oil
2 Tablespoons tomato paste
1 cup mayonnaise
¼ minced garlic clove
¼ teaspoon sugar
Pinch of salt

1. Char the skin of the peppers and peel when they have cooled; chop the peppers and sauté them in olive oil, drain, and cool. Add the peppers and tomato paste to the mayonnaise and season with garlic, sugar, and salt. Refrigerate until needed.
2. Remove the oysters from their shells, drain, and pat dry, reserving the oyster liquor for another use.
3. Combine the eggs, milk, oil, and seasonings, and mix well. Dip the oysters in the corn flour, then the egg mixture, and roll in crumbs.
4. Heat the oil to 375° in a deep fryer or a deep, heavy saucepan.
5. Lay a few oysters in a fryer basket, taking care not to crowd them. Lower the basket into the hot oil.

6. Fry the oysters until they are crisp golden brown. Remove and drain on a baking sheet lined with absorbent paper. Keep warm until all the oysters are fried.
7. Serve immediately with lemon wedges and a sauceboat of Andalouse sauce.

Serves 3

French-Fried Oysters Southern Style

24 shucked large oysters
Vegetable or peanut oil for frying
Lemon wedges
Tomato sauce (See p. 17)

Simple coating:
1 cup finely ground yellow cornmeal
Salt
1/2 teaspoon freshly ground pepper
Cayenne pepper
1/2 cup light cream

1. Remove the oysters from their shells, drain, and pat dry, reserving the oyster liquor for another use.
2. Mix the cornmeal and seasonings together on a large plate. Dip the oysters in the cream, drain, and coat with the cornmeal.
3. Heat the oil to 375° in a deep fryer or a heavy-gauge, deep saucepan.
4. Shake off the surplus cornmeal before placing the oysters, a few at a time, in the bottom of a fryer basket. Lower the oysters into the hot oil and fry until they are golden brown.
5. Remove and drain on a baking sheet lined with absorbent paper. Keep warm until all the oysters are fried.
6. Serve immediately with lemon wedges and a bowl of seasoned tomato sauce.

Serves 3

Firm chilled oysters rolled quickly in crumbs and dipped into good fat for almost no time at all, and then served quickly on hot plates with an honest tartar sauce or lemon slices, can be one of the best dishes anywhere.

M. F. K. Fisher, *Consider the Oyster*

French-Fried Oysters Japanese Style*

24 shucked large oysters
Vegetable or peanut oil for
    frying
Sour cream spinach sauce
    (See p. 19)
Lemon wedges

Batter coating:
  ½ cup flour
  ½ cup cornstarch
    Salt
1 beaten egg
⅔ cup ice water

1. Drain the oysters and pat them dry.
2. Heat the oil in a deep fryer or heavy saucepan to 375°.
3. Sift the flour, cornstarch, and salt into a bowl, and whisk in the egg and water. Keep the batter chilled by placing the bowl on ice.
4. Dip an oyster in the batter and coat it well; remove with a spoon, and drop into the hot oil. Cook for about 2 minutes, moving the oyster around occasionally so that all surfaces become golden brown.
5. Remove and drain on a baking sheet lined with absorbent paper. Keep warm.
6. Fry the oysters in small batches until all are cooked.
7. Serve immediately with the sour cream sauce and lemon wedges.

* Sixteenth-century Portuguese traders introduced the European notion of deep-frying to the Japanese. After four hundred years of refinement, Japanese tempura is probably the most delicate batter-fried food in the world.

Serves 3

French-Fried Oysters Chinese Style

24 shucked large oysters
Vegetable or peanut oil for
    frying
Sweet and sour sauce
    (See p. 175)

Coating:
3 Tablespoons cornstarch
¼ teaspoon sugar
    Salt
2 egg whites
1 cup white sesame seeds

Marinade:
2 teaspoons minced ginger root
 ½ cup water
 ½ cup dry white wine
1 Tablespoon lime juice

1. Make the marinade by soaking the ginger root in water for 30 minutes, and drain. Mix the ginger liquid with wine and lime juice.

2. Drain the oysters, reserving the liquor for another use. Marinate the oysters for about 15 minutes.
3. Mix the cornstarch, sugar, and salt, and whip in the egg whites.
4. Drain the oysters, dip them in the cornstarch mixture, roll in the sesame seeds, and allow to dry for 30 minutes.
5. Heat the oil to 300° in a deep fryer or heavy saucepan. Fry the oysters, a few at a time, until golden brown. Remove and drain on a baking sheet lined with absorbent paper. Keep warm in the oven until all the oysters are fried.
6. Serve immediately with a warm sweet and sour sauce.

Serves 3

French-Fried Oysters in Beer Batter with Hollandaise Sauce

24 shucked large oysters
1 cup corn flour
Oil for frying
Parsley sprigs
1 cup Hollandaise Moutarde Sauce*

Batter coating:
1 cup flour
Salt and freshly ground pepper
3 Tablespoons melted butter
²/₃ cup lukewarm water
½ cup beer
2 egg whites

1. Remove the oysters from their shells, pat them dry, roll in corn flour, and set aside.
2. Sift the flour, salt, and pepper into a 1½-quart bowl, whisk in the melted butter, water, and beer, and set aside for 10 minutes.
3. When it is time to fry the oysters, add a pinch of salt to the egg whites, beat them until stiff, and stir 2 tablespoons into the beer batter, then fold in the remaining whites.
4. Heat the oil to 375° in a deep fryer or heavy, deep saucepan.
5. Using a spoon, dip an oyster into the batter, lift out carefully, and drop it into the hot oil. Proceed to dip and drop several more oysters but do not crowd the pan. Remove with a slotted spoon when the oysters are golden brown, and drain on a baking sheet lined with absorbent paper. Keep warm.
6. Dip and fry the parsley sprigs in the same manner.
7. Serve the oysters with a garnish of the parsley and the Hollandaise sauce.

* Add 1 tablespoon of Dijon mustard to the warm Hollandaise sauce.

Serves 3

Oyster Croquettes with Tomato Sauce Provençale

1½ pints oysters and liquor
½ cup cream
3 Tablespoons butter
3 Tablespoons flour
¼ teaspoon mace
3 egg yolks
2 Tablespoons dry Sherry
¼ cup finely chopped parsley
Salt and freshly ground
pepper
Lemon juice
Vegetable or peanut oil for
frying

Simple coating:
2 cups seasoned fine bread
crumbs
1 egg
2 Tablespoons water

Sauce Provençale:
1½ cups tomato sauce
3 Tablespoons chopped parsley

Herb bouquet:
1 teaspoon dried basil
½ teaspoon fennel seeds
½ teaspoon powdered saffron

1. Drain the oysters and coarsely chop them; measure ½ cup of the oyster liquor and warm it in a small saucepan with the cream.
2. Melt the butter in another saucepan, stir in the flour and mace, and cook until bubbling. Remove from the heat and whisk in the cream. Return to heat and boil, stirring constantly, until the mixture thickens; simmer for 3 minutes.
3. Whisk the egg yolks in a bowl with the Sherry. Beat ½ cup of the hot mixture into the egg yolks, a spoonful at a time. Then slowly whisk in the remaining hot mixture. Transfer the enriched sauce back to the saucepan and, stirring carefully, bring to a boil.
4. Stir in the oysters, salt, pepper, parsley, and lemon juice, and heat thoroughly.
5. Spread the mixture on a large plate, cover it loosely with waxed paper, and set aside to cool.
6. Shape the mixture into 12 croquettes, roll them in bread crumbs, then in the egg beaten with water, and again in the crumbs. Dry for at least 2 hours.
7. Make the sauce by simmering the tomato sauce and herb bouquet for 30 minutes, discard the bouquet, and add the freshly chopped parsley.
8. Heat the oil to 375° in a deep fryer or deep, heavy-gauge saucepan.
9. Place the croquettes, a few at one time, in a fryer basket and lower into the hot oil. Fry until the croquettes are golden brown and remove to a baking sheet lined with absorbent paper. Keep warm in the oven until all are fried.
10. Serve the hot croquettes with a sauceboat of Tomato Sauce Provençale.

Serves 4

WELCOME TO OUR HOUSE BUFFET

Jardinière of Marinated Vegetables
Oyster Croquettes
Lemon Scalloped Potatoes
Arugula Salad
Apricot Mousse
Cappucino

Oyster and Corn Fritters

24	shucked medium oysters
6	slices diced bacon
1	cup cornmeal
1	cup flour
3	teaspoons baking powder
1/4	teaspoon mace
1/2	teaspoon salt
	Pinch of cayenne pepper
2	beaten eggs
1/2	cup milk
3/4	cup scraped corn
	Vegetable or peanut oil for frying

Sauce:

1	cup dry white wine
2	minced shallots
8	Tablespoons soft butter
2	Tablespoons *crème fraîche*
	Salt and freshly ground pepper
2	Tablespoons capers

1. Remove the oysters from their shells and set aside; reserve the liquor for another use.
2. Boil the wine and shallots in a small saucepan until reduced to 1/4 cup; strain and cool. Place a bowl of butter over warm water and whip the liquid into the butter, a spoonful at a time. Stir in the *crème fraîche*, seasonings, and capers.
3. Cook the bacon in a skillet or microwave oven until it is brown and crisp; drain on absorbent paper.
4. Sift the dry ingredients into a bowl, add the eggs and milk, and mix well. Stir in the corn, bacon, and oysters, and adjust the seasoning.
5. Heat the oil in a deep fryer or heavy saucepan to 350°. Drop a tablespoon of the batter, including 1 oyster, into the oil and fry from 2 to 3 minutes, moving the fritter around occasionally so the outside will be evenly browned.
6. Fry the fritters a few at a time, taking care not to overcrowd the pan. Drain on a baking sheet lined with layers of absorbent paper, and keep warm.
7. Serve immediately with the caper sauce on the side.

Serves 4

Oyster Fritters with Sweet and Sour Sauce

1   pint oysters and liquor
1½ cups flour
 ½ teaspoon baking powder
 ½ teaspoon salt
 ¼ teaspoon pepper
2   eggs
2   teaspoons minced ginger root
1   teaspoon sugar
1   Tablespoon soy sauce
 ¾ cup water
1   Tablespoon lemon juice

Vegetable or peanut oil for
   frying

Sauce:
1½ Tablespoons constarch
1   teaspoon dry mustard
 ¾ cup water
 ⅓ cup red wine vinegar
 ½ cup brown sugar
2   Tablespoons ketchup
2   Tablespoons soy sauce

1. Dissolve the cornstarch and mustard in 2 tablespoons of water. Pour into a small saucepan and combine with the remaining water and other sauce ingredients. Cook over moderate heat, stirring constantly, until the mixture thickens, and set aside.
2. Drain the oysters, chop them coarsely, and reserve ¼ cup of the liquor.
3. Sift the dry ingredients into a bowl. Separate the eggs; beat the yolks lightly and stir in the oyster liquor, ginger, sugar, soy sauce, and water. Add the dry ingredients, mixing well; stir in the oysters.
4. Beat the egg whites until stiff; stir one-fourth of them into the batter, then fold in the remaining whites.
5. Heat the oil to 350° in a deep fryer or heavy-gauge saucepan. Use a heaping tablespoon of the batter for each fritter and fry a few at one time until golden brown. Drain on absorbent paper and keep warm.
6. Serve immediately with a sauceboat of the hot sweet and sour sauce.

Serves 4

OYSTER FRITTERS

Drain off the liquor, and to each pint of oysters take a pint of milk, a salt-spoonful of salt, half as much pepper, and flour enough for a thin batter. Chop the oysters and stir in, and then fry in hot lard, a little salted, or in butter. Drop in one spoonful at a time. Some make the batter thicker, so as to put in one oyster at a time surrounded by the batter.

Catherine Esther Beecher, *Mrs. Beecher's Housekeeper and Healthkeeper*, 1876

Oyster and Crabmeat Fritters

1 pint oysters and liquor
Corn flake crumbs
2 eggs
½ cup milk
1 teaspoon grated lemon zest
¾ cup flour
1 teaspoon baking powder
¼ teaspoon salt
6 ounces crabmeat

Oil for frying

Curry Sauce:
1½ cups Sauterne
2 Tablespoons oyster liquor
¼ teaspoon curry powder
1½ Tablespoons cornstarch
3 Tablespoons cream
Freshly ground white pepper

1. Drain the oysters, cut them into quarters, and roll them in corn flake crumbs. Reserve 2 tablespoons of the liquor for the sauce.
2. Simmer the wine, oyster liquor, and curry in an uncovered saucepan for 15 minutes. Combine the cornstarch and cream, add them to the wine, and heat, stirring constantly, until the mixture thickens. Season to taste with pepper and keep the sauce warm.
3. Separate the eggs, and whisk the yolks, milk, and lemon zest in a bowl. Sift the flour, baking powder, and salt together, and add them to the eggs, mixing well.
4. Chop the crabmeat and stir it into the batter.
5. Add a pinch of salt to the egg whites and whip until stiff. Stir 2 tablespoons into the batter, fold in the remaining whites and oysters.
6. Heat a griddle or skillet* until a drop of water sizzles on the surface, brush lightly with oil. Cook no more than 4 fritters at one time, measuring the amount of batter with a large spoon. Turn once to brown both sides evenly, drain, and keep the fritters warm in the oven until all are cooked.
7. Serve immediately with the hot curry sauce.

* Or deep fry in oil heated to 350°.

Serves 4

TALLY-HO BRUNCH

Brandy Toddy
Chicken Almond Salad
Oyster and Corn Fritters
Spinach and Cheese Stuffed Tomatoes
Biscuits and Honey
Coffee

STIR-FRY

When innovative cooks "jumped out of the frying pan" and into the wok in the early seventies, a new trend in American cuisine began. Happily, it has survived the quick demise of less worthy culinary "fads," and for all the right reasons.

The wok is not only an age-old utensil, it is a symbol of a culinary style that has evolved for centuries. Behind all that steaming and stir-frying, all that slicing and shredding, is a cohesive philosophy of food, that every Chinese cook knows and respects.

Taoist belief that food should be eaten as close to its natural state as possible literally mandates "quick" cooking, capturing the natural flavors and juices of foods by tossing and stir-frying in as little oil as possible over high heat. And the etiquette of Chinese dining which dictates that food should be bite-sized and ceremoniously served is reason enough for cutting all the ingredients into appetizing pieces.

It seemed inevitable. The widespread appreciation of "cooking Chinese" led to imitation and, ultimately, to creation. Vegetables appeared on American tables tender-crisp and glowing with color. And the "sampling" of dishes that makes Chinese dining so distinctive has encouraged a movement away from the five-course meal to a freer pattern of serving several harmonious dishes together.

What an accommodating arrangement it all is for seafood cookery where light steaming or frying is so desirable, capturing the flavor of the sea so important, and variety so unexpected. If Oyster Egg Foo Yong and Oysters and

Vegetables on a bed of rice in company with abalone, sea bass, and "ginger fish" (flounder) are considered simple meals, think of the feasts!

And, while oysters cannot compete with shrimp as the principal seafood ingredient of Chinese dishes, they do add a special flavor and texture to some traditional recipes and some rather untraditional ones. Moreover, oysters play a substantial role in a special sauce that adapts to many basic foods. One way (stir-fry) or another (oyster sauce), Chinese cooking and oysters are something to rhapsodize about.

CHINESE NEW YEAR'S CELEBRATION

Rice Wine *or* *Champagne*	*Cold Spiced Eggplant* *Lobster Kew* *Oyster Egg Foo Yong* *Pressed Almond Duck* *Hot and Sour Soup* *Eight Precious Jewel Pudding*

---

*Oysters and Vegetables in Oyster Sauce**

24 shucked small oysters and liquor	*Marinade:*
1 small sweet red pepper	1 Tablespoon cornstarch
1 small green pepper	1½ Tablespoons oyster sauce
¼ pound mushrooms	1 Tablespoon dry Sherry
2 ribs Chinese cabbage	1 minced scallion
1 small onion	1 teaspoon peeled and grated fresh ginger root
½ cup water chestnuts	
½ cup fresh bean sprouts	*Sauce:*
2 Tablespoons peanut oil	2 teaspoons cornstarch
½ teaspoon Oriental sesame oil	1 Tablespoon oyster liquor
3 cups cooked long-grain rice	1 Tablespoon oyster sauce
	⅛ teaspoon freshly ground pepper

Preparation:
1. Remove the oysters from their shells, strain and reserve 1 tablespoon of the liquor for the sauce.
2. Combine the cornstarch, oyster sauce, Sherry, scallion, and ginger root in a

mixing bowl, add the oysters and marinate them while the vegetables are being prepared.

3. Cut the peppers in ³/₄-inch squares; slice the mushrooms with the grain, and finely slice the Chinese cabbage and onion across the grain. Thin-slice the water chestnuts.
4. Mix the cornstarch sauce and set aside.

Stir-fry:
1. Heat the oil in a wok until very hot.
2. Stir-fry the oysters in their marinade until they begin to curl at the edges. Remove and set aside in a warm heat-proof dish.
3. Add more oil, if necessary, and stir-fry the peppers for about 2 minutes; add the mushrooms, cabbage, onion, water chestnuts, and bean sprouts, and toss for another 2 minutes.
4. Add the cornstarch sauce, stir until thickened, return the oysters, add sesame oil, and remove the wok from the heat after 1 minute.
5. Spoon over hot rice and serve immediately.

* Oyster sauce may be purchased or made with fresh oysters and light soy sauce: simmer a dozen chopped oysters and a cup of oyster liquor for about 20 minutes. Strain through a fine sieve and discard the oysters. Add 3 tablespoons of light soy sauce, pour into a sterilized bottle, and refrigerate.

Serves 6 [†]

† If this and the following stir-fry recipes are offered as part of a four-or-five-dish Chinese menu, it will be sufficient for six or eight people. If a recipe is used as the main course, it will not serve more than four.

Oysters in Black Bean and Oyster Sauce

24	shucked small oysters and liquor
1	small sweet red pepper
1	Tablespoon grated lemon zest
2	teaspoons grated ginger root
2	finely chopped garlic cloves
2	Tablespoons peanut oil
2	cups cooked long-grain rice

Black bean sauce:

1¹/₂	Tablespoons fermented black beans
1	Tablespoon dry Sherry
¹/₂	teaspoon sugar
1	teaspoon light soy sauce
1	Tablespoon oyster sauce

Cornstarch mixture:

1	Tablespoon cornstarch
2	Tablespoons dry Sherry or water

Preparation:
1. Remove the oysters from their shells and set aside in a small bowl; strain and reserve 1 tablespoon of the liquor for the sauce.
2. Marinate the beans in Sherry for 15 minutes. Stir in the sugar, soy sauce, oyster sauce, and oyster liquor.
3. Cut the red pepper into fine julienne strips and set aside; combine the lemon zest, ginger root, and garlic in a small bowl.
4. Dissolve the cornstarch in Sherry and reserve.

Stir-fry:
1. Heat the oil in a wok until very hot and stir-fry the pepper, lemon zest, ginger, and garlic for 1 minute.
2. Add the black bean sauce and bring to a boil.
3. Stir in the oysters and stir-fry until the edges begin to curl.
4. Stir the cornstarch mixture into the wok, and continue to stir until the mixture thickens.
5. Spoon over hot rice and serve immediately.

Serves 4

AU REVOIR PARTY

Shrimp Toast
Rice Wine   Oysters in Black Bean and Oyster Sauce
Chicken with Broccoli
Cantonese Roast Pork
Egg Drop Soup
Rice Cake
Candied Apple Slices

Oysters and Chicken in Oyster Sauce

24 shucked small oysters
1 large green pepper
1/4 cup bamboo shoots
1/2 pound small mushrooms
1/2 peeled cucumber
1 chicken breast
2 Tablespoons peanut oil
1/2 teaspoon Oriental sesame oil
2 cups cooked long-grain rice

Sauce:
1 sliced small onion
1 Tablespoon soy sauce
2 Tablespoons oyster sauce
3/4 cup chicken stock (See p. 63)
1 teaspoon brown sugar
1 teaspoon freshly grated ginger root
1 Tablespoon cornstarch
2 Tablespoons dry Sherry

Preparation:
1. Mix all the ingredients for the sauce together and simmer for about 10 minutes, stirring occasionally.
2. Remove the oysters from their shells, reserving the liquor for another use.
3. Cut the green pepper and bamboo shoots into fine julienne strips; slice the mushrooms, and dice the cucumber, discarding the seeds.
4. Skin, bone, and cut the chicken breast into fine julienne strips.

Stir-fry:
1. Heat the oil in a wok until very hot.
2. Stir-fry the green pepper for 2 minutes and remove to a heated dish. Stir-fry the bamboo shoots and mushrooms for 2 minutes and reserve with the green pepper.
3. Add more oil if necessary and stir-fry the chicken for 3 or 4 minutes.
4. Pour the sauce into the wok, add the oysters and stir-fry until they begin to curl at the edges. Add the cucumber and return the reserved vegetables to the wok. Toss until all the ingredients are coated with the sauce. Stir in the sesame oil and remove from the heat.
5. Serve over hot rice.

Serves 4

The great point to be borne in mind in frying, is that the liquid must be hot enough to act instantaneously, as all the merit of this culinary operation lies in the invasion of the boiling liquid, which carbonizes or burns, at the very instant of the immersion of the body placed in it.

Beeton's Book of Household Management, 1861

Straw Mushrooms and Oysters

24	shucked small oysters and liquor
1	ounce straw mushrooms
4	scallions
1	teaspoon minced ginger root
2	Tablespoons peanut oil
2	cups cooked long-grain rice

Sauce:

1	Tablespoon cornstarch
1	teaspoon sugar
1	teaspoon white wine vinegar
2	Tablespoons dry Sherry
2	Tablespoons oyster sauce

Preparation:
1. Soak the mushrooms in hot water until they are soft, and rinse thoroughly in several changes of water to remove all sand and grit. Drain and squeeze out the excess water. Cut into matchstick-thin slices, and set aside.
2. Remove the oysters from their shells and set aside.
3. Strain ⅓ cup of the oyster liquor and combine with cornstarch, sugar, vinegar, Sherry, and oyster sauce.
4. Chop the scallions, including the green stems.

Stir-fry:
1. Heat the oil in a wok until very hot and stir-fry the scallions and ginger root for about 30 seconds.
2. Add the mushrooms and sauce and stir until the sauce thickens.
3. Stir-fry the oysters in the sauce until they begin to curl at the edges.
4. Spoon over hot rice and serve immediately.

Serves 4

Oysters and Steak Oriental

24 shucked small oysters and liquor	*Sauce:*
¾ pound boneless sirloin steak	1 Tablespoon cornstarch
1 small sweet red pepper	1 Tablespoon oyster sauce
¼ pound small mushrooms	
4 scallions	*Marinade:*
¼ pound snow peas	1 teaspoon cornstarch
2 Tablespoons peanut oil	1 Tablespoon soy sauce
1 teaspoon minced ginger root	Pinch of sugar
1 cup bean sprouts	2 Tablespoons Sherry
4 cups cooked long-grain rice	

Preparation:
1. Remove the oysters from their shells and set aside. Strain and reserve ¼ cup of the liquor for the sauce.
2. Combine the oyster liquor, cornstarch, and oyster sauce.
3. Mix the marinade. Cut the steak into ⅛-inch slices and marinate for at least 30 minutes.
4. Cut the pepper into thin julienne strips; slice the mushrooms; chop the scallions, including the stems. Trim and string the snow peas.

Stir-fry:
1. Heat the oil in the wok until very hot and stir-fry the pepper, scallions, and ginger for about a minute. Remove to a heated oven-proof dish.

2. Stir-fry the mushrooms and snow peas, adding the bean sprouts after about 30 seconds and toss for another 20 seconds. Remove the vegetables to the heated dish.
3. Add more oil if necessary and stir-fry the steak until the slices are browned on the outside but rare inside.
4. Return the vegetables to the wok.
5. Add the sauce and stir in the oysters while the sauce is thickening. When the edges of the oysters begin to curl, remove from the heat.
6. Spoon the steak and oysters over hot rice and serve immediately.

Serves 8

Pork and Dried Oysters in Oyster Sauce

½ pound dried oysters or two 3¾-ounce tins smoked oysters
½ cup diced lean raw pork
10 dried Chinese mushrooms
1 cup bamboo shoots
1 cup water chestnuts
2 ribs Chinese cabbage
2 Tablespoons peanut oil
1 garlic clove
3 cups Chinese noodles or cooked long-grain rice

Marinade:
1 teaspoon cornstarch
1 Tablespoon Saki or dry Sherry
1 Tablespoon soy sauce
1 teaspoon peeled and grated fresh ginger

Sauce:
1 Tablespoon cornstarch
½ teaspoon sugar
¼ cup white wine
2 Tablespoons oyster sauce
1 teaspoon grated lemon zest

Preparation:
1. Soak the dried oysters for 5 hours, drain, and dice; or rinse, drain, and dice the smoked oysters, and set them aside.
2. Mix the marinade and marinate the diced pork while the vegetables are being prepared.
3. Soak the mushrooms in warm water for about 15 minutes, drain, and dice.
4. Cut the bamboo shoots into fine julienne strips, slice the water chestnuts, and fine-slice the Chinese cabbage.
5. Mix the cornstarch, sugar, wine, oyster sauce, and lemon zest.

Stir-fry:
1. Heat the oil in a wok until very hot. Add the garlic clove and toss for 10 seconds. Remove and discard the garlic.
2. Add the pork and marinade, and stir-fry for about 3 minutes.

3. Add more oil if necessary and stir-fry the bamboo shoots, water chestnuts, cabbage, and mushrooms for about a minute.
4. Add the oysters and the sauce; stir until all the ingredients are evenly coated.
5. Serve over crisp Chinese noodles or freshly cooked long-grain rice.

Serves 6

Oyster Egg Foo Yong

1 pint oysters and liquor
3 Tablespoons peanut oil
½ cup chopped mushrooms
3 eggs
½ cup bean sprouts
½ cup cooked green peas

Sauce:
1 Tablespoon cornstarch
½ teaspoon sugar
½ cup chicken stock (See p. 63)
1 Tablespoon oyster sauce
2 Tablespoons dry Sherry

1. Drain the oysters, reserve half of them and ⅓ cup of liquor for the sauce. Pat dry and chop the remaining oysters for the omelets.
2. Heat 1 tablespoon of oil in a wok, stir-fry the mushrooms for about 30 seconds, and set aside to cool.
3. Add more oil if necessary and stir-fry the chopped oysters for about 30 seconds; remove and add to the mushrooms. Reduce the heat under the wok.
4. Combine the reserved oyster liquor with the cornstarch, sugar, stock, oyster sauce, and Sherry in a saucepan and cook, stirring constantly, until the mixture thickens; keep warm over low heat.
5. Break the eggs into a mixing bowl, beat well, and combine with the mushrooms and chopped oysters. Stir in the bean sprouts.
6. Add more oil to the wok and return to moderate heat.
7. Pour about ¼ cup of the egg mixture into the wok and fry without stirring for about a minute. Turn the omelet over and fry the other side to a light brown.
8. Transfer the omelet to a hot serving platter, add more oil if needed, and fry the other 5 omelets.
9. While the omelets are cooking, add the whole oysters and peas to the sauce and cook until the oysters are plump.
10. Spoon the oyster sauce over the omelets and serve immediately.

Serves 3

SAUTÉ

Lightly sautéed—does it sound familiar? Perhaps one of the most frequently used techniques for tender, quick-cooked food, this simple "browning in butter" method of frying is right for everything from boned chicken breasts and veal scallops to fish fillets and oysters. And it gives a full range of possibilities to coat, dip, dredge, and roll in seasoned flour, fresh bread, cracker, or corn flake crumbs.

But, undoubtedly, the greatest advantage of serving a sautéed entrée is the lure of the *saucière*. From a simple butter, lemon juice, and wine sauce spooned over perfectly fried oysters to a full-bodied tomato sauce that will spark up an Oyster Parmigiana, a creative cook can transform ordinary fried oysters into a beautifully realized dish.

The following recipes, including a contemporary adaptation of an Elizabethan "stew," suggest what is possible for every "accomplisht cook." The first step is always the same—dredge, dip, roll, and lightly sautée; the last step is sheer alchemy.

OPENING NIGHT SUPPER

Gazpacho
Spicy Cheese and Potato Soufflé
Saint-Satur *Oysters au Citron*
Watercress Salad
Pecan Tassies
Coffee

Oysters au Citron

24	shucked large oysters
2	eggs
2	Tablespoons milk
½	teaspoon salt
¼	teaspoon pepper
1	cup all-purpose flour
1	cup fine bread crumbs
	Clarified butter
	Lemon slices

Sauce:

1	cup dry white wine
1	minced garlic clove
1	teaspoon Worcestershire sauce
3	Tablespoons unsalted butter
2	Tablespoons lemon juice
2	Tablespoons minced parsley

1. Remove the oysters from their shells and pat them dry.
2. Beat the eggs in a bowl until frothy, whisk in the milk and seasonings. Combine the flour and bread crumbs in another bowl.
3. Roll the oysters, one by one, in the crumb mixture, dip in the egg, and roll again in crumbs. Set aside to dry for 30 minutes.
4. Melt enough clarified butter in a skillet to coat the bottom and prevent sticking. Sauté the oysters, a few at a time, adding more butter if necessary. Remove and drain the oysters on a baking sheet lined with absorbent paper. Keep warm until all the oysters are fried.
5. Add the wine, garlic, and Worcestershire to the pan juices, and boil until reduced by half. Swirl in the butter, a bit at a time. Remove from the heat and stir in the lemon juice and parsley.
6. Place the oysters on individual plates and serve immediately, garnished with lemon slices. Serve the sauce in a sauceboat.

Serves 4

Oysters Tarragon

24 shucked large oysters	1 cup fine cracker crumbs
1 cup flour	Butter
1/4 cup finely chopped fresh tarragon	Vegetable oil
Salt and freshly ground pepper	1 cup *crème fraîche*

1. Remove the oysters from the shells, drain the oysters and pat them dry.
2. Combine the flour, 1 tablespoon of the tarragon, and seasonings. Dust the oysters in the flour, roll them in crumbs, and set aside.
3. Heat enough butter and oil in a heavy skillet to prevent sticking. Sauté the oysters, about 6 at one time, turning them so both sides are lightly browned, and add butter and oil to the pan as necessary. Keep the oysters warm until all are cooked.
4. Heat the *crème fraîche* and add the remaining tarragon.
5. Arrange 6 oysters on individual plates and nap them with the sauce.

Serves 4

Bard's Oysters

12 shucked large oysters and liquor
¼ cup seasoned flour
½ cup fine bread crumbs
2 teaspoons grated orange zest
Clarified butter
4 thin orange slices

Sauce:
1 Tablespoon butter
1 cup red Bordeaux wine
1½ Tablespoons vinegar
Pinch of mace
½ Tablespoon cornstarch
2 Tablespoons orange juice

1. Remove the oysters from their shells; strain and reserve the oyster liquor for the sauce. Dust the oysters in flour, and roll them in crumbs seasoned with the orange zest.

2. Simmer the oyster liquor, butter, wine, vinegar, and mace in an uncovered saucepan for 20 minutes or until reduced by half. Dissolve the cornstarch in orange juice, add to the wine, and cook, stirring constantly, until the sauce thickens.

3. Melt enough clarified butter in a skillet to coat the bottom and prevent sticking. Without crowding the skillet, sauté the oysters for about 2 minutes on each side. Remove, drain on absorbent paper, and keep warm until all are sautéed.

4. Arrange 6 oysters in the center of 2 individual serving plates, surround with hot sauce, and garnish with orange slices.

Serves 2

TO STEW OYSTERS

Take a pottle [two quarts] of large oysters, parboil them in their own liquor, then wash them in warm water, wipe them dry, and pull away the fins, flour them and fry them in clarified butter fine and white, then take them up and put them in a large dish with some white or claret wine, a little vinegar, a quarter of a pound of sweet butter, some grated nutmeg, large mace, salt and two or three slices of an orange, stew them two or three walms [moments], then serve them in a large scoured [clean] dish, pour the sauce on them, and run them over with beaten butter, slic't lemon or orange, and sippets around the dish.

Robert May, *The Accomplisht Cook, or the Art and Mastery of Cooking,* 1660

SKI LODGE BUFFET

Pasta e Fagioli
Caesar Salad
Vermentino   *Oysters Parmigiana*
Melons in Sweet Vermouth
Expresso

Oysters Parmigiana

24	shucked large oysters		Vegetable oil
1	cup seasoned flour	1	cup Sauce Provençal*
2	beaten eggs		(See p. 172)
2	Tablespoons water	½	cup freshly grated Parmesan
1	cup fine corn flake crumbs		or Romano cheese
	Butter		

1. Remove the oysters from their shells and pat them dry, reserving the liquor for another use. Dust the oysters in flour, dip them one-by-one in the egg and water mixture, and roll in crumbs. Set aside to dry.
2. Heat a little butter and oil in a large skillet, and sauté the oysters, turning them once to brown both sides evenly. Do not overcrowd the skillet and use more oil and butter as needed. Keep the oysters warm in the oven until all are cooked.
3. Stir the sauce into the skillet and simmer until it is hot.
4. Arrange the oysters in individual serving dishes, spoon hot sauce over them, and serve a porringer of cheese on the side.

* Add ¾ cup sliced small mushrooms, if desired.

Serves 4

Oysters Cacciatore

24	shucked large oysters	1	cup cored and sliced fennel
1	cup flour	¼	cup chopped onion
	Salt and freshly ground	2	Tablespoons chopped red
	pepper		pepper
1	cup fine bread crumbs	3	Tablespoons white wine
	Butter		
	Vegetable oil		

(Oysters Cacciatore, *continued)*

1. Remove the oysters from their shells, drain, and pat dry. Roll them in flour seasoned with salt and pepper, and then in the bread crumbs.
2. Heat 1 tablespoon of butter and ½ tablespoon of oil in a saucepan and sauté the fennel about 10 minutes until it is soft. Add the onion and pepper and cook until tender; stir in the wine and season to taste.
3. Melt a tablespoon of butter and some oil in a large skillet and sauté the oysters, 6 at a time, for 2 minutes on each side, adding butter and oil if necessary. Remove with a slotted spoon and set aside in a warm oven until all are sautéed.
4. Arrange the oysters in a circle on heated plates and spoon the sauce into the center.

Serves 4

WELCOME HOME SUPPER

Bloody Mary Soup
Scalloped Oysters
Belgium Endive Salad
Beef Tenderloin Tips en Brochette
Pear Compote
Almond Coffee

BAKE

Whether as a hot appetizer on the half shell, in a vegetable casserole, or stuffed loaf, oysters are most frequently cooked in the oven. And there is no particular technique involved—only the reminder to set the timer or watch the clock to avoid over-cooking. And then move on to other things.

There's something comforting about the ease and simplicity of preparing oysters this way, something equally pleasant about the distinctive aroma emanating from the oven when guests arrive or children come home from school in the already-dark, late, fall afternoons. Perhaps that is why scalloped oyster recipes change so little, always seem to be what they were when made in grandmother's kitchen or when one of the subjects most frequently discussed by the Old Social Circle was whether or not to add Sherry.

Scalloped Oysters, Oyster Loaf, and Crumbed Oysters are the "plain Janes" of oyster cookery. But don't underestimate the drama of these light dishes—there may be a surprise or two under that golden brown topping. A dash of Sherry, pinch of nutmeg, some pungent fresh herbs, or a bit of this or that can, in almost no time at all, make one of these dishes the specialty of the house.

Scalloped Oysters

24 shucked medium oysters
    and liquor
8 Tablespoons melted butter
2 cups butter-cracker crumbs
    Salt and freshly ground
      pepper

1/4 cup heavy cream
3 Tablespoons dry Sherry
    (optional)

Oven Temperature: 325°

1. Remove the oysters from their shells and pat them dry; strain and reserve 1/4 cup of the liquor.
2. Mix the butter and crumbs, and line the bottom of a shallow buttered casserole or 9-inch pie dish with a third of them. Arrange half the oysters on top, sprinkle with salt, pepper, 2 tablespoons of both oyster liquor and cream, and half the Sherry. Repeat the layers, covering with the remaining crumbs.
3. Bake for 30 minutes until the top is golden brown.

Serves 4

SCALLOPED OYSTERS

Scallop was the old-time term for mixtures baked in milk or in a cream sauce and served in a scallop shell. The term scallop has since been extended to a number of dishes baked in milk or in a cream sauce, but not served in a scallop shell—scalloped potatoes, for example. This recipe is simple, old-fashioned, and very good.

The Yankee Magazine Cookbook

Scalloped Oysters with Herbs

24 shucked large oysters
    and liquor
8 Tablespoons unsalted butter
1 garlic clove
1 cup fresh bread crumbs
2 Tablespoons finely chopped
    parsley
1 Tablespoon finely chopped
    fresh dill

1 Tablespoon finely chopped
    fresh chervil
1 Tablespoon finely chopped
    fresh basil
    Salt and freshly ground
      pepper
1/4 cup heavy cream
    Lemon wedges

Oven Temperature: 375°

1. Remove the oysters from their shells and pat them dry; strain and reserve ¼ cup of the liquor.
2. Melt 4 tablespoons of butter in a saucepan and sauté the garlic until it is tender, and discard. Stir in the bread crumbs and parsley.
3. Blend the remaining butter with the herbs or process the butter and herbs in the work bowl of a food processor. Add a dash of salt and pepper to the butter.
4. Sprinkle half the crumbs on the bottom of a gratin dish or a 9 x 9-inch casserole. Arrange the oysters in a single layer, sprinkle with oyster liquor, dot with the herb butter. Cover with the remaining crumbs and drizzle with cream.
5. Bake for 15 minutes until the top is golden brown and bubbling.
6. Serve immediately with a small tray of lemon wedges.

Serves 4

Scalloped Oysters with Mushrooms

1 pint oysters and liquor	1 cup sliced small mushrooms
1¼ cups light cream	Salt and freshly ground
6 Tablespoons butter	pepper
3 Tablespoons flour	¼ cup fresh bread crumbs
1 teaspoon Worcestershire sauce	Paprika
2 teaspoons lemon juice	

Oven Temperature: 400°

1. Drain the oysters and set them aside. Measure ¼ cup of the oyster liquor and warm it in a small saucepan with the cream.
2. Melt the butter in another saucepan; remove and reserve 2 tablespoons for the crumbs. Stir in the flour and cook until bubbling. Remove from the heat and whisk in the cream. Return to heat, add the Worcestershire and lemon juice, and boil, stirring constantly, until the mixture thickens; simmer for 3 minutes. Stir in the mushrooms and simmer another minute.
3. Stir in the oysters and adjust seasonings.
4. Spoon the oyster mixture into large buttered scallop shells or individual gratin dishes; sprinkle with the buttered crumbs and paprika.
5. Place on a baking sheet and bake about 10 minutes until bubbling and golden brown.

Serves 4

Scalloped Oysters with Bacon

1 pint oysters	2 teaspoons chopped fresh tarragon
1/2 pound diced bacon	Celery salt
3 Tablespoons butter	Salt and freshly ground pepper
1/2 cup finely chopped shallots	
1/2 cup heavy cream	
1 cup unsalted cracker crumbs	3 Tablespoons lemon juice
1/4 cup chopped parsley	

Oven Temperature: 350°

1. Drain the oysters and pat them dry, reserving the liquor for another use.
2. Sauté the bacon in a skillet until almost crisp, remove with a slotted spoon, and set aside.
3. Pour off all but a tablespoon of fat from the skillet, melt the butter, and sauté the shallots until tender. Mix in one half of the bacon, the cream, crumbs, parsley, and tarragon.
4. Arrange the oysters in a buttered gratin dish or a 9 x 9-inch baking dish and season them with celery salt, salt and pepper. Sprinkle with lemon juice and top with the crumb mixture and remaining bacon.
5. Bake for about 15 minutes or until the bacon is crisp and brown.

Serves 4

Sag Harbor Scalloped Oysters

1 quart oysters	1/4 cup finely chopped parsley
1 loaf French bread	1/4 cup finely chopped chives
6 Tablespoons butter	2 Tablespoons lime juice
1/2 teaspoon anchovy paste	1/4 cup dry Sherry
1/2 cup finely chopped onion	1/2 cup heavy cream
Salt and freshly ground pepper	1/2 cup freshly grated Parmesan cheese

Oven Temperature: 325°

1. Trim the loaf and cut the pieces of crust into 1/4-inch cubes; measure and set aside 4 cups. Process some of the soft bread in a blender and reserve 1/2 cup of crumbs.
2. Melt the butter in a large skillet, stir in the anchovy paste, and sauté the onion until it is tender. Sauté the bread cubes in this mixture until they are crisp and brown.

3. Drain the oysters and pat them dry, reserving the liquor for another use.
4. Put 2 cups of the bread cubes in a large buttered casserole or gratin dish, cover with half of the oysters, season them with salt and pepper, and sprinkle with 2 tablespoons of parsley and 2 tablespoons of chives. Repeat the bread and oyster layers. Mix the lime juice, Sherry, and cream, and pour over. Add the reserved crumbs to the cheese, and sprinkle on top.
5. Bake for 30 minutes until the top is golden brown.

Serves 8

QUILTING BEE LUNCHEON

Mock Turtle Soup with Sherry
Oyster Loaf with Mushroom Sauce
Brussel Sprouts and Chestnuts
Fresh Lemon Mousse
Coffee

Well-Bred Oyster Loaf

1 pint oysters	2 Tablespoons lemon juice
1¼ cups milk	½ cup chopped parsley
4 Tablespoons butter	Strips of green pepper
1 teaspoon dry mustard	
½ cup finely chopped onion	*Sour cream sauce:*
3 Tablespoons flour	4 Tablespoons butter
¼ cup dry Sherry	¼ cup chopped green pepper
Salt and freshly ground pepper	1 cup chopped mushrooms
	1 cup sour cream
2 cups fine unsalted cracker crumbs	¼ cup cream
	Salt and freshly ground pepper
2 eggs	
1 teaspoon Worcestershire sauce	

Oven Temperature: 350°

1. Drain and coarsely chop the oysters, reserving the liquor for another use.
2. Warm 1 cup of the milk in a small saucepan.

3. Melt 3 tablespoons of butter in another saucepan, stir in the mustard and onion; and sauté the onion until tender. Add the flour and cook until bubbling. Remove from the heat and whisk in the milk. Return to heat, add the Sherry and seasonings, and boil, stirring constantly, until the mixture thickens. Simmer for 3 minutes.

4. Set aside 2 tablespoons of the crumbs for the topping, and stir the rest of the crumbs into the hot sauce.

5. Beat the eggs lightly in a bowl, stir in the remaining $1/4$ cup of milk, Worcestershire, lemon juice, parsley, oysters, and crumb mixture.

6. Spread the ingredients evenly in a buttered $4^{1}/_{2}$ x $8^{1}/_{2}$ x $2^{1}/_{2}$-inch glass baking dish, top with the reserved crumbs, and dot with the remaining butter.

7. Cover with foil and bake 20 minutes; uncover and bake another 20 minutes to brown the top.

8. Prepare the sauce while the loaf is baking. Melt the butter in a saucepan and sauté the pepper until tender. Stir in the mushrooms and cook for a minute or two until they are hot. Stir in the sour cream, cream, and season to taste. Just before serving, heat the sauce but do not allow it to boil.

9. Remove the loaf from the oven, run a knife around the sides of the baking dish, set a warm platter over the loaf and invert.

10. Garnish the loaf with strips of green pepper and serve with sour cream sauce.

Serves 6

Baked Expectations

$1^{1}/_{2}$ pints oysters
1 minced garlic clove
$1/4$ cup olive oil
$1/4$ cup vegetable oil
$3/4$ cup freshly grated Gruyère
    cheese

$1/2$ cup corn flake crumbs
Salt and freshly ground
    pepper
Paprika

Oven Temperature: 450°

1. Drain the oysters and pat them dry; reserve the liquor for another use.
2. Mix the garlic and oil in a bowl. In another bowl, combine the cheese, crumbs, and seasonings.
3. Dip the oysters in the oil and roll in the cheese mixture. Arrange them in a single layer in a shallow buttered casserole, and top with the remaining cheese and crumbs.
4. Reduce the oven temperature to 375° and bake the oysters about 10 minutes until the top is golden brown.

Serves 4

BROIL-GRILL

To define broiling or grilling as "putting oiled foods into or onto a preheated broiler or white-hot wood charcoal grill," probably tells the story of one of the oldest, and ironically, one of today's trendiest forms of oyster cookery. In 1876, to "roast" oysters meant to "put oysters in the shell, after washing them, upon the coals so that the flat side is uppermost, to save the liquor; and take them up when they begin to gape a little." That's a far cry from Chez Panisse and the perfectly reduced creamy fumet sauce and teaspoon of caviar that distinguish the mesquite wood *Charcoal-Grilled Oysters* on the Cafe's *carte du jour*. But it surely proves the point that oysters are forever.

Beginning with grilled oysters and including various broiled and skewered recipes suitable for an indoor grill or oven-broiler, the following recipes are presented with a bit of caution. Grilling is not an exact cooking technique. Wind, weather conditions, intensity of heat, and even the positioning of the oysters on the grill will vary the cooking time if an outdoor unit is used. And great care should be taken to remove the oyster from the grill at just the right moment. Yet, the pluses of preparing oysters this way definitely off-set the minuses, because there is something so light-hearted about the informality of dining outdoors that the effort of planning a successful "Oyster Roast" is amply rewarded.

Like the other high-heat methods of cooking oysters, broiling them will result in a tastier dish if the oysters are lightly coated, rolled in crumbs or basted, and counterpoised with other compatible ingredients. Served *en brochette* with bacon, sausages, or vegetables, oysters can be as casual or as glamorous as desired. So . . . *en garde*! Skewer away.

ORGIE

Wash, drain and dry the oysters. Butter the bottom of a shallow baking-dish and spread thickly with the oysters; sprinkle with dried cèpes powder and season with salt and cayenne. Have some very fine bread-crumbs that have been fried in olive-oil; mix with them double the quantity of grated cheese and cover the top of the oysters. Pour over a gill of champagne and brown in a quick oven.
May E. Southworth, *One Hundred & One Ways of Serving Oysters*, 1907

HARVEST MOON "OYSTER ROAST"

Martinis
Smoked Blue Fish Paté with Rye Rounds
Walnut, Orange, and Chicory Salad
Corn on the Grill
Dilled New Potatoes
Charcoal-Grilled Oysters with Shallot Butter Sauce
Herbed French Bread
A Cookie Basket
Coffee

Charcoal-Grilled Oysters

48   unshucked oysters
     Rock salt
     Lemon wedges

Sauce:
$1/4$ cup white wine vinegar
$1/4$ cup dry Vermouth
3   Tablespoons chopped shallots
$3/4$ pound ice-cold butter
     Grated lemon zest
     Salt and freshly ground
       pepper

1. Scrub and rinse the oysters and set aside.
2. Light the charcoal grill and allow 30 to 45 minutes for it to reach the proper temperature.
3. Reduce the vinegar, wine, and shallots in a saucepan over moderately high heat until only 2 tablespoons of liquid remain. Adjust to very low heat.
4. Cut the butter into $1/2$-inch slices and whisk one piece at a time into the reduced liquid; whisk constantly with each addition until the sauce is creamy and thick. Add the lemon zest and season to taste. Keep the sauce warm over water that is the same temperature as the sauce.
5. Line two large shallow pans with rock salt and heat in the oven.
6. Put the oysters, flat side up, directly on the grill when the coals are white hot.
7. Remove with tongs when the shells begin to open.* Shuck the oysters, discard the top shells, and place the oysters in their deep shells in the hot rock salt to keep warm.
8. Serve the oysters with the sauce and lemon wedges.

* Eastern oysters will toughen if heated too long; Pacific oysters remain tender in high heat.

Serves 6

Oysters in Burnt Onion Sauce

24 shucked medium oysters
 ½ cup corn flour
   Salt and freshly ground
     pepper
 4 Tablespoons butter
 4 Tablespoons vegetable oil

 1 Tablespoon lemon juice
 ½ cup thinly sliced scallions,
     including the green tops
 4 slices toasted white bread
     (optional)

Oven Temperature: High Broil

1. Remove the oysters from their shells, reserving the liquor for another use. Pat the oysters dry, dredge in seasoned flour, and set aside for 15 minutes.
2. Heat the butter and oil in a skillet and stir in the lemon juice. When the mixture is very hot, sauté the scallions quickly over moderately high heat until they turn dark, and set aside.
3. Heat an oiled broiling pan and arrange the oysters on it. Baste each with a teaspoon of the scallion-butter sauce.
4. Broil 4 inches from the heat source for 3 or 4 minutes.
5. Arrange 6 oysters on each plate and spoon the remaining sauce over them. Or, put a piece of toast on each plate and use it as a bed for the oysters and sauce.

Serves 4

Stage-Harbor Oysters

24 shucked large oysters
12 slices bacon
 1 cup fresh fine bread crumbs
 1 teaspoon dry mustard
 ¼ teaspoon paprika

   Salt
   Cayenne pepper
 ¼ cup melted butter
   Lemon slices
   Parsley sprigs

Oven Temperature: High Broil

1. Cut the bacon in half and cook in a skillet or microwave oven until crisp and brown. Drain on absorbent paper.
2. Remove the oysters from their shells, drain, and pat dry, reserving the liquor for another use.
3. Combine crumbs, mustard, paprika, salt, and cayenne, and roll the oysters.
4. Arrange oysters on an oiled baking pan and spoon melted butter over them.
5. Broil 5 inches from the heat until golden. Turn, nap with the remaining butter, and broil until the other side is golden.
6. Serve oysters and bacon garnished with lemon slices and parsley sprigs.

Serves 4

Oyster and Vegetable Kebabs

36	shucked medium oysters			Cayenne pepper
18	slices bacon		18	cherry tomatoes
1	large green pepper		18	blanched small white onions
1	large sweet red pepper			Corn flake crumbs
9	large mushroom caps		6	12-inch skewers
1/2	pound butter		4	cups cooked saffron rice
4	Tablespoons lemon juice			
	Salt and freshly ground pepper			

Oven Temperature: Medium Broil

1. Remove the oysters from their shells, drain, and pat dry. Reserve the oyster liquor for another use.
2. Cut the bacon in half and cook in a microwave oven for about 1 minute or pan fry until the edges begin to curl but it is still flexible. Drain well.
3. Cut the peppers into 1-inch squares and cut the mushroom caps in half.
4. Melt the butter in a large skillet and season with lemon juice, salt, pepper, and cayenne. Toss all the vegetables in the butter to coat them, and set aside.
5. Wrap each oyster in a half slice of bacon before skewering. Assemble the kebabs, alternating vegetables and oysters. Leave about 1 1/2 inches of the skewer exposed.
6. Brush melted butter over the vegetables and arrange the skewers on an oiled broiler pan.
7. Broil for 2 or 3 minutes, turn the skewers over, baste with more butter, and broil for 2 or 3 minutes longer, until the bacon is crisp.
8. Arrange the skewers on a bed of saffron rice and serve.

Serves 6

POST GAME VICTORY CELEBRATION

Cream of Carrot Soup
Oyster and Vegetable Kebabs on Saffron Rice
Tossed Green Salad with Goat's Cheese
Apple Flan
Irish Coffee

CLUB-CAR-SET BUFFET

Spicy Shrimp
Swiss Cheese Potato Gratin
Tomato and Basil Salad
Mixed Grill en Brochette
Fresh Asparagus in Lime and Ginger Sauce
Chocolate Mousse
Coffee

Mixed Grill en Brochette

24	shucked medium oysters
12	slices thick bacon
14	breakfast sausages
2	large onions
8	Tablespoons butter
1/4	cup minced parsley
1	garlic clove
	Salt and freshly ground pepper
	Cayenne pepper
	Corn flour
4	12-inch skewers
4	slices toasted white bread

Sauce:

4	Tablespoons butter
3/4	cup chili sauce
2	teaspoons Worcestershire sauce
1	teaspoon celery salt
1	Tablespoon grated lemon zest

Oven Temperature: High Broil

1. Remove the oysters from their shells, drain, and pat dry; reserve the liquor for another use.
2. Cut the bacon in half and place the bacon and sausages in a large saucepan of cold water. Bring to a boil and simmer for 5 minutes. Drain, rinse in cold water, and pat dry. Cut each of the sausages in half.
3. Peel the onions, cut into quarters, and use only the outer two layers of each quarter.
4. Melt the butter, add the parsley, garlic, and season with salt, pepper, and a pinch of cayenne. Lightly sauté the onion, remove with a slotted spoon and set aside on absorbent paper.
5. Allow the butter to cool slightly, dip the oysters, and roll them in corn flour.
6. Mix the ingredients for the sauce and simmer gently until the butter has melted. Remove the sauce from the heat and keep warm.

7. Wrap each oyster in a half slice of bacon. Skewer a piece of onion and sausage, then alternate the oysters and sausages, ending with sausage and onion. Place the skewers on an oiled broiler pan.
8. Broil about 5 inches from the heat for 3 or 4 minutes. Turn over when the bacon and sausage are golden brown and broil the other side until the bacon is crisp.
9. Place the toast slices on individual plates and slip the oysters and sausages from the skewers to the toast. Serve with a sauceboat of warm chili sauce.

Serves 4

Mustard-Glazed Oysters

24 shucked medium oysters
12 slices bacon
4 12-inch skewers
24 medium-sized mushroom caps
2½ cups cooked long-grain rice

Glaze:
⅓ cup Dijon mustard
½ teaspoon dry mustard
3 Tablespoons white wine vinegar
3 Tablespoons brown sugar
⅓ cup honey
2 teaspoons peanut oil
2 teaspoons dark soy sauce

Oven Temperature: Medium Broil

1. Blend the mustards together in a saucepan and gradually mix in the remaining glaze ingredients. Simmer for about 5 minutes over low heat. Cool to room temperature.
2. Remove the oysters from their shells, drain, and pat dry; reserve the liquor for another use.
3. Cut the bacon slices in half and wrap each oyster in one piece of bacon.
4. Thread the skewers with alternating oysters and mushroom caps.
5. Put the skewers on a platter and generously brush with the mustard glaze. Set aside for at least 15 minutes, turn the skewers and repeat the process. Transfer to an oiled broiler pan.
6. Broil about 6 inches from the heat for 5 to 8 minutes, turning to brown all sides evenly. Brush with more glaze, if desired.
7. Serve on a bed of rice.

Serves 4

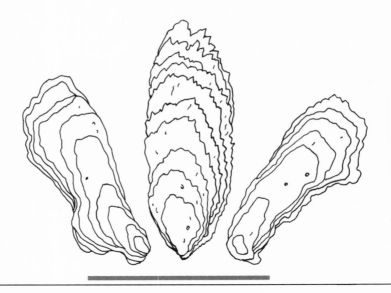

There are three kinds of oyster-eaters: those loose-minded sports who will eat anything, hot, cold, thin, thick, dead or alive, as long as it is *oyster*; those who will eat them raw and only raw; and those who with equal severity will eat them cooked and no way other.

The first group may perhaps have the most fun, although there is a white fire about the others' bigotry that can never warm the broadminded.

M. F. K. Fisher, *Consider the Oyster*

SMOTHERED FOWL AND OYSTERS

Dress a good, plump fowl as for roasting. Drain one pint of oysters and fill the fowl; sew up and set in a kettle to steam, put a rack under it to keep it out of the water. Put salt, pepper and some pieces of celery in the water. Boil hard until the fowl is tender but not broken. Serve with sauce made from the water in the kettle and one cup of cream thickened with flour. Add one pint of oysters and cook till they curl. Pour this over the fowl. An old-fashioned rule.

What We Cook on Cape Cod, 1916

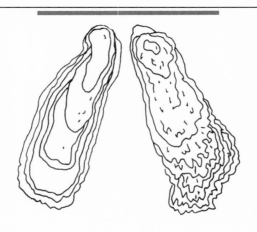

There is no better way to spend a rainy Saturday afternoon than to retreat to the attic or visit the browser's bookshop and pore over old cookbooks. They are the ones somebody's aunt added little marginal notes to before passing them along to a niece, the ones tucked away beneath the stairs of the local library to make way for the gloss and glamor of the new culinary tomes on display upstairs.

Explicit in instructions and no-nonsense in tone, the authors of those books were usually bent on more than a compilation of "receipts." They were concerned with the quality of culinary skill and never missed an opportunity to slip in a maxim here and a bit of homely wisdom there. The oft-repeated warning that "Many waters cannot quench love, but an incompetent cook can turn the flame into a heap of smouldering ashes," must have sent many a novice cook to the stove with alacrity. And, of course, the observation that "There was never an angel who wouldn't take off her wings and cook for the man she loved," surely spurred her on as well.

To please, always to please, was the message, and not an altogether outdated one. It inspired those stalwart guild ladies to assemble an awesome number of recipes that still have charm and more than a little currency. Understanding the possibilities and limitations of the "food convenient to [them]" was perhaps their greatest contribution. And using whatever was seasonal was their triumph. It might have been "an old-fashioned rule" to pour oyster sauce over a plump fowl, but it also made good sense—the oysters were in the bay, the chicken in the barn. Why not "Broil the steak, cover the top with raw oysters, and set it on the grate of the oven till the oysters curl," or take two dozen oysters chopped very fine for a "Delicious Stuffing for Fowl"? Call it thrift, call it a stroke of genius, the "huswive's affaires had never an end."

Yesterday's cooks were in many ways as cosmopolitan as they were committed to "What We Cook on Cape Cod" or elsewhere. The names of the recipes tell it all—Indian Pudding, German Apple Cake, Begorra, Portugese Fish Stew, and Spaghetti: An Italian Receipt Brought from Palermo—complete with the instruction, "To have a perfect dish, buy your spaghetti from the Italian dealers. And do not use bottled cheese." They learned from the Indians and later from the waves of *immigrées* who brought recipes, utensils, and a distinctive cuisine to the melting pot or perhaps it was the "Kettle-Ho."

The recipes in this chapter capture something of the past and reaffirm the strong conviction that innovative cooking will continue to be found in every family kitchen where an open cookbook and the contents of the refrigerator frequently determine the dinner to be served that evening. Ingredients are the "food convenient to [one]"—the eggs in a basket on the kitchen counter, a pound of sirloin in the meat compartment, some freshly made pasta, or a package of rice.

And the instructions for every entrée begin with *oysters*.

SUGGESTIONS:

- It is easier to cut pockets in steaks and chops if the meat has been placed in the freezer prior to cutting.
- Stuffing may be baked separately in a casserole dish, but it is necessary to add more liquid if baked this way. Use chicken or vegetable stock rather than oyster liquor to prevent over-salting.
- The recipe for oyster saúsage can be prepared as a terrine.
- Careful timing is essential in the preparation of fish and seafood. Overcooking reduces flavor and toughens.

HOW TO STEW OYSTERS

Straine the liquor from the Oysters, then wash them very clean, and put them into a pipkin with the liquor, a pinte of Wine to a quart of Oysters, two or three whole Onions, large Mace, Pepper, Ginger; let all the spices be whole, they will stew the whiter; put in Salt, a little Vinegar, a piece of butter and sweet Herbs; stew all these together till you think them enough, then take out some of that liquor and put to it a quarter of a pound of butter, a Lemmond minced, and beat it up thick, setting it on the fire, but let it not boyle; dreine the rest of the liquor from the Oysters thorow [through] a culender, and dish them; pour this sauce over them; garnish your dish with searced [sieved] Ginger, Lemmon, Orange, Barberries, or Grapes scalded; sippit it, and serve it up.
Joseph Cooper, *The Art of Cookery Refin'd and Augmented,* 1654

PASTIFICIO

The Italian legacy of a style of cooking totally allied with fresh, earthy, and wholesome flavors makes the venture into *ostriche cucina* as tempting today as exploring the Orient probably was for Marco Polo centuries ago. And the comparison may be less frivolous than it seems to be.

Allegedly the one who brought macaroni from China to his native land, the adventurous Venetian explorer may well have initiated the largesse of pasta available today. And he had more than a little to do with the succession of sauces that have been devised to accompany it.

In the beginning there was only an uncomplicated ginger-wine sauce and now there is an almost unbelievable range of full-bodied tomato, olive oil, basil, and garlic sauces that have come to be identified with the various regional cuisines of Italy. No ingredient, it seems, has been overlooked in the enduring partnership of pasta and vegetables, meats, and seafood.

For an excursion into this enticing world of pasta, follow the custom of generations of Italian fishermen who added clams to both white and red sauces. Substitute oysters for the clams, or serve oysters in a memorable pesto or "green" seafood sauce. The result can only be called *mescolando in gusto Italiano*, "getting it together, the Italian way."

. . . between 1775 and 1818 there lived and flourished (more or less) in Malta, Naples, Paris, and elsewhere, a notable composer, Nicolo Isouard, more generally known as Nicolo. He wrote many operas, all of which are now forgotten. Having lived in Naples he was a great macaroni eater, and prepared the dish himself in a somewhat original manner. He stuffed each tube of macaroni with a mixture of marrow, pâté de foi gras, chopped truffles, and cut-up oysters. He then heated up the preparation, and ate it with his left hand covering up his eyes, for he asserted that he could not afford to allow the beautiful thoughts engendered by such exquisite food to be disturbed by an extraneous sight. No wonder he died young.

Frank Schloesser, *The Greedy Book*

Oysters Paglia e Fieno

A platter of "straw and hay" pasta blanketed with a zesty white oyster sauce, a bottle of Lambrusco, and a shredded chicory salad are all one needs for an evening of *al fresco* dining that may well bring back the lingering memory of a little trattoria in the winding streets of Fiesole.

1	pint small oysters and liquor	2	teaspoons chopped fresh basil
1½	cups fish stock (See p. 62)	2	teaspoons chopped fresh oregano
2	Tablespoons lemon juice	½	cup minced parsley
1	teaspoon grated lemon zest		Salt and freshly ground white pepper
5	Tablespoons butter		
1	chopped medium onion	8	ounces egg fettuccini
2	minced garlic cloves	8	ounces spinach fettuccini
3	Tablespoons flour		
½	teaspoon nutmeg		

1. Drain the oysters and set aside. Mix ½ cup of oyster liquor with the stock, lemon juice, and zest in a small saucepan, and bring to a simmer.
2. Melt 3 tablespoons of butter in another saucepan, and sauté the onion and garlic until tender. Stir in the flour, nutmeg, basil, oregano, half the parsley, and cook, stirring constantly, for 3 minutes. Whisk in the hot stock and stir until the mixture thickens. Simmer for 10 minutes.
3. Fill a large saucepan with 4 quarts of cold water, add 1 tablespoon of salt, and bring to a boil. Cook the fettuccini *al dente*. Drain and toss with the remaining butter.
4. Reheat the sauce and add the oysters, remaining parsley, and adjust seasonings. When the oysters plump, spoon the sauce over the fettuccini and serve.

Serves 6

O woeful, weeping Walrus, your
tears are all a sham!
You're greedier for Oysters than
children are for jam.
You like to have an Oyster to give
the meal a zest—
Excuse me, wicked Walrus,
for stamping on your chest!
Lewis Carroll for Savile Clarke's *Alice*

Oysters Modena

The emphatic presence of pesto sauce casts a spell over the oysters and tortellini in this dish. Elegant as a first course, or *minestra*, and equally effective as a light entrée, these little curls of pasta wrapped around a special blend of veal forcemeat, spices, and eggs beautifully complement the sheer munificence of oysters.

1 pint small oysters and liquor	*Sauce:*
1 quart chicken stock (See p. 63)	4 Tablespoons butter
	1/2 cup olive oil
3 quarts water	2 cups chopped fresh basil
2 teaspoons salt	1 cup chopped broadleaf parsley
1 1/2 pounds stuffed (veal forcemeat) tortellini	1/2 cup freshly grated Asiago cheese
1 cup dry white wine	1/2 cup freshly grated Romano cheese
	1 Tablespoon pine nuts
	12 blanched chopped walnuts
	12 blanched halved almonds
	3 garlic cloves

1. Melt and cool the butter.
2. Process the butter, oil, basil, parsley, Asiago, Romano, nuts, and garlic in the work bowl of a food processor. Set aside.
3. Bring the stock and water to a boil, add the salt, and cook the tortellini until tender. Drain, and add 2 tablespoons of the cooking liquid to the pesto sauce.
4. When the tortellini is nearly cooked, poach the oysters in the liquor and wine until the edges begin to curl. Remove from the heat.
5. Divide the tortellini on individual plates, remove the oysters from the poaching liquid with a slotted spoon, and arange them on the tortellini. Spoon the pesto sauce over the oysters and serve.

Serves 6

Oysters Salsa Verde

A sauce that can be used with seafood, pasta, or artichokes, *salsa verde* boasts a pleasing color derived from all the chopped parsley and watercress used in its preparation and a revivifying scent from the simmering garlic and olive oil. Both make it utterly reliable for an oyster and pasta entrée.

1   pint oysters and liquor
1   Tablespoon salt
1   pound vermicelli
2   Tablespoons melted butter
1   cup dry white wine

Sauce:
2   Tablespoons chopped parsley
2   Tablespoons chopped
     watercress

2   Tablespoons capers
1   chopped garlic clove
1/2 teaspoon salt
1/4 teaspoon freshly ground
      pepper
3/4 cup olive oil
1/3 cup lemon juice

1. Make the sauce by combining the first six ingredients in the work bowl of a food processor fitted with the steel blade. Purée for 20 seconds and add the oil gradually. Add the lemon juice and process a few seconds longer. Transfer the sauce to a small saucepan and heat.
2. Boil 4 quarts of water in a large pot, add the salt, drop in the vermicelli, and stir. Cook *al dente*, drain, and toss with the melted butter.
3. Lightly poach the oysters in their own liquor and wine. Remove from the heat as soon as the edges curl, and drain.
4. Arrange the vermicelli on a large serving platter. Place the oysters in the center of the pasta, and spoon the hot sauce over them. Serve immediately.

Serves 6

Oysters Maruzzi

These shellfish and spinach-stuffed pasta shells are so redolent of the seashore that one will be tempted to serve them on a bed of seaweed. But, perhaps, asparagus spears in vinaigrette or a nest of julienned zucchini could create the same effect and please the palate more.

1   pint small oysters and liquor
1/2 cup milk
1/2 Tablespoon vegetable oil
     Salt
12 ounces large (2 1/2-inch) pasta
      shells
4   Tablespoons unsalted butter
12 ounces bay scallops
1   Tablespoon minced shallot
1/2 minced garlic clove
2   Tablespoons flour
2   teaspoons lemon juice
1/2 teaspoon grated lemon zest

1/8 teaspoon freshly ground
       pepper
     Cayenne pepper
10 ounces stemmed fresh spinach
1/2 cup heavy cream

Lemon sauce:
2   Tablespoons dry Vermouth
1   teaspoon lemon juice
1   teaspoon minced shallot
1/8 teaspoon saffron
1   cup heavy cream

(Oysters Maruzzi, continued)

Oven Temperature: 350°

1. Drain the oysters and set them aside. Mix ½ cup of the oyster liquor with the milk, and warm in a small saucepan.
2. Boil 3 quarts of water in a large saucepan, add the oil, 2 teaspoons of salt, and the shells. Cook the shells, stirring occasionally, until they are tender but firm. Drain in a colander and use the unbroken shells for the recipe.
3. Melt 2 tablespoons of the butter in a skillet over high heat. When the foam subsides, sauté the scallops and oysters for a minute or two; remove, quarter the oysters, and set aside.
4. Add 2 more tablespoons of butter to the skillet and lightly sauté the shallots and garlic. Stir in the flour and cook until bubbling. Remove from the heat and whisk in the warm milk. Return to heat and stir in the lemon juice, zest, pepper, cayenne, and salt to taste. Stir constantly until the mixture thickens and comes to a boil.
5. Blanch the spinach, drain, and chop fine.
6. Toss the spinach and seafood together. Add the sauce, stirring lightly until mixed. Fill 20 of the pasta shells with the mixture.
7. Place the shells in a buttered shallow baking dish and pour the cream into the bottom of the dish.
8. Cover and bake about 20 minutes until the shells are thoroughly heated.
9. While the shells are baking, combine the Vermouth, lemon juice, shallots, and saffron in a small saucepan. Cook, stirring frequently, until reduced to a tablespoon. Add the cream and cook until the sauce is reduced to ⅔ cup. Correct the seasoning.
10. Remove the shells from the oven and add the cream from the bottom of the dish to the sauce and additional cream if it is necessary to thin the sauce.
11. Arrange 5 shells on individual serving plates and pour some of the sauce over them. Serve immediately.

Serves 4

Ceres presents a plate of vermicelli,—
For love must be sustain'd like flesh and blood,
While Bacchus pours out wine, or hands a jelly:
Eggs, oysters, too, are amatory food.

    Lord Byron, *Don Juan*

Oysters Filetto

Patience is the joy of oysters.

Marge Piercy

In the continuing controversy about the suitability of red or white sauce for shellfish, the devotees of white (without a trace of cheese) will always oppose the champions of red (who insist on a spoonful of Parmesan or Pecorino). The "patient" oyster is happy in both.

1 pint oysters and liquor	Salt and freshly ground
3 Tablespoons olive oil	pepper
1 cup chopped onion	1 pound tomato linguini
2 garlic cloves	2 Tablespoons melted butter
1 quart fresh tomato pulp	
1/2 cup dry red wine	
1 teaspoon sugar	
1 Tablespoon chopped fresh basil	
1 teaspoon chopped fresh oregano	
1 teaspoon chopped fresh rosemary	
1/8 teaspoon hot red pepper flakes	

1. Drain the oysters and set them aside, reserving the liquor for the sauce.
2. Heat the oil in a saucepan and sauté the onion and garlic until tender; discard the garlic.
3. Stir in the oyster liquor, tomatoes, wine, sugar, basil, oregano, rosemary, pepper flakes, salt and pepper to taste. Simmer uncovered, stirring frequently, until the sauce is reduced by half, about 30 minutes.
4. Bring to a boil 4 quarts of water with 1 tablespoon of salt in a large pot. Drop in the pasta and stir during the cooking. Remove from the heat when cooked *al dente*, drain, and toss with the melted butter.
5. Reheat the sauce and stir in the oysters, adjust seasonings. Cook until the oysters begin to curl.
6. Ladle the sauce over the pasta and serve immediately.

Serves 6

Genoan Tagliatelle

All the bounty of the sea spills over the pasta in this recipe that is definitely in the spirit of the Italian Riviera although it was devised and served much closer to home.

1	pint oysters and liquor	1	cup dry white wine
	Salt		Freshly ground pepper
1	pound tagliatelli	1/4	cup Cognac
2	Tablespoons melted butter	1/4	pound cooked lobster
1/2	cup olive oil	1/2	pound cooked, shelled and deveined, medium shrimp
2	garlic cloves		
2	minced shallots	2	peeled, seeded, and chopped medium tomatoes
1	Tablespoon chopped fresh oregano	1	Tablespoon snipped chives

1. Bring 4 quarts of water to a boil in a large saucepan. Stir in 1 tablespoon of salt and drop in the pasta. Stir while the tagliatelli cooks and remove from the heat when tender but firm. Drain, toss with melted butter, and keep hot while preparing the sauce.
2. Heat the oil in a large saucepan and sauté the garlic and shallots until tender. Add the oregano, wine, and pepper to taste. Cook over moderately high heat until the liquid is reduced by half. Discard the garlic.
3. Add the oysters, oyster liquor, Cognac, pieces of lobster, shrimp, tomatoes, and chives, and adjust the seasoning. Cook until the mixture is thoroughly heated but do not boil.
4. Spoon the sauce over the tagliatelli and serve immediately.

Serves 6

Oyster Carbonara

It would be surprising, indeed, if the Guelfs and Ghibellines didn't feud over this dish in the 14th century because almost everyone else has done so since then. The number of eggs, the amount of bacon, cook or not cook, stir or toss—all are a matter of personal choice and conviction. So why not add a little more fuel to the fire and serve it with sautéed oysters.

1	pint small oysters	1/2	pound diced bacon
1/2	cup flour	4	Tablespoons butter
	Salt and freshly ground pepper	1	pound spaghetti
		1/3	cup chopped parsley
5	eggs	1/4	cup freshly grated Parmesan cheese (optional)
1	Tablespoon water		
1	cup fresh fine bread crumbs		

1. Drain the oysters, reserving the liquor for another use. Pat the oysters dry and dust with seasoned flour.
2. Beat 2 eggs in a bowl together with a tablespoon of water. Dip the oysters in the egg, roll in crumbs, and set aside.
3. Fry the bacon in a large skillet until crisp and brown. Remove and drain on absorbent paper spread on a baking sheet. Keep warm.
4. Pour off all but 1 tablespoon of bacon fat from the pan, add and heat 2 tablespoons of butter and sauté half the oysters over moderately high heat, turning them to brown both sides. Remove, keep warm, and sauté the remaining oysters, using more butter if needed.
5. Bring 4 quarts of water to a boil in a large pot, add a tablespoon of salt, and drop in the spaghetti. Stir while it is cooking, remove from the stove when tender but firm, and drain.
6. Beat the remaining 3 eggs in a large mixing bowl, pour in the spaghetti, and toss to coat the strands with egg. Sprinkle with bacon, parsley, and cheese, and toss again.
7. Spoon the pasta on individual serving plates and divide the oysters among the servings.

Serves 6

Oyster Tetrazzini

No telling what lengths a chef will go to in order to please a famous patron. This dish, named for Luisa Tetrazzini, an Italian coloratura soprano, was originally made with chicken. But think of the performance, if it had been made with oysters.

1 pint oysters and liquor	3 Tablespoons cream
2 cups chicken stock	1/4 cup dry Sherry
(See p. 63)	Salt and freshly ground
3/4 cup butter	pepper
1/2 pound sliced small	Tabasco
mushrooms	8 ounces spaghettini
4 Tablespoons flour	1/2 cup toasted almonds
2 egg yolks	

Oven Temperature: 400°

1. Drain the oysters and set them aside. Mix 1/2 cup of oyster liquor with the stock and heat in a small saucepan.
2. Melt the butter in another saucepan; spoon off and reserve 1/2 cup. Cook the mushrooms just long enough to heat them; remove with a slotted spoon and set aside. Stir the flour into the saucepan and cook until bubbling. Remove from the heat and whisk in the stock. Return to heat and boil, stirring constantly, until the mixture thickens. Simmer for 3 minutes.

3. Beat the egg yolks and cream in a bowl. Whisk in ½ cup of the hot mixture, a spoonful at a time. Gradually beat in a cup of the hot mixture, then transfer the enriched sauce back to the saucepan. Season with Sherry, salt, pepper, and Tabasco, and bring to a boil.
4. Stir the oysters and mushrooms into the sauce and immediately remove from the heat.
5. Boil 3 quarts of water in a large saucepan, add 2 teaspoons of salt, and drop in the spaghettini. Stir while it cooks, and remove from the stove as soon as it becomes limp. Drain the spaghettini and toss in a bowl with ¼ cup of the reserved melted butter.
6. Place half the pasta on the bottom of a buttered 2-quart baking dish. Cover with a layer of oyster sauce. Repeat the layers and drizzle with the remaining melted butter.
7. Cover the dish and bake for 20 minutes or until bubbling. Remove the cover and bake another 10 minutes.
8. Garnish with toasted almonds if desired.

Serves 6

RICE BOWL

From the ancient "paddy to pot" cuisines of China and India to the contemporary California-inspired style of cooking, rice dishes that have withstood the test of time are being recreated by cooks who have their own dining traditions and their own rules about how rice is cooked and served. Name a shallow pan of rice studded with seafood, paella or jambalaya; refer to a plate of curry-spiced rice and fish as kedgeree or the Indian *kitcherie*; or describe a dish of mushrooms and rice as *ris al forno*, or *riz duxelles*, and the ethnic differences as well as the universality of rice are reaffirmed.

Most of the following recipes come from a country or region known for both its cultivation of rice and long tradition of seafood cuisine. They emphasize the proverb that cooking with ingredients "convenient" to one is frequently a necessity and always can be the *art* of the possible.

Colony House Oysters

Tradition holds sway over this curried rice entrée. Call it Indian; call it British. Either way, the combination of all those "curry" spices with rice and oysters is really a roaring success.

1 pint oysters and liquor	1/4 teaspoon red pepper flakes
2 Tablespoons butter	1/2 teaspoon cinnamon
1 Tablespoon vegetable oil	1/4 teaspoon ground cloves
2 finely chopped medium onions	1/4 teaspoon coriander
1 teaspoon dry mustard	1/4 teaspoon cumin
1 teaspoon turmeric	1/2 cup cream
1 cup shredded dried coconut	Salt and freshly ground pepper
1 3/4 cups chicken stock (See p. 63)	3 cups cooked long-grain rice Chutney
1 crumbled bay leaf	

1. Drain the oysters and set them aside, reserving 1/4 cup of the liquor.
2. Heat the butter and oil in a skillet and sauté the onion until brown. Add the mustard, turmeric, and half of the coconut; cook and stir over moderately high heat until the coconut turns golden brown.
3. Reduce the heat under the skillet and mix in the oyster liquor, stock, bay leaf, and spices. Simmer, uncovered, for 15 minutes. Pour in the cream and simmer 5 minutes more.
4. Add the oysters and heat until the edges begin to curl. Season to taste with salt and pepper, and remove from the heat.
5. Spoon the hot rice into individual bowls and then add the oyster curry. Serve with porringers of peach or mango chutney and the remaining coconut.

Serves 4

CURRIED OYSTERS

Put one tablespoonful of butter, one teaspoonful of grated onion, one-half teaspoonful of curry powder and one tablespoonful of flour in a hot chafing dish. When blended add the oyster liquor and cook a minute, stirring, add the oysters and when they curl serve on toast.

What We Cook on Cape Cod, compiled by Amy L. Handy, 1911.

Patchen Place Oysters

In this entrée both the rice and the seafood are prepared with the "trinity" of Creole cookery—green pepper, celery, and onions. The vegetables are as common to the garden patches that dot the Louisiana countryside as the rice fields are to the rich low lands of the delta. And then there are all those oysters. Glory be. . . .

1   pint oysters and liquor
1½ cups long-grain rice
3½ cups chicken stock
        (See p. 63)
1½ Tablespoons corn oil
   ⅓ cup finely chopped celery
   ⅓ cup finely chopped green
        pepper
   ⅓ cup finely chopped onion
        Salt and freshly ground
           pepper
        Cayenne
2   Tablespoons butter

1   cup fish stock (See p. 62)
   ½ cup tomato purée
2   garlic cloves
        Pinch of thyme
   ½ cup cream
6   ounces lump crabmeat
1   pound shelled and deveined
        raw medium shrimp

Oven Temperature: 350°

1. Combine the rice, chicken stock, corn oil, and 3 tablespoons each of the celery, green pepper, and onion. Season with pepper, cayenne, and a pinch of salt. Bake in a tightly covered, buttered casserole for about an hour until the rice is tender.
2. Drain the oysters and set aside, reserving ⅓ cup of the liquor.
3. Melt the butter in a skillet, add the oyster liquor, fish stock, tomato purée, garlic, thyme, and the remaining chopped vegetables. Simmer uncovered for 15 minutes, stirring occasionally. Discard the garlic.
4. Stir in the cream and crabmeat and simmer 5 minutes more.
5. Add the oysters and shrimp and cook until the edges of the oysters begin to curl and the shrimp are pink. Adjust the seasonings.
6. Spoon some of the rice into one side of individual serving bowls and the seafood mixture into the other side.

Serves 6

Jambalaya

Situated between New Orleans and Baton Rouge, Gonzales is one of the oldest Spanish settlements in Louisiana. Because the crown jewel of its local cuisine is a jambalaya that is heir apparent to Spain's own *paella*, it is well worth traveling to Gonzales to sample this one-dish meal in its authentic setting. Or try this recipe in a copper paella pan if a visit to Gonzales is impossible.

1	pint oysters and liquor	4	chopped medium onions
12	cherry stone clams in shells	3	chopped scallions, including green parts
1	pound lean pork		
1	pound smoked mild sausage	2	minced garlic cloves
3	Tablespoons butter	1	cup finely chopped ham
½	teaspoon chili powder	1½	cups long-grain rice
¼	teaspoon thyme	3	cups beef stock (See p. 64)
¼	teaspoon ground cloves		Salt
1	crumbled bay leaf	2	Tablespoons chopped parsley
¼	teaspoon freshly ground pepper		
	Pinch of cayenne pepper		

Oven Temperature: 325°

1. Drain the oysters and set them aside, reserving ⅓ cup of the liquor. Scrub the clams thoroughly.
2. Cut the pork into ½-inch cubes and the sausage into ⅜-inch slices.
3. Melt the butter in a large skillet over low heat and stir in the chili powder, thyme, cloves, bay leaf, and pepper. Sauté the onions, scallions, garlic, ham, and pork about 15 minutes until they are brown, stirring frequently.
4. Stir in the sausage and cook for 20 minutes.
5. Transfer the contents of the skillet to a bowl, and keep warm.
6. Add more butter and the rice to the skillet, cook and stir over medium heat for 5 minutes until the rice is golden brown.
7. Pour in the oyster liquor and beef stock, and season to taste. When boiling, reduce the heat so the mixture simmers *very slowly*. Cover and cook for 20 minutes or until the rice is almost tender and most of the liquid has been absorbed.
8. Spoon one-third of the rice into a large buttered baking dish or paella pan. Place the meat in a single layer and spoon in more rice. Distribute the oysters, cover with the remaining rice, and add the clams to the top layer. Pour in more stock if the rice seems dry.
9. Cover and bake about 15 minutes until the clams open.
10. Garnish with parsley and serve.

Serves 6

Delight of Three

The combination of ham, shrimp, and oysters in a dish of Oriental fried rice will certainly cause a division of loyalty between those epicures who prefer *chow fan* made with chicken rather than ham. But perhaps the "particularity" of oysters will bridge the gap.

1	pint oysters	½	pound diced ham
	Vegetable or peanut oil	½	cup shelled peas
2	lightly beaten eggs	3	cups cooked long-grain rice
8	minced scallions, including green parts	2	Tablespoons soy sauce
1	minced slice fresh ginger root		
½	pound shelled, deveined raw medium shrimp		

1. Drain the oysters, pat dry, and set aside, reserving the liquor for another use.
2. Heat a wok to high heat and swirl 2 tablespoons of oil around the bottom and sides until well coated. Lower the heat.
3. Pour in the beaten eggs mixed with a few scallions. Cook until the eggs set. Transfer the eggs to a warm bowl and break the eggs into small pieces with a fork.
4. Add 1 tablespoon more oil to the wok and raise the temperature to medium high. Add the ginger and the remaining scallions and stir-fry for 1 minute.
5. Add the shrimp and stir-fry them until they turn pink. Add the ham and peas and stir-fry another minute. Remove all the ingredients from the wok to a warm bowl.
6. Add another tablespoon of oil to the wok and heat. Toss and stir-fry the cooked rice and oysters for 2 minutes; stir in the soy sauce.
7. Return all the ingredients to the wok, toss and mix together.
8. Remove the wok from the heat and spoon the rice onto a platter. Serve immediately as an entrée or as part of a Chinese dinner.

Serves 4

Oysters are the usual opening to a winter breakfast. . . . Indeed,
they are almost indispensable.
Almanach des Gourmandes, 1803

Oysters Paglia e Fieno (Page 205)

Oysters Casanova Grill (Page 236)

Crazy Oats

What's in a name? Indians called it *manomin*, settlers called it water rice, French explorers called it "crazy oats," and now everyone calls it wild rice. For a truly "fare-thee-well," mix it with almonds, chicken livers, and oysters, and it will never be called anything less than provocative.

1 pint small oysters	¼ cup orange juice
1 cup wild rice	1 Tablespoon grated orange zest
6 Tablespoons butter	1 cup golden raisins
½ cup chopped scallions, including green parts	½ teaspoon salt
1 cup blanched almonds	⅛ teaspoon freshly ground pepper
2¾ cups chicken stock (See p. 63)	½ pound chicken livers

Oven Temperature: 325°

1. Rinse the rice in several changes of water, and drain.
2. Melt 4 tablespoons of butter in a large skillet. Stir and sauté the rice, scallions, and almonds for 15 minutes.
3. Add the stock, orange juice, zest, raisins, and seasonings, and bring to a boil.
4. Transfer to a buttered 1½-quart casserole, cover, and bake 1 hour.
5. Drain the oysters and set aside, reserving the liquor for another use.
6. Cut the livers in 1-inch pieces and sauté them quickly in a skillet in the remaining 2 tablespoons of butter. Remove with a slotted spoon when the livers begin to brown, and set aside.
7. After the casserole has been in the oven for an hour, stir in the oysters and livers, and fluff the rice with a fork. Cover and bake another 30 minutes.

Serves 6

FROM THE EGG BASKET

Probably no other food has as much versatility as the dependable egg. It binds together, enriches, puffs up, thickens, fluffs, and enhances everything from sauces, custards, and pancakes to vegetables and cheese. And no other food is as comforting. An affirmative answer to the question: "Are there any eggs in the refrigerator?" virtually guarantees a meal that will stave off hunger any time of the day or night.

No longer regarded as the "autocrat of the breakfast table," the egg can perform dramatically at a festive brunch, lunch, dinner, or late supper, and it can be prepared in almost every imaginable way. As an added fillip, the absolute neutrality of its flavor makes an egg combined with fruit and sugar as delicious as it is zesty when mixed with spices and herbs.

Definitely a principal in a cast of two or more, an egg is at its best when partnered with other ingredients. So, from the inspired soufflé to the baked egg on a breakfast tray, here are the "egg plus" recipes that work with oysters.

Oysters Si Bon

Anything as regal as Oysters Si Bon incurs a debt of gratitude. So, thank you, Catherine de Medici, for introducing the Florentine *sformata* to the royal court of France and making the soufflé a dish fit for a king.

½ pint oysters	¼ teaspoon salt
2 Tablespoons butter	Pinch of freshly ground
3 Tablespoons flour	pepper
¼ teaspoon nutmeg	2 teaspoons chopped fresh dill
1½ cups hot milk	4 egg whites
3 slices smoked salmon	
3 egg yolks	

Oven Temperature: 375°

1. Melt the butter in a 1½-quart saucepan; stir in the flour and nutmeg, and cook until bubbling. Remove from the heat and whisk in the hot milk. Return to heat and stir constantly while the mixture boils for 1 minute, and then allow to cool.
2. Drain and coarsely chop the oysters, reserving the liquor for another use. Cut the salmon into ¼-inch strips, and set aside.
3. Beat the egg yolks lightly; add the salt, pepper, and dill. Whisk the yolks into the cooled sauce, one spoonful at a time.
4. Beat the egg whites until stiff in a large bowl. Stir ¼ of them into the yolk mixture. Fold the rest of the whites in quickly in order not to deflate or diminish their volume.
5. Spread an inch of the mixture on the bottom of a well-buttered and floured 1½-quart soufflé dish. Arrange the oysters and salmon on top of it and spoon in the rest of the mixture.
6. Bake in the center of the oven for 25–30 minutes, and serve immediately.

Serves 4

Smokehouse Soufflé

This mock soufflé is a little treasure of ruffles and flourishes to serve at a brunch or late evening supper. Easy to do ahead and bake just before serving, it wants only a tossed green salad, perhaps an oyster sausage or two, and a glass of Chablis for accompaniment.

2	3¾-ounce tins smoked oysters	¼	cup dry Sherry
10	thin slices firm white bread	½	teaspoon salt
3	Tablespoons soft butter	⅛	teaspoon freshly ground pepper
1	large tomato		
4	eggs	½	pound grated Brie or herbed Brie cheese
1¾	cups milk		

Oven Temperature: 350°

1. Rinse the oysters, drain, pat dry, and coarsely chop them.
2. Remove the bread crusts. Butter 2 slices, trim them to fit, and place them, buttered-side down, on the bottom of a 2-quart buttered casserole. Make butter sandwiches of the remaining slices, cut them in half diagonally, and place them in spoke-fashion around the dish. Prop the tomato slices against the sides of the dish between the slices of bread.
3. Beat the eggs in a bowl with the milk, Sherry, salt and pepper. Stir in the cheese and oysters.
4. Spoon the mixture into the dish, spreading it evenly between the bread points. Cover loosely with plastic wrap and refrigerate for at least an hour. The dish may also be frozen but bring to room temperature before baking.
5. Bake uncovered for 1 hour until the egg is set and the bread points are golden.

Serves 6

Oyster Surprise

Good things come in French brioches. Just open the lid and find the oysters and scrambled eggs inside. Marvelous with Kir Royale or Mimosa on one of those revving-up-for-the-week-ahead Sunday mornings.

12	shucked small oysters	8	eggs
½	cup corn flour	2	Tablespoons cream
	Salt and freshly ground pepper		Tabasco
	Cayenne pepper	4	heated 3½-inch brioches
6	Tablespoons unsalted butter		Parsley sprigs
			Thin orange slices

1. Remove the oysters from their shells and pat dry, reserving the liquor for another use. Dip the oysters in flour seasoned with salt, pepper, and cayenne.
2. Melt 2 tablespoons of the butter in a skillet and sauté the oysters over moderately high heat, browning both sides quickly. Set the oysters aside on absorbent paper.
3. Beat the eggs and cream in a bowl, but do not homogenize. Season with pepper, Tabasco, and ¼ teaspoon salt.
4. Melt 3 tablespoons of butter in a large skillet over low heat, add the eggs, and stir, scraping the bottom of the pan, until the eggs begin to thicken. Swirl in the remaining tablespoon of butter. Add the oysters and cook until the eggs are firm but not dry.
5. Remove the "lid" from each brioche and hollow it out. Place the bottoms on heated plates and fill each with the scrambled eggs and oysters. Replace the tops and serve immediately with a garnish of parsley sprigs and orange slices.

Serves 4

Oyster Aphrodisia

Everyone dreams of that "betwixt the sheets" breakfast when ambience is the magic word, and Venus is in the kitchen preparing a feast of mangos and melons, followed by scrambled eggs napped with an oyster and lobster sauce . . . and "love was the pearl of his oyster/ And Venus rose red out of wine." * Here is the recipe.

½ pint oysters and liquor	½ teaspoon tomato paste
¾ cup cream	½ cup coarsely chopped cooked
5 Tablespoons butter	lobster meat
2 Tablespoons chopped shallots	Salt and freshly ground
1½ Tablespoons flour	pepper
2 teaspoons chopped fresh	8 eggs
tarragon	
2 Tablespoons dry Vermouth	
1 teaspoon lemon juice	

1. Drain the oysters, reserving the liquor. If the oysters are large, cut them in halves or quarters, and set aside. Mix ¼ cup of the liquor with the cream, and warm in a saucepan.
2. Melt 2 tablespoons of butter in another saucepan and sauté the shallots until tender. Stir in the flour and cook until bubbling. Remove from the heat and whisk in the cream. Return to heat, add the tarragon, Vermouth, lemon

juice, and tomato paste. Boil, stirring constantly, until the mixture thickens; simmer for 3 minutes.

4. Stir the oysters and lobster into the sauce and adjust seasonings. Heat the sauce thoroughly and keep it warm while scrambling the eggs, but do not allow it to boil.

5. Beat the eggs in a bowl and season with ¼ teaspoon of salt and pepper.

6. Melt the remaining butter in a skillet over low heat, add the eggs, and stir until they start to thicken; increase the heat, and stir rapidly until the eggs reach the desired consistency.

7. Serve immediately on hot plates, napping the eggs with the oyster and lobster sauce.

* Algernon Charles Swinburne, *Dolores*

Serves 4

OYSTER OMELET, (Very Fine.)

Take twelve large oysters chopped fine. Mix the beaten yolks of six eggs into a tea-cupful of milk, and add the oysters. Then put in a spoonful of melted butter, and lastly add the whites of the eggs beated to a stiff froth. Fry this in hot butter or salted lard, and do not stir it while cooking. Slip a knife around the edges while cooking, that the centre may cook equally, and turn it out so that the brown side be uppermost.

Catherine Esther Beecher, *Mrs. Beecher's Housekeeper and Healthkeeper, 1876*

Incredible Omelet

Two eggs and two tablespoons of filling, and the Incredible Omelet becomes an edible masterpiece. Make and serve it individually like a precious *objet d'art*. It's the ultimate compliment to a guest.

2 fresh eggs	1 Tablespoon unsalted butter
Salt	¼ cup of one of the following
1 teaspoon water	oyster fillings
Freshly ground pepper	

1. Crack the eggs into a small bowl, add a pinch of salt and water. Lightly beat the eggs with a fork, but do not homogenize the texture of the eggs. Crack in a bit of pepper and set aside.

2. Melt the butter in a 6-inch skillet over high heat. Pour in the eggs when the butter starts to foam.
3. Stir the eggs briefly with the flat of the fork; allow them to set, tipping the skillet to permit the uncooked egg to run to the bottom.
4. Spoon the filling across the center of the omelet while it is still moist. Fold the omelet over and tip it onto a warm plate. Garnish and serve.

Serves 1

CREAMED MUSHROOM FILLING*

½ pint oysters
2 Tablespoons unsalted butter
¼ teaspoon mace
¼ pound sliced small
 mushrooms
¼ cup cream

3 Tablespoons dry Madeira
2 Tablespoons finely chopped
 parsley
Salt and freshly ground
 pepper

1. Drain and coarsely chop the oysters, reserving the liquor for another use.
2. Melt the butter in a skillet, stir in the mace, and sauté the mushrooms over moderately high heat until the liquid has evaporated. Remove the mushrooms with a slotted spoon and set aside.
3. Lower the heat under the skillet, add the cream and Madeira, and simmer until reduced by half.
4. When it is time to prepare the omelets, return the mushrooms to the skillet. Stir in the oysters, parsley, seasoning, and heat thoroughly.

* The amount of filling in each of the following recipes is sufficient for 4 individual omelets or an 8-egg omelet to serve 4 people.

APPLE FILLING

½ pint oysters
1 large tart apple
4 Tablespoons butter
¼ cup chopped celery

3 Tablespoons brown sugar
2 Tablespoons Calvados
¼ cup golden raisins

1. Drain and coarsely chop the oysters, reserving the liquor for another use.
2. Peel and core the apple, and cut into ⅜-inch wedge-shaped pieces.
3. Melt 2 tablespoons of butter in a skillet and sauté the apple over moderately high heat, turning often to brown all sides. Remove with a slotted spoon and set aside.
4. Reduce the heat under the skillet and add the remaining butter. Sauté the celery until tender, and stir in the brown sugar. Cook until the sugar has

dissolved, add the Calvados and raisins. Cook, stirring frequently, for 5 minutes.

5. When it is time to prepare the omelets, return the apples to the pan, add the oysters, and cook until the filling is hot.

BACON AND POTATO FILLING

1/2 pint oysters	1/2 cup sliced onion
2 slices diced bacon	Salt and freshly ground
2 Tablespoons butter	pepper
1 cup diced cooked potato	

1. Drain and coarsely chop the oysters, reserving the liquor for another use.
2. Fry the bacon in a skillet until brown and crisp. Remove with a slotted spoon and drain on absorbent paper. Pour off the drippings from the pan.
3. Add and melt the butter; sauté the potato and onion until well browned. Season to taste.
4. When it is time to prepare the omelets, return the bacon to the pan. Stir in the oysters and move them around quickly with a spatula to heat them.

Hangtown Fry

Dry Diggings, Hangtown, and Placerville—all names for one small California town. And rumor has it that it wasn't gold, or desperadoes, or the Chamber of Commerce that put it on the map, but a certain cook at the Blue Bell restaurant who added a few oysters and bacon to a skillet of scrambled eggs. Another story of another golden egg!

24 shucked medium oysters	1 cup fine unsalted cracker crumbs
8 slices bacon	
10 eggs	4 Tablespoons cream
1/2 cup flour	Dash of Tabasco (optional)
Salt and freshly ground pepper	6 Tablespoons butter

1. Cook the bacon in a skillet or microwave oven until brown and crisp. Drain on absorbent paper and set aside.
2. Beat 2 of the eggs in a bowl.
3. Remove the oysters from their shells, drain, pat them dry, and coat with seasoned flour. Dip the oysters in the egg, and roll in cracker crumbs.
4. Beat the remaining eggs with the cream and seasonings.
5. Melt half the butter in a large skillet over moderately high heat and sauté

the oysters quickly on both sides. Add the remaining butter, pour the egg mixture over the oysters, reduce the heat to low, and cook until the eggs are set and the bottom of the omelet is lightly browned.

6.   Fold the omelet and serve on a warm platter with the bacon slices.

Serves 4

Pampered Oysters

Cosseted under this light crabmeat sauce, an oyster timbale will pamper even a reluctant diner and remind him of all those custards surrounded by cream sauce that were served in auntie's kitchen.

1½ pints oysters and liquor
2   cups milk
4   Tablespoons butter
4   Tablespoons flour
2   eggs
2   egg yolks
  ¼ teaspoon salt
  ⅛ teaspoon freshly ground white
      pepper

½ cup heavy cream
2   Tablespoons Cognac
6   ounces lump crabmeat
2   teaspoons lemon juice

Oven Temperature: 350°

1.   Drain the oysters and set them aside. Measure ½ cup of the oyster liquor, mix with the milk, and warm in a saucepan.
2.   Melt the butter in another saucepan, stir in the flour, and cook until bubbling. Remove from the heat and whisk in the warm milk. Return to heat and boil, stirring constantly, for 1 minute. Remove from the stove and allow the sauce to cool.
3.   Place the eggs, yolks, salt, pepper, and oysters in a blender, and process at high speed for 1 minute. Add 1 cup of the sauce, 5 tablespoons of cream, and the Cognac, and process for 15 seconds.
4.   Pour the mixture into 6 buttered ramekins.* Place in a pan of boiling water and bake for about 30 minutes or until set.
5.   While the timbales are baking, stir 3 tablespoons of cream, the crabmeat, and lemon juice into the remaining sauce. Adjust the seasonings and heat.
6.   Unmold the timbales and serve the crabmeat sauce in a sauceboat.

  * Or use a 1½-quart buttered ringmold.

Serves 6

CHICKEN, TURKEY,
AND A REPERTOIRE OF STUFFING

Looking over the "old" recipes for chicken stifle, deep-dish pie, and cream gravy is happily nostalgic, and there is a rightness about the honest, uncluttered instructions to "add butter the size of an egg," and "pour over the fowl right away," that makes one wonder if these recipes can really be improved upon. There is also a certain reluctance to expose them to too much light, or too much scrutiny for fear of losing something precious.

Undoubtedly, it is important to take what they have to offer, to join in the spirit of prodigality that existed at a time when it was commonplace and certainly nutritious to serve many chicken dishes with an oyster sauce or gravy and to stuff a brace of quail or a cavernous turkey with dozens of oysters. Important to remember, too, that it was considered a tad racy to add a pinch of thyme or a drop or two of Sherry.

The word "memories" best describes the repertoire of stuffings collected here. Thyme-sage-and-onion bread stuffing is such an "over the river and through the woods" kind of thing; it cannot be forgotten. And there are many who still believe that half the pleasure of a nicely roasted bird is the partnership that exists between the stuffing and the intrinsic flavor of the meat. So, here are a few not-so-familiar stuffing combinations for the cook who wants to preserve an old-fashioned, authentic recipe and still use the wondrous selection of ingredients available today.

Some of these are festive entrées for special holidays, some are Sunday fare, all of them are seasoned with oysters and . . . .

[Rosemary] . . . is so frequently used to flavour roasted meat or chicken that in Italy the fragrance of rosemary in the house almost invariably means that there is a roast in progress in the kitchen. It is an easy herb to grow in a window box and is as common a wild plant in southern Europe as it is a garden plant in northern Europe.

Marcella Hazan, *The Classic Italian Cookbook*

Carriage Trade Oysters

Anyone who keeps a dinner diary will record this one with four stars. The emphatic flavoring of the oysters, scallops, and shrimp adds a slight Southern accent to a dish that needs only a potato puff or lemony artichoke for completion.

1	pint small oysters and liquor	3	Tablespoons brandy
4	whole chicken breasts		Lime wedges
8	Tablespoons butter		Parsley sprigs
2½	cups chicken stock (See p. 63)		*Coating:*
¼	cup finely julienned leeks		Salt and freshly ground pepper
¼	cup chopped shallots		Flour
2	Tablespoons flour	2	eggs
½	cup heavy cream	1	teaspoon water
8	ounces bay scallops	2	cups fine fresh bread crumbs
8	ounces peeled and deveined raw shrimp		

1. Split the chicken breasts, remove the skin and bones. Flatten each piece by pounding between sheets of waxed paper. Season with salt and pepper, and dredge with flour.
2. Beat the eggs lightly with water; dip the chicken pieces, and roll in crumbs. Set aside to dry for 30 minutes.
3. Melt 5 tablespoons of butter in a large skillet and sauté the chicken on each side until golden. Remove to a platter, and keep warm.
4. Drain the oysters and set aside. Heat ½ cup of the liquor with the stock in a saucepan.
5. Melt the remaining butter in another saucepan, stir in the leeks, cover the pan, and cook over low heat for 5 minutes. Add the shallots and cook another minute. Stir in the flour and cook until bubbling. Remove from the heat and whisk in the stock. Return to heat and boil, stirring constantly, until the mixture thickens.
6. Stir in the cream and simmer uncovered for 10 minutes, stirring occasionally.
7. Add the scallops, shrimp, and brandy, and simmer for a minute until the shrimp turn pink.
8. Add the oysters and season to taste; and heat until the oysters curl.
9. Nap some of the sauce over the chicken, garnish with lime wedges and parsley, and serve the remaining sauce in a sauceboat.

Serves 6

Tailgate Turkey Croquettes

It's Wedgewood and sterling for this game. And may the best team win.

1 pint oysters and liquor	1 cup finely chopped cooked turkey
²⁄₃ cup chicken stock (See p. 63)	
3 Tablespoons butter	¹⁄₄ cup minced parsley
1 Tablespoon chopped fresh tarragon	Peanut or vegetable oil for frying
2 Tablespoons chopped shallots	Cranberry sauce
3 Tablespoons flour	
3 egg yolks	*Coating:*
¹⁄₄ cup heavy cream	2 cups seasoned fine bread crumbs
Salt and freshly ground pepper	1 egg
Cayenne pepper	2 Tablespoons water

1. Drain the oysters, coarsely chop, and set them aside. Measure ¹⁄₃ cup of the liquor and warm it with the stock in a small saucepan.
2. Melt the butter in another saucepan, add the tarragon, and sauté the shallots until tender. Stir in the flour and cook until bubbling. Remove from the heat and whisk in the stock. Return to heat and boil, stirring constantly, until the mixture thickens. Simmer for 3 minutes.
3. Beat the egg yolks and cream in a bowl. Whisk ¹⁄₂ cup of the hot mixture into the yolks, a spoonful at a time. Then slowly beat in the remaining hot mixture. Transfer the enriched sauce back to the saucepan and, stirring carefully, bring to a boil.
4. Stir in the oysters, season to taste, and heat thoroughly.
5. Remove from the stove and stir in the turkey and parsley; adjust seasonings. Spread the mixture on a large plate, cover loosely with waxed paper, and set aside to cool.
6. Shape the mixture into 12 croquettes, roll them in bread crumbs, then in the egg beaten with water, and again in the crumbs. Dry for at least 2 hours.
7. Heat the oil to 375° in a deep fryer or heavy-gauge saucepan.
8. Place the croquettes in a fryer basket, a few at a time, and lower into the hot oil. Fry until the croquettes are golden brown and remove to a baking sheet lined with absorbent paper. Keep warm until all are cooked, or make ahead of time and reheat in a 400° oven.
9. Serve the croquettes with a sauceboat of cranberry sauce.

Serves 4

Rushy Marsh Bake

When the wind blows ripples across the marsh, the November clouds dull the sky, and the swans and ducks socialize in polite groups in the pond, then it's the time of year to build a fire in the fireplace, put the chicken in the oven, and stir up a little cranberry chutney.

1/2 pint oysters and liquor	1 Tablespoon butter
1 small chicken	2 cups chicken stock
1/3 cup dry pancake mix	(See p. 63)
1 Tablespoon chopped fresh	1 cup domestic Sauterne
rosemary	1 1/2 Tablespoons flour
Salt and freshly ground	1/2 cup chopped mushrooms
pepper	1/2 cup frozen pearl onions

Oven Temperature: 350°

1. Cut the chicken into quarters and coat with dry pancake mix that has been seasoned with rosemary, salt and pepper.
2. Place the chicken in a small roasting pan, dot with butter, and bake for about an hour until tender and browned.
3. While the chicken is baking, drain the oysters and set aside. Mix the oyster liquor, stock, and wine in a saucepan, and simmer uncovered until reduced by half.
4. Remove the chicken from the pan to a platter and keep warm while the sauce is being prepared.
5. Place the baking pan with chicken drippings over moderate heat. Stir in the flour, scraping the bottom of the pan, and cook until bubbling. Whisk in the stock and cook, stirring constantly, until the mixture thickens.

6. Lower the heat, add the mushrooms, onions, salt and pepper to taste, and simmer 5 minutes.
7. Before serving, stir in the oysters and heat until they plump.
8. Serve the chicken on the platter or individual plates, and nap with the oyster sauce.

Serves 4

Eagle Pond Pie

After a skating party at one of the nearby ponds, a hot toddy and an oyster and chicken pie crested with fluffy biscuits is relaxation and reward all rolled into one.

1	pint small oysters and liquor	1	cup chopped celery
1	6-pound roasting chicken	6	Tablespoons flour
1	bay leaf	3	egg yolks
1	garlic clove	1/4	cup chopped parsley
	Salt		Freshly ground pepper
8	Tablespoons butter		Biscuit dough for top crust
1/2	teaspoon mace		
1	cup chopped leeks		

Oven Temperature: 425°

1. Cut the chicken into large pieces, place in a pot, cover with water, add the bay leaf, garlic, 1½ teaspoons of salt, and simmer until tender, about 1½ hours.
2. Remove the chicken when it is cool enough to handle; skin, bone, and cut it into ½-inch cubes. Chill the broth and skim the fat.
3. Boil the broth in an uncovered saucepan until it is reduced to 4 cups. Keep the stock warm until needed for the sauce.
4. Drain the oysters and set aside, reserving ½ cup of the liquor.
5. Melt the butter in a large saucepan, stir in the mace, and sauté the leeks and celery for 5 minutes. Remove the vegetables with a slotted spoon and set aside.
6. Stir in the flour and cook until bubbling. Remove from the heat and whisk in the hot broth. Return to heat and boil, stirring constantly, until the mixture thickens; simmer for 3 minutes.
7. Whisk the egg yolks and oyster liquor together in a large bowl. Beat in ½ cup of the hot mixture, a spoonful at a time. Gradually whisk in the remaining hot mixture. Stir in the oysters, chicken, parsley, reserved vegetables, and adjust seasonings.
8. Pour into a buttered 2½-quart casserole. Cover with biscuit dough rolled ¼-inch thick and trimmed to fit the dish. Cut decorative slits.
9. Bake about 25 minutes until the crust is golden.

Serves 8

Chanticleer Stifle

This saucy stifle really struts its stuff and has been doing so for a long time. Although it's in a class by itself, brussels sprouts and chestnuts or honey-glazed carrots do it proud.

1 quart small oysters and liquor	1 Tablespoon oil
2½ cups half-and-half	4 Tablespoons flour
5 whole chicken breasts	½ cup dry Sherry
Salt and freshly ground	¼ cup chopped parsley
pepper	
Dry mustard	
4 Tablespoons butter	

Oven Temperature: 325°

1. Drain the oysters and set them aside. Mix ½ cup of the liquor with half-and-half and warm in a saucepan.
2. Split the chicken breasts and season with salt, pepper, and mustard.
3. Heat the butter and oil in a large skillet. When the foam subsides, cook the chicken, a few pieces at a time, until golden brown on all sides. Arrange the pieces in one layer in a buttered baking dish or roasting pan.
4. Stir the flour into the skillet and cook until bubbling. Slowly stir in the half-and-half, and boil, stirring constantly, until the mixture thickens. Add the Sherry, and pour the sauce over the chicken.
5. Cover the baking dish and bake for 1½ hours. Baste at least twice during the baking time.
6. Remove the chicken to a hot platter and keep warm.
7. Pour the sauce from the pan into a blender and process to reblend the fat which has separated during the baking.
8. Transfer the sauce to a saucepan, stir in the oysters, and parsley. Adjust the seasonings and heat until the oysters begin to curl.
9. The sauce may be poured over the chicken breasts or served in a sauceboat.

Serves 10

What is sauce for the goose may be sauce for the gander, but it is not necessarily sauce for the chicken, the duck, the turkey or the Guinea hen.

Alice B. Toklas

Whoever eats oysters on St. James Day will never want money.
Proverb

Stuffing

From the land of cotton plantations and bluegrass horse-racing to the windswept bluffs and weathered captains' houses on Plymouth Bay, dressing a bird is part of a holiday ritual. Whether the stuffing base is bread, chestnuts, noodles, dried fruits, rice, or dozens of combinations of meat or seafood is often a matter of tradition, sometimes a matter of taste. But making it an integral part of the presentation of an entrée and not a taken-for-granted-background is always a matter of care.

HERB AND OYSTER BREAD STUFFING FOR POULTRY*

1	pint oysters and liquor	1/2	teaspoon ground marjoram
1	cup unsalted butter	1/2	teaspoon dried rosemary
1	cup chopped onion	1	cup chopped fresh parsley
1	cup chopped celery		Salt and freshly ground
8	cups cubed day-old bread		pepper
2	well beaten eggs		
1/2	teaspoon ground sage		
1/2	teaspoon dried thyme		

1. Drain and coarsely chop the oysters, reserving 1/2 cup of the liquor.
2. Melt the butter in a skillet, pour off and reserve 1/2 cup.
3. Sauté the onion and celery in the skillet until tender. Stir in the oyster liquor and simmer for 10 minutes.
4. Toss the bread cubes and vegetable mixture together in a large bowl, and allow the mixture to cool slightly.
5. Add the eggs and herbs, and mix until well blended. Gradually add the reserved butter to moisten and toss with a fork to coat evenly.
6. Add the oysters, and salt and pepper to taste.
7. Allow the stuffing to cool before using.

* This stuffing can also be used for fish, boned breast of veal, and boneless loin of pork.

Yield: 10 cups

CORN BREAD, APPLE, AND OYSTER STUFFING
FOR TURKEY*

1	pint small oysters and liquor	3	peeled, cored, and coarsely chopped tart apples
12	Tablespoons unsalted butter		
1	coarsely chopped sweet onion	½	cup currants
6	cups crumbled corn bread		Salt and freshly ground pepper

1. Melt the butter in a skillet; pour off and reserve ½ cup to moisten the stuffing. Sauté the onion until tender, and remove the skillet from the heat.
2. Add the apples to the skillet and stir until well coated with butter.
3. Drain the oysters and reserve the liquor.
4. Toss the corn bread, oysters, apple mixture, and currants in a large bowl. Moisten with the reserved butter, add oyster liquor if needed, and mix well. Season with salt and pepper.
5. Allow the stuffing to cool before using.

* This stuffing can be served with ham and medallions of pork or veal.

Yield: 8 cups

OYSTER AND ARTICHOKE STUFFING
FOR CHICKEN AND CAPON*

1½	pints oysters and liquor	1	cup chopped onion
8	cups day-old white bread crumbs	½	cup pine nuts
		½	teaspoon nutmeg
2	9-ounce packages frozen artichoke hearts	1	teaspoon grated lemon zest
	Salt		Salt and freshly ground pepper
½	cup unsalted butter		

1. Drain the oysters, reserving the liquor. Coarsely chop the oysters and toss them with the crumbs in a large bowl.
2. Cook the artichokes for 5 minutes in ½ cup of boiling salted water; refresh in cold water and drain. Coarsely chop the artichokes and toss with the stuffing.
3. Melt the butter in a skillet, add the onions and pine nuts, and sauté until the onions are golden.
4. Toss the onion mixture, nutmeg, and lemon zest with the stuffing. Add enough oyster liquor and water to make the mixture moist. Season to taste with salt and pepper. Let the stuffing cool.

* This stuffing is excellent with veal scallops and beef or veal roulades.

Yield: 10 cups

Oyster Sausages (Page 237)

Neptune's Delight (Page 247)

OYSTER AND FENNEL STUFFING
FOR CORNISH HENS AND GAME BIRDS*

1	pint small oysters and liquor	5	Tablespoons butter
14	slices day-old white bread	2	Tablespoons oil
1	1-pound fennel bulb with leaves	1/4	cup dry Vermouth
2	chopped shallots		Salt and freshly ground pepper

1. Tear the bread into 1/2-inch pieces and place in a large bowl.
2. Drain the oysters, reserving the liquor. Toss the oysters with the bread.
3. Wash and trim the fennel, discard the core, and chop the bulb. Chop 3 tablespoons of the leaves.
4. Heat the butter and oil in a skillet. Add the chopped fennel and shallots, cover and cook about 10 minutes until tender. Stir occasionally and do not allow the mixture to brown.
5. Mix the contents of the skillet with the bread and oysters.
6. Add the Vermouth and oyster liquor as needed to bind the stuffing. Season with salt and pepper, and allow the stuffing to cool.

* This stuffing is especially suitable for stuffing a large fish or fish fillets.

Yield: 8 cups

OYSTER AND BRATWURST STUFFING FOR GOOSE*

1	pint small oysters and liquor	1/4	cup dry white wine
5	cups stale bread crumbs	1	teaspoon chopped fresh sage
1	pound bratwurst	1	teaspoon chopped fresh rosemary
4	Tablespoons butter		Salt and freshly ground pepper
1	chopped medium onion		
1	crushed garlic clove		

1. Drain the oysters and toss them in a bowl with the crumbs. Reserve the liquor to moisten the stuffing.
2. Poach the bratwurst in water for 3 minutes. When cool, remove the casing and coarsely chop the sausage.
3. Melt the butter in a skillet and sauté the bratwurst, onion, and garlic for 5 minutes until lightly browned; remove from the stove. Mix the bratwurst and onion with the stuffing.
4. Return the skillet to the stove, stir in the wine, sage, and rosemary; scrape the pan to loosen bits of sausage, and cook until the liquid is reduced by half. Add this to the stuffing.
5. Use the reserved oyster liquor to moisten the stuffing to the desired consistency. Season with salt and pepper and cool completely before using.

* This stuffing can also be used for a boned leg or shoulder of lamb.

Yield: 8 cups

RICE, PECAN, AND OYSTER STUFFING
FOR CHICKEN AND TURKEY*

1   pint small oysters and liquor
3   cups cooked long-grain rice
1   cup coarsely chopped pecans
1   Tablespoon chopped fresh
      tarragon
 ¼ cup chopped parsley
4   Tablespoons unsalted butter

½ cup chopped onion
½ cup chopped celery
¼ cup Cognac
    Salt and freshly ground
      pepper

1. Drain the oysters and reserve the liquor to moisten the stuffing. Toss the
    oysters in a large bowl with the rice, pecans, tarragon, and parsley.
2. Melt the butter in a skillet and sauté the onion and celery until tender but
    do not allow it to brown. Toss the onion mixture with the stuffing.
3. Add the Cognac and a little of the oyster liquor if the stuffing seems dry.
    Season with salt and pepper.
4. Allow the stuffing to cool completely.

* This stuffing is suitable for fish, shellfish, and crown roast of pork.

Yield: 7 cups

WILD RICE STUFFING FOR DUCK*

1   pint oysters and liquor
1   cup wild rice
4   cups chicken stock
      (See p. 63)
3   Tablespoons butter
 ½ cup chopped onion
 ½ cup chopped celery

1   cup chopped mushrooms
 ¼ cup Madeira
    Dash of Tabasco
    Salt and freshly ground
      pepper

1. Drain and coarsely chop the oysters, reserving the liquor.
2. Rinse the rice in several changes of water, and drain. Simmer the rice in
    stock for 45 minutes or until tender. Uncover the pan, fluff the rice with a
    fork, and simmer to evaporate excess liquid. Set aside to cool.
3. Melt the butter in a saucepan and sauté the onion and celery until tender.
    Stir in the oyster liquor, mushrooms, Madeira, and Tabasco, and simmer
    uncovered until the liquid has evaporated.
4. Add the vegetable mixture to the rice, stir in the oysters, and adjust
    seasonings.
5. Cool the dressing before using.

* This is an excellent stuffing for all poultry.

Yield: 6 cups

BEEF, VEAL, LAMB, AND PORK

What respectable member of the polo club would decline oysters and chopped sirloin on pumpernickel for a lunch that's as pukka as a chukka? And what finer way to give a real boost to a dinner for the Chairman of the Board than with beef fillets broiled to perfection and sauced with oysters in a glorious Bearnaise? There may be a better way to start the day than with a rasher of bacon and oyster sausages, but one wonders if anyone has discovered it.

The accommodation of oyster cookery to the meat-eating propensity of generations of Americans has been going on for years. And it's difficult, if not impossible, to ignore the appeal of a stuffed pork chop, a tempting serving of Steak and Oyster Tartare, or a sizzling Oyster and Steak au Poivre. The votes are in—the togetherness of oysters and meat will always have an across the board appeal.

One cannot think well, love well, sleep well if one has not dined well.
Virginia Woolf

Steak and Oyster Tartare (A Gentleman's Dish)

This recipe, like "private stock," is only for the few. Decidedly decadent but not altogether disreputable, it's ideal for lunching in pub or club.

12	shucked oysters	1	Tablespoon capers
1	pound chopped strip sirloin	1	fresh egg (optional)
4	finely sliced scallions or chopped shallots	2	Tablespoons minced fresh parsley
	Salt and freshly ground pepper		Lime wedges
			Homemade rye bread

1. Drain, pat dry, and coarsely chop the oysters.
2. Combine the steak and scallions with a fork. Lightly mix in the capers and oysters, and season to taste. Handle gently and shape into a patty. Garnish with a raw egg if desired.
3. Place the patty in the center of a serving plate. Sprinkle with parsley and surround with a ring of lime wedges.
4. Serve with a basket of homemade rye bread cut into thin slices.

Serves 4

Oysters Casanova Grill

"What becomes a legend most?" Steak and oysters, and, perhaps, the pleasure of his company.

8 shucked medium oysters and liquor	3 Tablespoons butter
¹/₂ cup dry white wine	¹/₄ pound sliced small mushrooms
4 1-inch thick strip steaks or fillets	1 Tablespoon lemon juice
Salt and freshly ground pepper	¹/₂ cup Cognac
	¹/₄ cup chopped parsley

1. Lightly poach the oysters in their own liquor and wine, drain, and pat dry.
2. Cut a deep pocket in the side of each steak with a sharp knife. Sprinkle the pocket with salt and pepper and insert 2 oysters. Rub the outside of the steaks with salt and pepper.
3. Melt the butter in a large skillet until it foams and begins to brown. Pan fry the steaks to the desired degree of doneness. Remove the steaks to a heated platter and keep warm.
4. Sauté the mushrooms in the skillet for 1 minute. Stir in the lemon juice, Cognac, and parsley, and cook briefly over high heat.
5. Spoon the pan juices and mushrooms over the steaks and serve immediately.

Serves 4

Soho Oysters

Here is the recipe for all those who have an unswerving appetite for hamburgers. Serve with a wine sauce or cushion on a sesame roll with grilled onions, tomato chutney, bacon, or mushrooms and rediscover "village" cuisine.

6 shucked medium oysters	4 Tablespoons butter
2 eggs	¹/₂ cup thinly sliced onion
1¹/₂ pounds chopped sirloin	¹/₂ cup thinly sliced green and red sweet peppers
¹/₄ cup fresh bread crumbs	¹/₄ cup dry Sherry
¹/₂ teaspoon Worcestershire sauce	Dash of steak sauce
Salt and fresh cracked pepper	

Oven Temperature: High Broil

1. Beat the eggs lightly in a bowl and combine with the beef, bread crumbs, Worcestershire, and seasonings.
2. Form into 6 oval-shaped patties and pocket an oyster in the center of each.

3. Broil the patties to the desired degree of doneness.
4. Melt the butter in a saucepan and sauté the onion and peppers until brown. Stir in the Sherry, steak sauce, and some cracked pepper. Simmer for a minute or two.
5. Serve the patties immediately, napped with the hot sauce.

Serves 6

Oyster Sausages

These sausages introduce oysters into contemporary charcuterie with uncompromising authority. As chic breakfast or brunch fare, they can be served with any number of egg recipes. And they can also be grilled over charcoal and enjoyed with a piquant sauce at lunch or supper.

1 pint oysters and liquor	1/2 teaspoon white pepper
1³/₄ pounds marbled pork butt or shoulder	1 teaspoon brown sugar
1³/₄ pounds veal	1/2 teaspoon freshly grated nutmeg
2 cups *crème fraîche*, milk, or water*	1/4 teaspoon powdered ginger
2 Tablespoons minced onion	1/4 teaspoon coriander seed
2 Tablespoons minced parsley or chives	1 teaspoon lemon zest
Salt †	10 feet good quality sausage casing

1. Drain the oysters and reserve 2 tablespoons of the liquor.
2. Cut the pork and veal into 1-inch cubes. Be sure the meat is below 65° in temperature before grinding in a food processor fitted with the steel blade.
3. Add the oyster liquor, *crème fraîche*, onion, and parsley, and mix thoroughly.
4. Coarse chop the oysters by hand, and add to the sausage mixture.
5. Sauté a spoonful of the mixture, taste, and adjust seasonings.
6. Using a sausage stuffer, stuff into the casing, making each sausage about 4 inches long. Twist and tie.
7. Heat a large saucepan of water to 180° and cook the sausages for about 15 minutes.
8. Remove from the water, and allow to come to room temperature.
9. Grill the sausages or sauté in unsalted butter until golden brown.

* If made with milk, the sausages should be eaten immediately or frozen for later use. If made with *crème fraîche* or water, they will keep about a week in the refrigerator.

† Use 1/2 teaspoon of salt and adjust after tasting. The amount of salt depends upon the salinity of the oysters.

Yield: 24

OYSTER SAUSAGES

Beard, rinse well in their strained liquor, and mince, but not finely, three dozens and a half of plump oysters, and mix them with ten ounces of fine bread-crumbs, and ten of beef-suet chopped extremely small; add a saltspoonful of salt, and one of pepper, or less than half the quantity of cayenne, twice as much pounded mace, and the third of a small nutmeg grated; moisten the whole with two unbeaten eggs, or with the yolks only of three, and a dessert spoonful of the whites. When these ingredients have been well worked together, and are perfectly blended, set the mixture in a cool place for two or three hours before it is used; make it into the form of small sausages or sausage-cakes, flour and fry them in butter of a fine light brown; or throw them into boiling water for three minutes, drain, and let them become cold, dip them into egg and bread-crumbs, and broil them gently until they are lightly coloured. A small bit should be cooked and tasted before the whole is put aside, that the seasoning may be heightened if required. The sausages thus made are very good.

Small plump oysters, 3½ dozens; bread-crumbs, 10 ozs.; beef-suet, 10 ozs.; seasoning of salt, cayenne, pounded mace, and nutmeg; unbeaten eggs 2, or yolks of 3.

Obs.—The fingers should be well floured for making up these sausages.

Eliza Acton, *Modern Cookery, in all its Branches,* 1858

Veal Roulades

Especially attractive served on a bed of homemade parsleyed noodles, these stuffed veal scallops are parcels of pure flavor seasoned with oyster forcemeat and herbs. A light Beaujolais seems just right for this veal entrée.

1½ pints oysters
3 slices diced bacon
12 veal scallops
    Mace
    Ground cloves
    Salt and freshly ground black pepper
    Flour
4 ounces ground veal
3 Tablespoons chopped parsley

1 teaspoon chopped fresh thyme
2 Tablespoons butter
2 Tablespoons oil
1 cup white wine
3 Tablespoons chopped shallots
½ cup heavy cream
8 Tablespoons soft unsalted butter

1. Drain the oysters and set them aside, reserving the liquor for another use.
2. Blanch the bacon in boiling water for 5 minutes, and drain on absorbent paper.
3. Season the veal scallops lightly with mace, cloves, salt and pepper. Dip in flour, and pound flat between pieces of waxed paper.
4. Place the oysters, bacon, and ground veal in the work bowl of a food processor fitted with the steel blade and process for a minute. Add the parsley, thyme, a pinch of salt and pepper, and process for 30 seconds more.
5. Spread some forcemeat on each veal scallop; fold up the ends, and make a rolled package, securing with skewers or string.
6. Melt the butter and oil in a large skillet and sauté the veal quickly on all sides. Add the wine and shallots, cover, and simmer for 20 minutes.
7. Place the veal scallops on a heated platter, remove the skewers or string, and keep warm while the sauce is being prepared.
8. Boil down the pan juices until reduced to about 3 tablespoons. Stir in the cream and reduce again.
9. Strain the liquid into a saucepan. Place the pan over low heat and whisk in the soft butter, one spoonful at a time. Keep moving the pan on and off the burner to avoid overheating which would melt the butter. Adjust seasoning.
10. Nap the veal scallops with the sauce and serve immediately.

Serves 6

Bayswater Pie

This is a recipe that may well go back to the one found in *The Virginia House-Wife* written by Mary Randolph in 1824. Madeira seems to accent the flavors more subtly than Sherry; the shallots are more appropriate than onions. But more than a hundred and fifty years later, the recipe still pleases.

1	pint oysters and liquor	1	Tablespoon flour
	Salt	2	Tablespoons Madeira
1	teaspoon lemon juice	3	egg yolks
1	pair sweetbreads		Freshly ground white pepper
1	cup heavy cream		Unbaked pastry for a 2-crust
2	Tablespoons butter		pie
2	Tablespoons finely chopped shallots		

Oven Temperature: 450°

1. Mix 1 teaspoon of salt and the lemon juice in water, bring to a boil and simmer the sweetbreads for 20 minutes. Drain, and plunge into a bowl of cold water. Remove the skin and membranes, and cut into bite-sized cubes.

2. Drain the oysters and set aside. Mix ⅓ cup of the liquor with ¾ cup of cream and warm in a small saucepan.
3. Melt the butter in another saucepan and sauté the shallots until tender. Stir in the flour and cook until bubbling. Remove from the heat and whisk in the cream. Return to heat, add the Madeira, and boil, stirring constantly, until the mixture thickens. Simmer for 3 minutes.
4. Beat the egg yolks in a bowl with the remaining ¼ cup of cream. Whisk in ½ cup of the hot mixture, one spoonful at a time. Gradually beat in the remaining hot mixture. Transfer the enriched sauce back to the saucepan and, stirring carefully, bring to boil.
5. Remove from the stove and, when the sauce has cooled slightly, stir in the oysters and adjust seasonings.
6. Line a deep 1½-quart casserole with pastry and crimp the edges.
7. Spoon a third of the oyster mixture into the casserole and cover with half the sweetbreads. Repeat the layers, topping with the oyster mixture. Put the top crust in place; seal and crimp the edges. Cut a hole in the center to allow steam to escape.
8. Bake in the upper third of the oven for 10 minutes. Reduce the oven temperature to 325° and continue baking for an additional 15 minutes until the crust is golden.

Serves 4

Peace and Plenty Oysters

It will take a little sleuthing to discover the oysters hidden inside the pork chops in this satisfying casserole of baked apples, onions, and caraway seeds, but they're there. And this entrée will surely reinforce the old wive's tale about the power of caraway to bring anyone back to the place where one ate it.

16	small or 8 large freshly shucked oysters	8	trimmed and butterflied 1-inch thick pork chops
1	thinly sliced large onion	½	cup bread stuffing (See p. 231)
3	Granny Smith apples		Salt and freshly ground pepper
1	Tablespoon caraway seeds		
1	Tablespoon honey	2	Tablespoons Dijon mustard
2	Tablespoons Calvados		

Oven Temperature: 350°

1. Remove the oysters from their shells, drain, and pat them dry. Reserve the liquor for another use.
2. Butter a large baking dish and layer the onion slices over the bottom. Peel, core, and slice the apples; cover the onion slices with apples. Sprinkle half

the caraway seeds, spoon the honey, and pour the Calvados over the apples.

3. Cut a deep pocket in each pork chop and fill with 1 large or 2 small oysters, and a tablespoon of bread stuffing. Season the chops with salt and pepper, and coat both sides with mustard. Arrange the chops in a single layer over the apples and sprinkle with the remaining caraway seeds.
4. Bake uncovered for about 1 hour. After a half hour, add more Calvados or water to the baking dish if no liquid has accumulated.
5. Serve the stuffed pork chops on a bed of apples and onions.

Serves 8

Drover's Inn Scallop

New England cooking at its tastiest . . . After a day of cross-country skiing, scalloped oysters and ham are as inviting as a blazing fire and hot rum punch.

1 pint oysters	6 ³/₈-inch thick slices baked ham
4 Tablespoons butter	1 cup sliced small mushrooms
2 Tablespoons flour	1 cup fresh bread crumbs
1½ cups scalded cream	¼ cup chopped parsley
¼ cup dry Sherry	
Salt and freshly ground pepper	

Oven Temperature: 350°

1. Drain the oysters, pat them dry, and set aside. Reserve the liquor for another use.
2. Melt the butter in a saucepan; stir in the flour and cook until bubbling. Remove from the heat and gradually whisk in the cream. Return to heat, add the Sherry, season to taste, and stir vigorously while the mixture comes to a boil and thickens. Simmer for 3 minutes.
3. Arrange the ham slices on the bottom of a 12 x 8-inch buttered baking dish. Distribute the oysters and mushrooms over the ham, and cover with the sauce. Sprinkle with crumbs.
4. Bake about 25 minutes until bubbling and brown.
5. Garnish with parsley and serve immediately.

Serves 6

A loaf baked without love, feeds only half a man's hunger.
Proverb

Oysters and Kidneys en Brochette

Combining the best of all possible "grills," these bacon-oyster and kidney kebabs gallop to the rescue of the bored diner.

16	shucked large oysters	8	small white onions
6	lamb or veal kidneys	8	cherry tomatoes
8	slices bacon	4	12-inch skewers
2	Tablespoons butter	3	cups cooked herbed rice
1	Tablespoon lemon juice		

Oven Temperature: High Broil

1. Trim the fat from the kidneys, cut them in half, and soak for 30 minutes in salted water. Drain on absorbent paper.
2. Cut the bacon strips in half and partially cook in a skillet or for 1 minute in a microwave oven. Remove when still pliable and drain on absorbent paper.
3. Melt the butter in a skillet, stir in the lemon juice, and sauté the kidneys and onions. Remove the kidneys after 30 seconds. Cover the pan, reduce the heat, and cook the onions for 5 more minutes, turning them occasionally. Remove the onions with a slotted spoon and set aside.
4. Remove the skillet from the stove and stir the tomatoes in the pan juices so they are well coated.
5. Drain the oysters, pat them dry, and wrap each one in a piece of bacon.
6. Thread the oysters, alternating with the kidneys, onions, and tomatoes on 12-inch skewers.
7. Broil on a heated, oiled broiling rack for 3 minutes. Turn and broil for 2 more minutes.
8. Serve on a bed of hot rice.

Serves 4

The oyster is the most disinherited of mollusks . . . Being acephalous—that is to say, having no head, it has no organ of sight, no organ of hearing, no organ of smell. Neither has it any organ of locomotion. Its only exercise is sleep; its only pleasure eating.
Alexander Dumas

DOWN TO THE SEA

Along the Grand Banks of Newfoundland, up and down the Atlantic and Pacific coasts, in the Gulf of Mexico, Long Island Sound, and Chesapeake Bay, the sea talks to the fisherman in his trawler in a more intimate way than it talks to the people who walk along the shore, and it shares its bounty with him. From the lobster traps, clam baskets, and nets of the men who go down to the sea in ships, come the ingredients for a score of seafood dishes.

The following recipes are specifically for the "catch of the day," for shellfish just out of the water and fillets of sole, haddock, and flounder so fresh that only the minimal embellishments of a brush of butter, a dash of wine, and a wedge of lemon are needed by way of preparation.

Lemon Tree Oyster Gratin

Freshly shucked oysters and Maryland lump crabmeat are absolutely necessary in this recipe which depends on the freshness of every ingredient, including the lemons, for its success.

24	shucked medium oysters and liquor	1/4	cup chopped onion
1/2	cup dry white wine	1/4	cup chopped parsley
1 1/2	cups light cream	2	teaspoons Worcestershire sauce
6	Tablespoons butter		Salt and freshly ground pepper
4	Tablespoons flour		Tabasco
1	cup chopped scallions, including green parts	8	ounces lump crabmeat
		1/2	cup buttered bread crumbs
			Lemon wedges

Oven Temperature: High Broil

1. Remove the oysters from their shells; strain 1/2 cup of the liquor and heat it in a saucepan with the wine. Poach the oysters until the edges begin to curl, remove with a slotted spoon, and set aside. Add the cream to the poaching liquid and warm it.
2. Melt the butter in another saucepan, stir in the flour, and cook until bubbling. Add the scallions, onion, and parsley, and cook until they are tender. Remove from the heat and whisk in the liquids. Return to heat, add the Worcestershire, season to taste, and boil, stirring constantly, until the mixture thickens.
3. Add the crabmeat and simmer 15 minutes, stirring occasionally.
4. Arrange 6 oysters in each of 4 buttered individual gratin dishes, divide the crabmeat sauce over them, and cover with crumbs.
5. Place under the broiler until bubbling and golden. Garnish with lemon wedges and serve immediately.

Serves 4

Oysters Dulcinea

If an elegant seafood entrée prepared in less than thirty minutes seems like "an impossible dream," or a feckless Quixotic gesture, Oysters Dulcinea is a likely recipe.

16 shucked medium oysters	1 Tablespoon chopped parsley
16 medium raw shrimp	1/4 cup dry Sherry
1/2 pound bay scallops	1 pound steamed snow peas
8 Tablespoons butter	Lemon butter
1 Tablespoon chopped fresh tarragon	

Oven Temperature: 325°

1. Remove the oysters from their shells and pat them dry; shell and devein the shrimp, and rinse and pat dry the scallops.
2. Arrange the shellfish in a lightly buttered gratin dish.
3. Melt the butter in a saucepan; stir in the tarragon, parsley, and Sherry, and simmer briefly. Pour the sauce over the shellfish.
4. Bake about 15 minutes until the oysters begin to plump and the shrimp turn pink.
5. Spoon over a bed of steamed snow peas and serve with a sauceboat of lemon butter.

Serves 4

There is no spectacle on earth more appealing than that of a beautiful woman in the act of cooking dinner for someone she loves.

Thomas Wolfe

Port of Call Newburg

Not one but six "gifts of the sea" add to the pleasure of this creamy Newburg. It can be served on waffles or in patty shells, but using shredded potato baskets adds a flavor and texture to the dish that is *non pareil*.

1	pint oysters and liquor	2	egg yolks
1	cup dry white wine	1/4	cup Cognac
4	ounces bay scallops		Salt and freshly ground white pepper
4	ounces haddock or flounder fillets	6	French-fried shredded potato baskets
4	ounces raw medium shrimp		Lemon slices
4	ounces cooked crabmeat		Parsley sprigs
4	ounces coarsely chopped cooked lobster		
2	cups light cream		
5	Tablespoons butter		
3	Tablespoons flour		

1. Drain the oysters and mix the liquor and wine in a 1½-quart saucepan. Bring to a boil and lightly poach the oysters. Remove when the edges begin to curl, drain, and set aside.
2. Use the same liquid to poach the scallops, fish, and shrimp. Set the scallops aside; coarsely flake the fish; shell and devein the shrimp. Add to the crabmeat and lobster and set aside. Strain and reserve the poaching liquid for another use.
3. Scald 1½ cups of the cream in a small saucepan.
4. Melt the butter in another saucepan, stir in the flour, and cook until boiling. Remove from the heat and whisk in the hot cream. Return to heat and boil, stirring constantly, until the mixture thickens. Simmer for 3 minutes.
5. Lightly beat the egg yolks and remaining ½ cup of cream in a bowl. Whisk in ½ cup of the hot mixture, one spoonful at a time. Gradually beat in the remaining hot mixture. Transfer the enriched sauce back to the saucepan, add the Cognac and, stirring carefully, bring to a boil.
6. Stir in the seafood, season to taste, and reheat.
7. Spoon the Newburg into warm potato baskets, garnish with lemon slices and parsley, and serve.

Serves 6

Snooty Fox Oysters

It's a sly hostess who will have this recipe for oyster-stuffed fish fillets tucked away in a safe place. French beans and almonds or stir-fried zucchini are colorful accompaniments.

1/2 pint oysters
4 Tablespoons butter
Pinch of thyme
1 garlic clove
3 Tablespoons chopped scallions, including green parts
Salt and freshly ground pepper
Cayenne pepper
Fresh bread crumbs
2 1/2 pounds fillet of sole
White wine
1 1/2 cups Béarnaise sauce

12 cooked, shelled, and deveined medium shrimp
2 Tablespoons minced shallots
1 Tablespoon finely chopped fresh tarragon
1 Tablespoon chopped parsley
Lemon wedges

Oven Temperature: 350°

1. Drain the oysters, chop coarsely, and set them aside.
2. Melt the butter in a saucepan, add the thyme, garlic, and scallions, and sauté until tender; discard the garlic.
3. Stir in the oysters, season to taste, and cook briefly; remove the skillet from the stove as soon as the oysters are hot.
4. Stir in enough bread crumbs to absorb most of the liquid, but the stuffing should remain moist.
5. Cut the sole fillets lengthwise if they are large. Each of the 12 fillets should not be wider than 2 or 3 inches.
6. Spoon some stuffing over each fillet, roll, and stand on end in a buttered, large muffin pan. Moisten each one with some white wine.
7. Place in the oven and bake about 25 minutes.
8. While the fillets are baking, mix the Béarnaise sauce; add shrimp, shallots, tarragon, and parsley, and heat.
9. Place 2 fillets on each plate, nap with the sauce, and garnish with lemon wedges.

Serves 6

Neptune's Delight

The god of the sea himself would approve the simplicity and pure flavor of this dish. On one of those warm, early, spring evenings, serve with a dry Chablis and an herbed cherry tomato salad for an impeccable seafood supper.

12	shucked oysters and liquor	1½	Tablespoons flour
2	pounds flounder, sole or sea bass fillets	½	cup heavy cream
2	Tablespoons lime juice	½	Tablespoon lemon juice
1	Tablespoon finely chopped shallots		Salt and freshly ground pepper
½	cup dry Vermouth		
3	Tablespoons butter		

Oven Temperature: 350°

1. Remove the oysters from their shells and set aside, reserving the liquor.
2. Rinse and dry the fillets. Place in a buttered, shallow, baking dish, or fish-poaching pan, sprinkle with lime juice, and set aside for an hour.
3. Add the shallots, Vermouth, and enough water to cover the fillets. Cover the dish loosely, bring to a boil on top of the stove, then poach the fish in the oven for about 10 minutes until the flesh is opaque but not flaky.
4. Remove the fillets to a heated platter, cover with a piece of buttered waxed paper, and keep warm on a hot tray or over hot water.
5. Add the oyster liquor to the poaching dish and quickly reduce the liquids to 1 cup.
6. Melt the butter in a saucepan, stir in the flour, and cook until bubbling. Remove from the heat and whisk in the poaching liquid. Return to heat, add the cream, lemon juice, salt and pepper to taste, and boil, stirring constantly, until the mixture thickens. Simmer for 3 minutes.
7. Add the oysters and heat until the edges begin to curl.
8. Spoon off any liquids which may have accumulated on the platter, nap the fish with oyster sauce, and serve immediately.

Serves 4

Top of the Cove Kebabs

Oysters wrapped in leek leaves alternating with peppers, cherry tomatoes, and swordfish cubes, broiled, and served on a bed of rice—something for everyone, especially the swordfish devotee.

24	shucked medium oysters	1	large sweet red pepper
2	large leeks	3	Tablespoons lemon juice
	Salt and freshly ground	8	cherry tomatoes
	pepper	4	12-inch skewers
1	pound swordfish	3	cups cooked long-grain rice
3	Tablespoons lime juice	2	Tablespoons minced parsley
1	cup butter		
1	large green pepper		

Oven Temperature: Medium Broil

1. Remove the oysters from their shells, pat dry, and set them aside, reserving the liquor for another use.
2. Separate and rinse the leek leaves; blanch them in boiling salted water for 2 minutes; drain and chill in ice water. Drain again and pat dry.
3. Open the leaves and spread on a flat surface. Cut to the width of the oysters and roll the oysters in the leaves before skewering.
4. Cut some of the remaining leeks into fine julienne strips to use in the sauce.
5. Cut the swordfish into 1-inch cubes, sprinkle with lime juice, salt and pepper.
6. Melt 2 tablespoons of the butter in a skillet, lightly sauté the swordfish on all sides, and set aside.
7. Cut the peppers into 1-inch squares.
8. Heat the remaining butter and lemon juice in a saucepan.
9. Thread the oysters, fish, peppers, and tomatoes on 4 skewers, and brush with lemon butter.
10. Place the skewers on a hot, oiled broiling pan and broil for 2 minutes. Turn the skewers and broil on the other side for another 2 minutes.
11. Serve the kebabs on a bed of hot rice. Mix the parsley and reserved leeks with the melted butter, and spoon the sauce over the top, or serve it in a sauceboat.

Serves 4

COTUIT HOLIDAY

. . . for all of us Cotuit seemed the repository of our happiest hours. In it was contained summer, childhood, family life, and for me it must always hold more poignant memories still.

Helen Howe, *The Gentle Americans*

BREAKFAST

Cranberry Kir
Apple and Vermont Cheddar Omelet
Oyster Sausages
Fluffy Biscuits and Beach Plum Jelly
Café au Lait

DINNER

Champagne	Oysters on the Half Shell with Mignonette Sauce
	Squash Bisque
	Orange, Endive and Watercress Trillium Salad
	Cranberry Citrus Relish
Pinot Noir '80	Native Duck with Oyster and Wild Rice Stuffing
	Brussels Sprouts and Chestnuts
	Scalloped Sweet Potatoes
Johannisberg Riesling '79	Brandied Mincemeat Pie
	Coffee

LATE SUPPER

Creamed Mushrooms
Oyster Loaf
Daisy Wine *

* 1 quart daisies crowded full; to every quart of daisies, 1 quart boiling water; put down one day and strain off the next. To every quart juice, 1 pound sugar. Put it up and leave the corks loose about a week, then cork tight.

Mrs. Horace Fish, *Ladies P.M. Cook Book*, Cotuit, 1910

OYSTER GLOSSARY

Adductor: The single muscle, popularly called the "heart;" extends from the center of one valve, or shell, through the oyster to the other shell. When the adductor is relaxed, the shells open; under water, the shells remain partly open at all times unless counteracted.

American: See *Crassostrea virginica*.

Apalachicola: Oyster from the Gulf side of the Florida coast; 2 to 3-inch curved shell, deep body.

Aquaculture: Oyster farming; the oysterman considers himself a farmer of the sea, rather than a fisherman. Oysters are seeded, cultivated, moved from bed to bed, and harvested by means of rakes, tongs, drags, dredges, and by divers. Oyster farming off the coast of Greece dates from the 4th century B.C. In the United States oysters may not be harvested before they reach a size of 3 inches; 5-inch oysters are at peak maturity.

Atlantic: See *Crassostrea virginica*.

"Banana": Name given by commercial oystermen to an elongated oyster; used only for stews and soups.

Bank: Oyster bed; oysters growing naturally, profusely, permanently.

Beak: Hinged, narrow end of the oyster.

Beard: Gills of the oyster, sometimes removed before cooking.

Belon: Oyster of France, round shell, slim body; has been introduced to the Maine and New Hampshire coasts.

Bill: Thin end of the oyster shell.

Blue Point: Oyster from Great South Bay, Long Island, New York; 2½ to 3-inch shell, plump body; also, a collective term for a medium-sized American oyster.

Box: 4 to 10 year-old oyster from Gardiner's Bay, Long Island, New York; 5 to 6-inch square-shaped shell, large body.

Bras d'Or: Oyster from Cape Breton, Nova Scotia; curved shell, flattish body.

Bristol: Oyster from South Bristol, Maine; 2½-inch round shell, plump body.

Brood: Seed oyster; a 1 to 3 year-old adult which is ready to spawn.

Buying: Raw shucked oysters constitute 80% of the oyster market, another 15% are sold in the shell, and the remaining 5% are frozen, canned, or processed for frozen or canned soups and stews. Of the shucked category, 90% are sold in fish markets and grocery stores, with the remainder going to restaurants. Bulk shucked oysters are graded as follows: Standards 30–40 to the pint; Selects 26–30 to the pint; Extra Selects 21–26 to the pint. Fresh shell oysters should be tightly closed when purchased.

Chambering: Process by which a pocket inside the shell, started by water, or a worm, or grain of sand, is sealed off with a chalky substance manufactured by the oyster. Within the pocket, the foreign substance putrifies and creates an odor.

Chatham: Oyster of Chatham, Cape Cod, Massachusetts; 3½ to 4-inch shell, fat body, somewhat flat in flavor.

Chincoteague: Oyster from Chincoteague Bay, Maryland, or an oyster from other waters which is placed in Chincoteague Bay before harvesting to improve its flavor.

Colchester: Famous oyster from Colchester, England; also known as a Walflete oyster in Elizabethan times.

Collector: Culch, or the solid substance to which a free-swimming 2-week-old oyster may attach himself. The collectors may be tree roots, asbestos shingles, styrofoam, or other man-made substances. They may be vertical rafts of shells or tiles strung on poles, or horizontal beds of rock or shells on the sea bottom.

Coon: See *Crassostrea frons.*

Cotuit: Oyster of Cotuit, Cape Cod, Massachusetts; 3 to 3½-inch shell, plump body, moderately salty.

Crassostrea angulata: (L.) The rough, cupped-shell oyster known as the Portuguese oyster. Of Asian origin, it is presumed to have been carried to Portugal on the hulls of explorers' ships, and was introduced to the coastal waters of southwestern France in the middle of the last century.

Crassostrea frons: (L.) A small oyster which attaches itself to tree roots and grows along the Carolina shores and southward. It is called the coon oyster because raccoons eat them when the oysters are exposed at low tides.

Crassostrea gigas: (L.) The large, cupped Pacific oyster of Asian origin, introduced to the northwest American coast in 1905.

Crassostrea virginica: (L.) also *C. virginiana.* The cupped, common oyster of the Atlantic and Gulf coasts of North America, known as the American, Atlantic, and Eastern oyster.

Culch: also cultch. See Collector.

Dégorgeoir: (Fr.) A stone or cement basin used in Brittany to prepare oysters for shipment to distant markets. The oysters are placed in the basin for three or four days and water and food are withheld intermittently. The oysters respond to this treatment by keeping their shells closed during the intervals when they are exposed to air; they keep themselves alive by retaining their liquids. Thus, when they are packaged and in transit to market, they remain closed and in prime condition.

Eastern: See *Crassostrea virginica.*

European: See *Ostrea edulis.*

Freezing: Shuck the oysters and pack in plastic containers with tight fitting lids; allow ½-inch of head space. Storage life in a freezer at 0°F is about six months.

Frilled: Broad end of an oyster.

Fringe: End of oyster opposite the hinge.

Galway: Famous oyster from the west coast of Ireland. International oyster festivals are held annually in Galway.

Gender: Some oysters are hermaphrodites, may change sex once a year. The female is capable of laying 60,000,000 eggs at one time. *C. virginica* and *C. angulata* female oysters eject the eggs directly into the sea where they are fertilized by the male sperm; *O. edulis* egg is fertilized within the shell.

Gill: Organ for obtaining oxygen from water. Also called the beard, it lies along the broad end of the shells where they open. The gill filters from ten to twelve gallons of water each hour, retaining microscopic plankton for food.

Golden Mantle: Oyster from Puget Sound, Vancouver, British Columbia; long oval shell, plump body.

Greening: Process by which the oyster's gills become colored when the oyster is placed in water with minute marine algae-like animals, a treatment that lasts from three weeks to one year; considered by oyster epicures especially delicious.

Half-ware: Name for the 2 to 3 year-old oyster.

Ho Tsee: (Ch.) Dried oyster.

Kent: Oyster from Kent Island, Chesapeake Bay; 3 to 3½-inch shell, plump body.

Malpeque: Oyster from Malpeque Bay, Prince Edward Island, Canada; narrow, curved shell.

Mantle: Membrane embracing the oyster and lining the shell, it secretes shell-building material.

Meleagrina margaritifera: (L.) Pearl oyster. It is not a true oyster; it is more closely related to the mussel; widely distributed in the Indian Ocean, Red Sea, Pacific, Gulf of California, Caribbean; the oldest fisheries are in Ceylon. The pearl substance is aragonite.

MSX: *Minchinia nelsoni;* microorganism fatal to mollusks; destroyed large portions of the Virginia, Maryland, and New Jersey oyster populations twenty years ago, and more recently appeared in Long Island bays.

Nutrition: Six oysters contain: 59 calories, 1.6 grams fat, 66 mgs. sodium, 45 mgs. cholesterol. Oysters have significant quantities of A, B complex, and C vitamins, and are valuable for minerals: iron, copper, iodine, some calcium, phosphorus, and zinc. The Eastern oyster measures 74.7 mgs. zinc per 100 grams of weight; the Pacific oyster measures 9.0 mgs.

Olympia: See *Ostrea lurida.*

Ostends: Belgium oyster of the *O. edulis* species.

Ostiones: (Sp.) Oyster; in the Caribbean, a small 2-inch narrow oyster which grows on tree roots.

Ostrea edulis: (L.) The oldest genus of oyster, known as the European oyster; flat, smooth shell; many varieties in the rivers and coastal inlets of the British Isles and Europe.

Ostrea lurida: (L.) Olympia oyster of North America's Pacific coast, it is being cultivated again after near extinction due to pollution. Olympias are tiny in size: over 200 are required to make one pint.

Oyster: Classified in the phylum *Mollusca,* class *Pelecypoda,* family *Ostreidae;* an edible bivalve mollusk; the shell is made up of two valves, the upper one flat and the lower convex. Said to be the most prolific of all living creatures, there are 70 different species of oysters around the world and over 300 different varieties.

Oyster Catcher: Any of certain wading birds of the widely distributed genus *Haematopus;* 16 to 20-inches in length; stout legs and heavy wedge-shaped bill are usually pinkish or bright red. Its bill is used to open bivalves; usual habitat is mudflats, sandy beaches, and rocky shores.

Oyster Crab: *Pinnotheres ostreum*; a crab which lives as a commensal in the gill cavity of the oyster; approximately ³/₈-inch shell diameter.

Oysterleaf: Sea mertensia (*Mertensia maritima*); a seaside plant of the Forget-me-not family; the fleshy, glaucous leaves taste of oysters.

Oyster Mushroom: An edible agaricaceous fungus or mushroom (*Pleurotus ostreatus*) growing in shelving masses on dead wood; the thallus resembles the form of an oyster shell, and smells like an oyster.

Oyster Plant: Salsify; a fusiform root; when boiled, it tastes like oysters.

Pacific: See *Crassostrea gigas*.

Park: Pond for farming oysters as opposed to a natural bed; tidal waters may be controlled by sluices and floodgates.

Pearl: See *Meleagrina margaritifera*.

Petticoats: Shoots, rings, or layers of the oyster shell which help establish its age.

***Pinctada margaritifera*:**   A pearl oyster; a non-conformist genus of *Ostrea*.

Plaquemines Parish: Oyster of Louisiana growing in estuaries along the Gulf coast.

Plumping: Moving oysters just before harvesting to a lower density water for a few days; they fatten, but lose flavor.

Portuguese: See *Crassostrea angulata*.

Prairie Oyster: Chaser for hangover, made with one raw egg, measure of Sherry, dash of Worcestershire sauce, salt and pepper.

Predators: Starfish, oyster drills, whelk tingles, certain species of crab, shrimp fish, and worms, oyster catchers, and herons.

Puget Sound: Oyster from Puget Sound, Washington; 3-inch shell, pronounced coppery flavor similar to that of the European oyster.

Red coloration: May appear in the liquor of shucked oysters within 48 hours after shucking or after freezing.

Rocky Mountain Oysters: Cooked lamb's testicles which, allegedly, resemble fried oysters.

Salsify: See oyster plant.

Seed: Brood oyster; name for the 1 to 2-year-old oyster which is approximately 1-inch in size; used for transplanting purposes.

Set: n., Newly settled oyster; spat.

Shelf life: 2 weeks for shell oysters placed cupped shell down on ice or under refrigeration at 35°F; 7 days for shucked oysters in the refrigerator.

Shell: Substance of the oyster shell is calcium carbonate. The shell-building material is secreted by the oyster's mantle and extruded in rings which help define the oyster's age. Historically, oyster shells have been used for road surfacing, to make a type of cement, and for chicken feed.

Shuck: n., shell; v., to remove the shell. To open an oyster, scrub the shell under cold running water, wear a glove on the hand holding the oyster or protect the hand with a towel. Hold the oyster flat side up, grip the broad edge with the fingers, and insert the tip of a shucking knife or beer can opener directly into the hinge; twist, and pry the shells apart. Or chip off a piece of the thin edge of the shell with pliers or a sharp blow of a hammer;

insert the knife and pry open. Run the knife under the top shell and sever the muscle. Taking care not to spill the liquor, sever the part of the muscle that attaches the oyster to the lower shell, and turn the oyster over in the shell to serve.

Shucking can be facilitated by relaxing the muscle of the oyster by heat or by extreme cold, or by covering the oysters with carbonated water. These methods are not as satisfactory as hand shucking when oysters are to be served on the half shell.

Shucking knife: A sharp stainless steel knife with a strong 3-inch blade that may be straight, slightly curved, and protected by a flange.

Spat: Young oyster up to the age of one year.

Spatting: Ejecting of spat by the parent oyster.

Trochosphere: Larva of a fertilized egg. In the oyster it swims freely by means of a rudder and ciliated velum, or foot. After a week or so, the young oyster secretes a limey deposit through its foot, positions itself on its left side and attaches itself to a smooth surface, to which it clings for the rest of its life.

Vase: (Fr.) Dark sea mud of an oyster bed, made "gluish" from the mucous excreted by the oysters.

Ware: An oyster that is more than three years old.

Wellfleet: Oyster of Wellfleet, Cape Cod, Massachusetts; oval shell, plump body, firm texture, moderately salty.

Wheaton Shucking Machine: Infrared-light machine used to open oysters at the rate of 60 per minute; designed by F. W. Wheaton at the University of Maryland, 1968.

Whitstable: Famous English oyster of the flat European (*O. edulis*) species.

Zeeland: *O. edulis* of Holland.

SELECTED BIBLIOGRAPHY

Beard, James. *James Beard's Fish Cookery*. Boston: Little, Brown & Co., 1954.

> The culinary "grand marshall" at the beginning of the parade of cookbook authors who really have made a difference, James Beard gives a thorough-going presentation of the usual oyster recipes in this cookbook which is devoted exclusively to seafood.

Bolitho, Hector. *The Glorious Oyster*. Chapters by Maurice Burton, and W. A. Bentley. New York: Horizon Press, 1961.

> One of the better raconteurs of oyster legends and lore, Bolitho concentrates on the history of oysters in ancient times and in England, adding entertaining literary references and thirty-nine traditional recipes.

Child, Julia; Beck, Simone; and Bertholle, Louisette. *Mastering the Art of French Cooking*, vol. 1. New York: Alfred A. Knopf, Inc., 1973.

> Certainly the author-television chef who has literally made French cooking accessible to a generation of American cooks, Julia Child is at her best in this early volume which thoroughly explains the skills and techniques basic to French cuisine.

Claiborne, Craig. *Cooking with Herbs & Spices*. New York: Harper & Row, Publishers, Inc., 1970.

> Because it is a cookbook rather than a book on herbs, this collection of recipes is an effective way to venture into the art of cooking with suitable herbs and spices.

Claiborne, Craig, ed. *The New York Times Cook Book*. New York: Harper & Row, Publishers, Inc., 1961.

> The cookbook that has contributed more toward the general principles of good cooking than any other cookbook published in America in the sixties and seventies, Claiborne's first book is critically unassailable and a very important book in any cookbook collection.

Claiborne, Craig, and Lee, Virginia. *The Chinese Cookbook*. Philadelphia and New York: J. B. Lippincott Co., 1977.

> This is a cookbook that not only puts Chinese cooking within the range of every cook, but it also serves as a valuable source book for an understanding of Chinese cuisine.

Clark, Eleanor. *The Oysters of Locmariaquer*. New York: Pantheon Books, Inc., 1964.

> A truly literate study of the science, history, legends, and cultivation of oysters with a special emphasis on the human dimensions of oystering in northern France.

Clayton, Bernard, Jr. *The Breads of France*. Indianapolis and New York: Bobbs-Merrill Co., Inc., 1978.

> Although devoted to the regional breads of France, there is so much information about bread-baking in this book that it will inspire confidence in every cook who values the art of baking.

Collin, Rima, and Richard. *The Pleasures of Seafood*. New York: Holt, Rinehart & Winston, CBS, Inc., 1976.

> Though not an unqualified success in terms of clear cooking instructions, this book offers many unusual and creative recipes for the experienced seafood cook who can read between the lines.

De Gouy, Louis P. *The Oyster Book*. New York: Greenberg, Publisher, 1951.

> Neither "old" nor innovative, this book of oyster recipes covers the traditional appetizers, soups, and entrées associated with oyster cookery before the introduction of food processors, blenders, microwave and convection ovens and does it well.

Fisher, Mary Frances (Kennedy). *Consider the Oyster*. New York: Duell, Sloan & Pearce, 1941.

> Undoubtedly the most interesting book that an American writer has ever written about oysters, this volume proves once more that M. F. K. Fisher writes about food in a way that is unforgettably and uniquely her own.

Franey, Pierre. *The New York Times 60-Minute Gourmet*. New York: Fawcett Columbine, 1979.

Franey, Pierre. *The New York Times More 60-Minute Gourmet*. New York: Times Books, 1981.

> These two volumes bring the principles of good cooking and balanced menus into the kitchen of every cook. Of special interest are the number of oyster and pasta recipes that are as delicious as they are easy to make.

The Grand Central Oyster Bar & Restaurant Seafood Cookbook. Introduction by Jerome Brody. New York: Crown Publishers, Inc., 1977.

> One of the better "restaurant" cookbooks, this collection of recipes from New York's most famous seafood restaurant is more valuable for general seafood recipes than for oyster recipes.

Guste, Roy E., Jr. *The Restaurants of New Orleans*. New York: W. W. Norton & Co., Inc., 1982.

> Devotees of Cajun and Creole cooking will find the recipes in this "restaurant" book to their taste although the clarity of some of the recipes is uneven. Because of the introductory information about each restaurant, the book also doubles as a guide to the renowned bistros of the "crescent city."

Hazan, Marcella. *The Classic Italian Cookbook*. London and New York: Macmillan, Inc., 1980.

> This cookbook simply conveys the comfortable feeling that whatever Marcella Hazan says about Italian cooking is the right thing. Following her instructions is a pleasure and so is the food.

Hering's Dictionary of Classical and Modern Cookery. 7th English Edition by Walter Bickel. London: Virtue & Co., Ltd., 1981.

> Basically a reference manual for the restaurant trade, this valuable book includes brief descriptive recipes, professional information about wine, menus, and table service, as well as the appropriate names for English, French, German, Italian, and Spanish dishes.

Hooker, Richard J. *A History of Food and Drink in America*. Indianapolis and New York: Bobbs-Merrill Co., Inc., 1981.

> An up-to-date annotated history of America's changing taste in food and drink, this book is as readable as it is informative.

Hurlburt, Sarah. *The Mussel Cookbook*. Cambridge, Massachusetts: Harvard University Press, 1977.

> An excellent example of what a "single-subject" cookbook should be, this competent and complete guide to mussel cookery is a treasure. The 96 recipes are clear, explicit, and attractively presented.

Jones, Evan. *The World of Cheese*. New York: Alfred A. Knopf, Inc., 1976.

> With the availability of so many varieties of Continental and domestic cheeses today, a guide to the different cheese "families," clear instructions about appropriate use, and reliable recipes are absolutely necessary. This volume comes closer than any of its predecessors to filling that need with thoroughness and style.

Jones, Judith, and Evan. *The Book of Bread*. New York: Harper and Row, Publishers, Inc., 1982.

> This newest book on the subject of bread strikes a wonderful balance between interesting historical information and clear, uncluttered recipes. What is even more creditable, it expands the parameters of its subject to include recipes using less conventional grains, as well as recipes for yeast breads, muffins, pastries, and dumplings.

Lach, Alma. *Hows and Whys of French Cooking*. Chicago and London: University of Chicago Press, 1974.

> A revised and expanded edition of the author's *Cooking à la Cordon Bleu*, this book is a very helpful guide to the art of French cooking with the added bonus of 45 pages of provincial menus and recipes along with a useful section on wine service.

Maryland's Way. The Hammond-Harwood House Cook Book. Annapolis, Maryland: Hammond-Harwood House Assn., 1963.

> The value of this collection of Southern recipes which includes a number of traditional oyster recipes is somewhat negligible, but the book contains interesting culinary footnotes, menus, and regional lore.

Mitcham, Howard. *Creole Gumbo and All That Jazz: A New Orleans Seafood Cookbook*. Reading, Massachusetts: Addison-Wesley Publishing Co., 1978.

> This is the author's second cookbook, and it incorporates many of the recipes that appeared in the earlier *Provincetown Cookbook*. As might be expected, the emphasis is on shellfish, including many of the usual oyster soup, stew, and gumbo recipes.

Morasch, Marian. *The Victory Garden Cookbook*. New York: Alfred A. Knopf, Inc., 1982.

> The ultimate in vegetable cookbooks, there are almost no words to describe the wealth of information Morasch has assembled in this book, including basic information about growing, preserving, and cooking vegetables. The recipes are nutritious and delicious and are accompanied by useful serving hints.

Rombauer, Irma S. *The Joy of Cooking*. Indianapolis and New York: Bobbs-Merrill Co., 1936.

It is as difficult to evaluate the value of this cookbook as it is to put a price tag on a favorite tea kettle. It's simply there whenever a recipe, oven temperature, baking time or any other necessary information is needed.

Root, Waverley. *Food: An Authoritative and Visual History and Dictionary of the Foods of the World*. New York: Simon and Schuster, 1980.

The author intended this lengthy and quite readable history of food to be called *Food: An Informal Dictionary*, and it is unfortunate that the publishers didn't use that title because it perfectly describes the nature of this indispensable reference work.

Rosengarten, Frederic, Jr. *The Book of Spices*. New York: Jove Publications, 1973.

A handy reference manual for spices, this compact volume gives background information, characteristics, and simple guidelines and some recipes for the use of spices.

Rosso, Julee, and Lukins, Sheila, with McLaughlin, Michael. *The Silver Palate Cookbook*. New York: Workman Publishing Co., Inc., 1982.

One of the most imaginative cookbooks published in the early eighties, this cookbook supplies recipes for many of the purchasable items at The Silver Palate gourmet shop in New York, and it offers a great deal more—cooking hints, ideas for entertaining, suggested menus, and information about imported and domestic ingredients.

Rydon, John. *Oysters with Love*. London: Peter Owen, 1968.

In another history-plus-recipes volume devoted to oysters, Rydon weaves 26 oyster recipes in between chapters devoted to the legends, lore, aphrodisiac myths, science, and history of the oyster.

Southworth, May E., comp. *One Hundred & One Ways of Serving Oysters*. San Francisco: Paul Elder, 1907.

This early twentieth-century cookbook of recipes devoted to the single subject of oysters is an amazingly original group of recipes for its time. With very little change, many of the recipes are quite workable today.

Stockli, Albert. *Splendid Fare: The Albert Stockli Cookbook*. New York: Alfred A. Knopf, Inc., 1970.

Written by the famous Swiss-born chef, this cookbook shares his recipes for many of the dishes that made Four Seasons restaurant in New York and Stockli's own Stonehenge Inn at Ridgefield, Connecticut, famous for good food.

Tedone, David. *The Complete Shellfisherman's Guide, Maine to Chesapeake Bay*. Old Saybrook, Connecticut: Peregrine Press, 1981.

This book is a current and helpful guide to the information essential to every shellfisherman including coastal regulations, fees for licenses, and shellfish habitats.

Vanderbilt, Amy. *Amy Vanderbilt's Complete Cookbook*. New York: Doubleday & Co., Inc., 1961.

For recipes a cut above the ordinary all-purpose cookbook, this cookbook is particularly useful in providing interesting variations and serving suggestions for specific dishes.

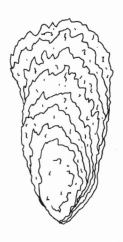